PERPETUAL **WAR**

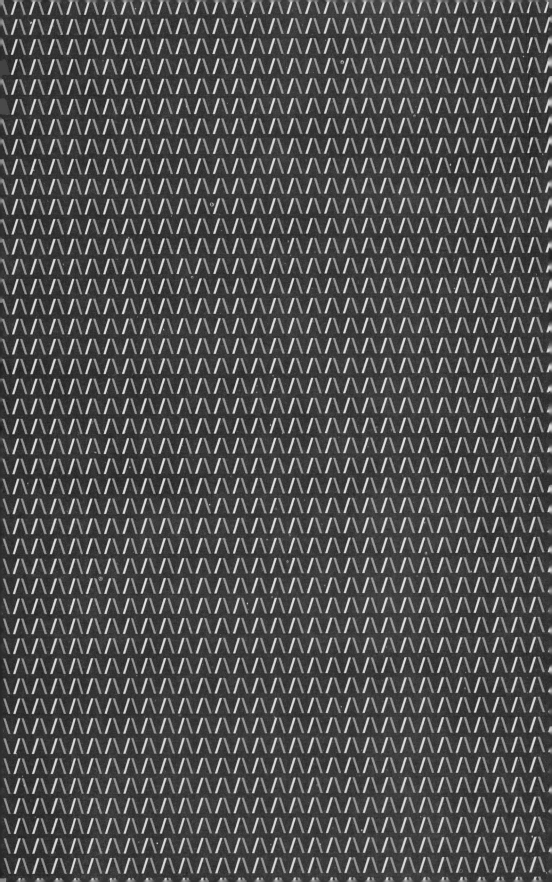

BRUCE ROBBINS

# PERPETUAL WAR

COSMOPOLITANISM *from the*
VIEWPOINT *of* VIOLENCE

Duke University Press   Durham and London   2012

## ACKNOWLEDGMENTS

Among the colleagues and friends to whom I have incurred debts of various sorts in writing this book I would like to offer very special thanks to Etienne Balibar, Ali Behdad, Leonard Cassuto, Amanda Claybaugh, Bill Connolly, Eleni Coundouriotis, Rita Felski, Susan Stanford Friedman, Hannah Gurman, Bonnie Honig, Stephen Howe, Andreas Huyysen, Ann Kaplan, David Kastan, Laura Kipnis, George Levine, Jim Livingston, Denilson Lopes, Christina Lupton, Steve Mailloux, Sharon Marcus, John McClure, Aamir Mufti, David Palumbo-Liu, Martin Puchner, Rajeswari Sunder Rajan, Lynne Segal, Helen Small, Gayatri Chakravorty Spivak, Elsa Stamatopoulou, Nirvana Tanoukhi, QS Tong, Fengzhen Wang, Richard Wilson, and Robert Young. For sustained interrogation and support I am grateful to the editorial board of the journal *boundary 2*, headed by Paul Bove, and to the faculty and participants at the School of Criticism and Theory at Cornell in 2007, then directed by Dominick LaCapra, especially Ray Hsu, Shashi Thandra, Alexa Weik, and Pei-Ju Wu. In a period when he had other things on his plate, Jeffrey Williams repeatedly gave me the benefit of his notoriously acute editorial insights. Amanda Anderson took the time to read the entire manuscript with even more than her customary care and passion; I only wish I could have done more of what she wanted me to do. It's hard for me to imagine this book would have been completed at all without the unending intelligence and generosity of Jonathan Arac and Ken Wissoker.

I am grateful to the following publications for permission to reprint:
*boundary 2* 34:3 (fall 2007), for "Cosmopolitanism: New and Newer";
David Palumbo-Liu, Bruce Robbins, and Nirvana Tanoukhi, eds., *Immanuel Wallerstein and the Problem of the World* (Durham: Duke University Press, 2011), for "Blaming the System: Immanuel Wallerstein";
PMLA 117:1 (January 2002), for "The Sweatshop Sublime"; also Helen Small, ed., *The Public Intellectual* (Oxford: Blackwell, 2002);
*Modern Intellectual History* 5:1 (2008), for "Intellectuals in Public, or Elsewhere";
Sor-hoon Tan and John Whalen-Bridge, eds., *Democracy as Culture: Deweyan Pragmatism in a Globalizing World* (Albany: SUNY Press, 2008), for "War without Belief: Louis Menand's *The Metaphysical Club*";
Austin Sarat and Nasser Hussain, eds., *Forgiveness, Mercy, and Clemency* (Stanford: Stanford University Press, 2007), for "Comparative National Blaming: W. G. Sebald on the Bombing of Germany."

An earlier version of chapter 2 was published in *New Literary History* 40:3 (summer 2009).
An earlier version of chapter 5 was published in Mina Karavantas and Nina Morgan, eds., *Edward Said and Jacques Derrida: Reconstellating Humanism and the Global Hybrid* (Cambridge: CSP, 2008).

When my son was ten I took him to see the movie *Three Kings* (1999). A dark caper-comedy set in the final days of the first Gulf War, *Three Kings* presents that war as a meaningless spectacle performed largely for the benefit of the television cameras, a war that nevertheless killed a lot of people and, after encouraging resistance to Saddam Hussein, left those Iraqis who rose against him to be slaughtered by the Republican Guard.[1] One of the film's characteristic sequences follows the path of a bullet through the inner organs of the person who's been shot. Another, this one memorable enough to have been parodied on *South Park*, shows a flagrantly decent American soldier, played by Mark Wahlberg, who is captured and tortured by electric shock in a basement bunker. Wahlberg's Iraqi interrogator, speaking accented but highly idiomatic American, says that his house has been hit by an American bomb. His child is dead and his wife has had her legs blown off. He asks the strapped-down Wahlberg how he would like it if the Iraqis came to America and bombed *his* house. The scene suddenly shifts to a tranquil American home with a mother cradling a baby in her arms. There is an explosion, and darkness fills the screen.

As we were leaving the theater I asked my son what he thought of the movie. He said he liked it. I asked him why. He thought for a minute and said, "Well, it's not one of those 'I'm great, you stink' movies."

Cosmopolitanism has never been so popular. Across a variety of academic disciplines and in the more respectable regions of the press the concept is repeatedly evoked whenever attention is paid to the movement of peoples and cultures and the creative mixtures that emerge as they interact. Since cultural mixture is now understood to be more or less universal and something that only the wrong people, xenophobes, racists, and so on, would want to resist, neither the pervasiveness of the term *cosmopolitanism* nor the whiff of pious euphoria it gives off should be surprising. What *is* surprising is that the concept's runaway popularity does not seem to have resulted in a general practice of exposing "I'm great, you stink" stories, especially the ones we ourselves tell, even when such stories emerge in contexts like Iraq and Afghanistan, where war making is more than a hypothetical option and where the stories will therefore bear responsibility for inciting or justifying large-scale loss of life.[2] Cosmopolitanism's original meaning—the overriding of local loyalties by a cosmic, transnational, or species-wide perspective—has tended to fade into the background, and it has taken with it the prospect that cosmopolitanism will interfere with the perpetrating of violence. This book tries to bring that prospect into the foreground again. With the Long Gulf War (the war against Iraq) now over, at least formally, but the war in Afghanistan celebrating its tenth anniversary in 2011, and others like these plausibly waiting around the corner, priority on the cosmopolitan agenda should go to the problem of transnational aggression, especially ours. Here is a challenge to face or, for those who disagree, to dispute: either cosmopolitanism detaches Americans from their nation and does so in time of war, when the price of such detachment rises precipitously, or it is not worth getting very excited about.

In recalling an older, more restrictive sense of cosmopolitanism, my purpose is not to reproach recent theorists for reframing the concept as a cultural particular, thereby allowing it to proliferate widely. The philosophical debate over the particular and the universal is one that for various reasons I prefer not to be drawn into and that I think can be legitimately avoided. I take the cultural relativizing of cosmopolitanism as a significant event in the recent intellectual history of the United States. It would be erroneous to think of it as a simple error. I myself would be badly placed to wish it away, having propagandized for it (with some mixed feelings, but on the whole more positive than negative ones) over some twenty years. But there are two objections to the strong culturalist program which, though only partial, I would like to see factored back in. The first concerns timing. What we need from cosmopolitanism does not stand still. The sophist Gorgias of Leontini said that no one has ever been able to define "the art of the right moment." At the time, this was probably an argument against Socratic universalism, but in the present moment it supplies a motive for reconsidering the virtues of cosmopolitanism's universalist impulse, which is to say, its impulse toward global justice. Cosmopolitanism behaves differently when it is applied at different times and places, and above all as it is applied (as I will argue it has been, most often unconsciously) at different scales. Working from what seems to be the same principle, that is, saying no to "I'm great, you stink," the scales of the classroom, neighborhood, city, region, nation, and world of nations can produce different results.

Lessons learned on a school playground may work pretty well when raised to the scale of a military conflict between the United States and Iraq, but the translation is never automatic; it's not hard to imagine how the casual equation of one scale with another could go very, very wrong. I have heard a thirteen-year-old defend the Israelites' ethnic cleansing of the Midianites by very implausible analogy with the problem of dealing with a lunchroom bully. In the second decade of the twenty-first century, and perhaps this will hold for some time to come, the crucial instance of nonidentity of scales seems to me the line dividing cosmopolitanism at the national level from cosmopolitanism at the transnational level. These two scales, each claiming to embody cosmopolitanism, in fact produce distinct cosmopolitanisms, which is to say, distinct and perhaps even antithetical politics.[3] We (by "we" I mean the category to which likely readers of this book might belong, however it is named) have to be ready to take account of this difference and to balance our priorities accordingly.

My second objection is to the influential, if only implicit, assumption that these different scales are themselves incommensurable particulars, parallels which by definition will never cross or contradict each other. My point is not that cosmopolitanism and patriotism are always and inevitably antithetical to one another. They aren't. Cosmopolitan politics of the pragmatic sort that I argue for throughout this book would be much more difficult if political projects could not draw on loyalties and affiliations functioning simultaneously at diverse scales. On the other hand, cosmopolitics is absolutely inconceivable if the dilemma of having to choose between different affiliations is not at least a theoretical possibility. Let us at least entertain the notion that the scales might one day collide—that the moment might come when it would be necessary to choose. I myself believe that Americans inhabit such a moment. Today, I think, the larger, planetary scale trumps the smaller, national scale—not because it is larger, as if arithmetically greater meant normatively superior, but as a matter of present politics, a matter of timing.

I will argue, accordingly, that the cosmopolitan explorations and debates that have preoccupied the cultural disciplines for the past two decades can be clarified, and with them the responsibilities of intellectuals, by a focus on "I'm great, you stink" at the transnational scale. My proposal is that what we write and teach should be guided by the impulse to expose and shame narratives that organize the world of nations, often with great subtlety, according to that principle. At the very least we should be open to sharing my son's delight and approval when "I'm great, you stink" narratives are replaced, as in *Three Kings*, by others that organize the world of nations in some more self-implicating and ethically balanced way.

This may not seem to be asking for very much. The basic insight was within the capacities of a ten-year-old—albeit a ten-year-old who was attending the United Nations International School and who, after seeing a science fiction movie, had already observed, "You know, dad, to the aliens *we're* the aliens." But given the general disinclination to factor in the possible viewpoints of aliens, the recognition and rejection of "I'm great, you stink" seems after all to set quite a high standard for cosmopolitanism. And if you take into account, on the one hand, the increasingly routinized self-satisfaction of today's cosmopolitanism studies and, on the other hand, the confusions and imperatives, some unprecedented and some all too predictable, brought to us by the present conjuncture, nothing less strenuous would seem to do.

What conjuncture is that? For the purpose of assessing the responsibilities of intellectuals, whose work today is genuinely urgent and also necessarily slower than that of the talking head or real-time blogger, conjunctures require duration; they cannot take their cue from last week's sensational headlines. The sense of the present moment implied here starts with topical events that, in the absence of a closure called for and promised, have metamorphosed into long-term and self-perpetuating conditions. I mean, first of all, the violence in the Middle East that has been initiated and supported by the United States. By the time this book is published, all U.S. troops may have finally left Iraq. One can hope. But habitual Israeli brutality against Palestinians will almost certainly not have ended, sustained as it is by the calm, long-term assurance that, whatever the number of casualties, the American government will never show more than token displeasure against its closest regional ally. Nor, despite all the excitement and uncertainty over Tunisia and Egypt, will we have seen the end of U.S. support for monarchical dictatorships in Saudi Arabia and elsewhere. The so-called war on terror, which likewise has proved to be stubbornly bipartisan, even in an era that declares the end of bipartisanship, will continue to offer geopolitical strategists a blank check.[4] The prospect of U.S. forces withdrawing from Afghanistan has been announced, but that still seems distant. It is unlikely that missiles from U.S. planes and drones will have stopped killing civilians in their beds in Pakistan as well as Afghanistan and then time after time becoming the objects of an apology or an investigation.

Behind all these bits of news and the many others I have not mentioned there is a more widespread object that calls for investigation, apology, and, like any real apology, a change in our ways. I mean the common sense that reduces background news like this to background noise. What is it that enables all this inflicting of pain on people outside our borders to go on and on? As in the case of Abu Ghraib, the question is, Why has there been no regime-toppling scandal? What allows such things to seem structural, hence more or less acceptable? The best name for this body of largely unconscious and often self-contradictory presuppositions, propositions that may push in very different directions from official truths and official values, even plain-as-day values like "I think torture is never justified," is also the simplest name available: nationalism.

"I'm great, you stink" doesn't usually take the form of bloodthirsty enthusiasm for the long-distance murder of foreign civilians. These days, at least, nationalism is not so self-flaunting or loudly belligerent. On the contrary, it usually seems a quiet default setting that relishes an intermittent solidarity with fellow nationals and wishes no harm to anyone. At the same time, however, it assumes, or is not quite ready to dispute, the principle that people far away don't matter as much as Americans do or don't matter as much as Americans do as long as Americans' survival is at stake—or perhaps merely their self-interest. This assumption seems to hold even if, as is so richly and incontrovertibly the case for Americans, the things done in their name by their government and their corporations end up killing their children, maiming their wives or husbands, or having other seriously injurious effects on them for which these particular acts of violence can stand as metaphors. It is this long-term common sense that is the proper object of polemic or even of reeducation on the part of teachers, scholars, and other cultural workers: the indifference, the ignorance, the lazy habits of backing one's own and of not thinking too much about the other side that maintain a sort of perpetual rehearsal for future military interventions while they also legitimate and enable ongoing ones.

Physical aggression is only the most visible way in which suffering is visited first and foremost on foreigners. Subsidies to U.S. agribusiness, which make it impossible for small farmers abroad to compete with prices in the United States and drive them off their land and into the slums, are one example among many. Why is it that such subsidies seem vulnerable to critique, to the extent that they are, only on the grounds of hypocrisy, that is, because we preach free trade but don't practice it? Why are they not denounced on the stronger grounds of their consequences for the planet's non-American inhabitants? If asked, we would probably not respond that non-Americans don't matter. Yet what other conclusion can be drawn from the fact that the question is *not* asked? Global violence is also at work, to take up one instance among many, in the U.S.-backed regime of intellectual property. Large numbers of people in undeveloped nations are dying of AIDS for lack of affordable medications that in the United States have drastically cut the mortality rate of that disease. But when the governments of Thailand and Argentina recently tried to import cheaper, generic drugs to treat their populations, the U.S. House of Representatives put them on its priority watch list of countries that do not respect intellectual property rights.[5] This is not just the familiar weighing of profits against lives, but a weighing of American profits against Thai and Argentinian lives. No lesser word than *nationalism* will serve to describe this state of affairs.

In the United States the habit of blaming other nations—these days, most often China, followed by other nations of Asia and the Middle East, though Africa and Latin America are close behind, and even European countries are potentially fair game—makes it utterly uncontroversial to export everyday economic suffering as much as possible to regions of the world that do not vote in U.S. elections and indeed can be mocked as anti-American if they protest. Even the BP oil spill in the Gulf of Mexico in 2010 is often blamed not on the oil industry and the government's deregulation of it but indirectly on Arab states and America's dependence on them. The fact that perceived dependence on products from elsewhere sounds like a pathological condition, even to progressives, and indeed is opposed by almost no one except champions of unfettered free trade capitalism, shows how profoundly nationalistic common sense remains. So-called lost jobs in the United States are similarly blamed on foreign states, which are supposed to be stealing those jobs, rather than on, say, American corporations that ship them offshore. There is no historical questioning of the process by which Americans obtained those jobs in the first place. No one asks whether, judging by the same standard, other countries would have been equally justified in reporting a theft of jobs back in the nineteenth century when certain manufacturing industries moved from Europe to the United States, or whether non-Americans are wrong to depend on commodities produced here in order to be sold over there, giving Americans many of those jobs they still have. In all the to-do over China's supposed manipulation of its exchange rate, has anyone been publicly inquiring as to whether the policy of the United States on exchange rates has worked against the U.S. national interest as Washington and Wall Street understand it? Who wrote the supposedly neutral rules that China is supposedly breaking? And who follows them? And, again, why is no one even asking these questions? The shameless, infantile clinging to a double standard, one for the United States and another for every other country, is predictable and sensible from a nationalist perspective but unacceptable from a cosmopolitan perspective.

What I've described so far, deeply corrupt as I hope it sounds, is only business as usual. But there is also new business on the agenda. Looking forward, it seems likely that people in the United States are on the verge of a new wave of nationalism, nationalism that may well take politically disorienting forms, that may well show up in unexpected constituencies, and that will put to the test the commitments of those who assume themselves not to be nationalists. On the "Styles" page for 6 September 2007 the *New York Times* ran a story on a new fashion for "Made in America" labels—new not in the sense that the moral imperative to "buy American" is new (as Dana Frank shows in her book of that name, economic nationalism has been going strong since the Boston Tea Party), but new in the sense that it is appealing to a new market: sophisticated progressives. "Made in the U.S.A.," the *Times* story says, "used to be a label primarily flaunted by consumers in the Rust Belt and rural regions. Increasingly, it is a status symbol for cosmopolitan bobos." The reason most often given for such behavior is unimpeachable: "heightened concern for workplace and environmental issues" (c1). But such concern would have to target American products as well, and perhaps primarily. That doesn't seem to be the tendency. This "move by the affluent left to conspicuously 'Buy American,'" an inversion of the internationalist sensibility that it always wore as a badge of distinction, is also about "supporting the United States economy" (c6). In other words, "the National Public Radio demographic" is flirting "with a cause long associated with the Rush Limbaugh crowd" (c6).[6]

If you're a conscientious, paid-up member of the NPR demographic, it's easy enough to wrinkle your nose at the ravings of a Limbaugh or, before his banishment from CNN, an anti-immigrant hysteric like Lou Dobbs. Feelings may be less clear, however, when the subject under discussion is, say, Michael Moore, who came close to blaming the Saudi Arabian government for 9/11, or William Greider of *The Nation*, who has taken up Ross Perot's phrase "that giant sucking sound," or a commentator on MSNBC. Progressives, too, have their reasons for putting their countrymen first and economizing on concern about others, even if those others are going to be immediately affected by decisions taken in the United States. Nationalism can be a very democratic impulse as long as what you mean by *democracy* refers only to what goes on inside your own borders. Consider the slew of books that have recently appeared, before as well as during the economic crisis that began in 2008, which mix ecological virtue—how to have less of an impact on the planet—with more or less undisguised xenophobia or anti-Chinese racism, as in Sara Bongiorni's *A Year without "Made in China"* (John Wiley, 2007), the story of the Bongiorni family's "yearlong boycott of Chinese goods" (1). The fact that this title was considered acceptable to a mainstream publisher is itself worthy of thought. Imagine the reaction if Americans were told of titles like *A Year without "Made in USA."* Faith that the divine will intends the inhabitants of the middle latitudes of the North

American continent to get the lion's share of the world's goods and services is equally apparent in Roger Simmermaker's *How Americans Can Buy American: The Power of Consumer Patriotism* (2008), now in its third edition. But even an infinitely more enlightened book like Barbara Kingsolver's *Animal, Vegetable, Miracle: A Year of Food Life* (Harper, 2007) seems to assume that Americans would be better off if they did not trade with other countries at all. What that might mean to their level of employment or standard of living goes unquestioned. Ecological virtue is enlisted (abusively, in my view) in support of an ideal of self-sufficiency, and the ideal of self-sufficiency then does a passive-aggressive flip-flop into economic nationalism. Americans alone, Americans first.

With the rise of East Asia and America's loss of its once-unchallenged economic preeminence, the sentiment of economic nationalism in the United States can only be expected to intensify, and as it intensifies it can be expected to make itself available for conversion into a more openly belligerent, overtly militarist nationalism. A nation that has lost or is losing its economic hegemony but still possesses a high-tech arsenal of conventional and nuclear weapons out of all proportion to that of any other nation, and indeed has never kicked the habit of using military force whenever a glimmer of opportunity presented itself, is a very, very dangerous nation. Passive nationalism, which not only bucks at any criticism of what American men and women in uniform do once they are placed in harm's way but also refrains from asking how they got there, awaits only the proper occasion to rear up into a more proactive, less harmless state of mind. And occasions are sure to present themselves.

This view of the conjuncture would seem to require some stock taking on the part of American intellectuals. If America is a wounded giant, likely to writhe and flail in all directions as it is beset by pesky debtors and competitors, it may be that American humanists should start training themselves for a more modest and appropriate pedagogy. They might, for example, try backing off a bit from the project of instructing the world in how to wear its identities lightly—this is one way in which cosmopolitanism is often conceived—and instead try defending the world as far as possible against the destruction that the American behemoth is likely to inflict as it staggers, bumps, and smashes. Even if the giant makes a recovery, which is possible— this book does not rest its claims on a confidently negative prognosis—it seems hard to imagine that there will not be a good deal of damage in the meantime.[7] Under such circumstances it may be that education of any sort simply cannot do much practical good. But to the extent that it can, there is a strong case to be made that teachers' first, crude, and unavoidable task is to teach American citizens that they are also citizens of a larger world, a world that they should do their best to treat more carefully and equitably; in other words, to teach cosmopolitanism, understood first and foremost as the ability to detach Americans from the national self-interest as it has been presented to them.

This brings me to the question of how cosmopolitanism *has* been understood. Some of the answer has already been alluded to above, and more will be explained below. But to summarize: over the past two decades cosmopolitanism has been understood (1) at smaller rather than larger scales. In part for that reason it has been understood (2) as an attitude that offers no necessary or significant challenge to nationalism.

In the years after the Cold War, probably in part because the binaries of that war were no longer imposing their fearful symmetry, the definition of cosmopolitanism suddenly loosened. For antiquity and the Enlightenment (I speak roughly here), cosmopolitanism had meant a relatively straightforward antithesis to local loyalties. On the whole, the term signified an attitude of detachment from one's place of origin and a transfer of primary loyalty to a larger social collectivity.[8] Those who saw cosmopolitanism as courageously ethical and those who saw it as treasonous, perverse, or politically evasive tended to agree that it was rare, a category destined to remain underpopulated, if not socially empty. Since around 1989, however, it has filled up. Two decades later, the question is how this filling up should be weighed and measured.

Whether it is associated with the transnational turn or with the rise of international civil society, this redefinition of cosmopolitanism was, first of all, a democratization. Membership in the once exclusively Western, exclusively upper-class club was now open to a much less privileged cast of characters. The shift first struck me as I followed the always interesting intellectual trajectory of the historian of anthropology James Clifford. In 1980, in an influential review of Edward Said's *Orientalism*, Clifford had used the term *cosmopolitan* to describe the humanist side of Said, of which he strongly disapproved. This was the side that claimed "the privilege of standing above cultural particularism, of aspiring to the universalist power that speaks for humanity," a privilege "invented by a totalizing Western liberalism." Ten years later, in Clifford's essay "Traveling Cultures," the term *cosmopolitan* had migrated from Western anthropologists and travelers to "the host of servants, helpers, companions, guides, bearers, etc. [who had] been discursively excluded from the role of proper travelers because of their race and class" (106). These too, Clifford now said, had "their specific cosmopolitan viewpoints" (107), viewpoints that were well worth retrieving. *Cosmopolitanism* had become a term of approval.

This discovery of "cosmopolitanism from below" brought a great deal of excitement to me and to many others in the 1990s.[9] The concept was genuinely fruitful, and one could only be glad when it multiplied. In the cultural disciplines in particular it opened up what would turn out to be a very productive program of work, most of it empirical research into the transnational subjectivity of particular cultures, subaltern groups, diasporas, and so forth, some of it philosophical meditation on that research. "Unrecorded Lives," the title John C. Hawley gives to the introduction of his *India in Africa, Africa in India: Indian Ocean Cosmopolitanism*, defines the characteristic emphasis. Here, as in many other writings, a term weighty with distinguished associations from classical Greece and the European Enlightenment is brought forward in order to confer honor on unrecorded lives, especially non-Western lives, which, as was now noticed, had not merely stayed in place in order to be studied by visiting cosmopolitan westerners but were themselves mobile and cross-cultural.[10]

Because the vectors of mobility and the cultures crossed were themselves so various, this democratizing could also be described as a pluralizing of cosmopolitanism. When Diogenes called himself a *kosmo-politis*, or "citizen of the world," all the plurality seemed to be on the side of the polis, or city-state. Of city-states there were many examples, and each was distinguished in various ways from the others. But there seemed to be only one way to be a citizen of the world. Cosmopolitanism had a singular essence: it meant refusing particular political affiliations and obligations, as Diogenes refused to serve Sinope, and declaring loyalty instead to a more universal community, however hypothetical. Now, however, instead of a single, definitive criterion the concept indicated a variety of social borders, a variety of crossings, a variety of attachments newly acquired and transformed as well as attachments broken.[11] There was suddenly perceived to be a variety of cosmopolitanisms. Logically enough, the term came to be modified by an ever-increasing number of adjectives—rooted, vernacular, discrepant, patriotic, actually existing, and so on—each insisting in its own way that cosmopolitanism was particular, situated, and irreducibly plural. Just as logically, however, such pluralization put into question the value of these cosmopolitanisms. The move from singular to plural thereby could also be expressed as a shift from normative to descriptive cosmopolitanism. This phrasing suggests that cosmopolitanism is no longer a self-evident honorific, no longer realizes a predetermined positive value, but can be described only in its empirical detail, with decisions as to its value provisionally suspended.

At the same time, all signs suggested that a celebration was in full swing. But if this cosmopolitanism was indeed descriptive rather than normative, then what exactly was there to celebrate? This question was implicit in Clifford's about-face, though I myself took some years to recognize it. How much of a change was there, in fact, between Clifford's use of the word *cosmopolitan* in 1990 and his use of it in 1980? In the second statement and in the new efforts of description and retrieval that it helped stimulate, *cosmopolitan* was no longer being used as a term of disapproval. But if it had become a term of praise, exactly how much of what Clifford had disapproved of in the original, normative concept was being praised now? Did the new, nonelite cosmopolitans protest, like Said, against Orientalism or neo-imperialism? Did they claim the same privilege that Clifford had chastised Said for claiming, the privilege of speaking for humanity? Or, agreeing with Clifford's critique of Said from 1980, did they unite with nationalists in a new, small-is-beautiful, anti-universalist coalition opposed to all those who falsely made translocal claims? To put these questions somewhat differently: Were they cosmopolitans merely by virtue of their mobility, whether they had learned something from that mobility or not? Or were they also cosmopolitans in the more demanding sense of having fashioned their transnational experience and multiple loyalties into a worldview that, like Said's, differed from that of any of the nations where they had lived, a worldview that was somehow more responsible to the bigger picture? The latter possibility would suggest that they, like Said, took nationalism as an implicit antagonist. The former would suggest that Said's task had been silently repudiated: that the new, nonelite cosmopolitans instead favored particular experiences of border crossing they might desire to see publicly expressed but would not want to see generalized. In short, it was now an open question whether the experiences that "guides, assistants, translators, carriers, etc." (107) were now seen as sharing had anything at all to do with Said's demands for global justice.[12]

Uncertainty as to cosmopolitanism's normative payoff, whether it still had one, and if so what it might be, was perhaps the inevitable result of an inflated conceptual currency. Once a great many people were perceived to possess it, cosmopolitanism could hardly be expected to sustain the high market value it had been assigned when, though controversial, it was considered elitist or not for the faint of heart or simply scarce. As it expanded, one might have predicted that it would forfeit some of its ethical prestige. And that is what has happened. In the past twenty years the population of those described as cosmopolitan has increased so rapidly as to make some wonder whether anyone is left whom the concept does not cover, and this has been recognized as a problem for what Pnina Werbner calls its "ethical grounding." "At the present cosmopolitan moment in anthropology," Werbner writes, "there is a temptation to label almost anyone—African labour migrants, urbanites, Pentecostals, traders, diasporics—'cosmopolitan.' This obscures the ethical grounding of the new cosmopolitan anthropology in ideas of tolerance, inclusiveness, hospitality, personal autonomy, emancipation" (17).[13] Werbner understates the problem. Tolerance, inclusiveness, hospitality, and so on are nice ideas, but were they ever enough of an "ethical grounding"? This question has also been posed outside the academy. True, usage in the press, which is plentiful and largely enthusiastic, tends to be even less normatively demanding than Werbner's. Many references to cosmopolitanism content themselves with connecting diversity of cuisine to desirability of real estate. Describing locations where it's not as hard as you might think to find couscous, tofu, decaf latte, or some other nonnative comestible, they tend to imply that these are stylish, pleasant places to live because cultural difference is tolerated and encouraged.[14] Appreciation of cultural difference seems to be the concept's outer limit as it is popularly understood. But this does not lead to universal satisfaction. Murmurs can be overheard asking whether cosmopolitanism really entails anything more than "let's be nice and respect each other." In other words, it's a fine injunction as far as it goes—but how far is that? Has the concept been evacuated of all ethical substance, leaving nothing more than a marker of transnational movement?

Once it came to refer to mobility as such and to the forms of complex and simultaneous belonging that mobility was held to produce, thus inviting discovery by scholars in an ever-proliferating variety of contact zones, trade routes, diasporic affiliations, culinary and musical and sexual styles, premodern and prenational political regimes, and unlikely tourist destinations, cosmopolitanism surrendered much of its focus on conflict with the nation and, by logical extension, on resistance to conflict between nations. Once it could be seen as happening at scales smaller than the nation but also within nation formation itself, where subidentities are pressured to adapt or dissolve, it could no longer be identified by its friction with the nation. The dominant motive in the discussions of the 1990s seems to have been, on the contrary, a desire for reconciliation with the nation. In 1994 the former poet laureate Robert Pinsky presented Martha Nussbaum's cosmopolitanism as "a view of the world that would be true only if people were not driven by emotions" (87). By the end of the decade, the truth of cosmopolitanism no longer seemed to preclude the emotions, even emotions as particularistic and apparently inconsequential as rooting for a local team. Pinsky rejected cosmopolitanism in favor of passionate patriotism. But for many writers patriotism itself could now be redescribed as a variant of cosmopolitanism. Or at least American patriotism could. For the historian David Hollinger and the literary critic Ross Posnock, for example, cosmopolitanism referred to a multicultural America's ability to hold its separate racial and ethnic identities at arm's length and rise above them. In *Postethnic America*, Hollinger argued his preference for a cosmopolitan rather than a pluralist vision of multiculturalism, an ideal of America that, while appreciating diversity, "is willing to put the future of every culture at risk through the sympathetic but critical scrutiny of other cultures" (85). In *Color and Culture* Posnock argued for a deracialized culture, or what he called, citing the legal philosopher Jeremy Waldron, "the cosmopolitan recognition that one lives as a 'mixed-up self' 'in a mixed-up world' where ancestral imperatives do not exert a preordained authority" (3).[15]

In 2001, laying out the results of a decade's insights and spirited controversies, Hollinger drew a line between the old cosmopolitanism, which he designated as empty, and a new cosmopolitanism, which he described as full and stocked with a great number of examples. On the old, empty, rootless side was the cosmopolitanism of Nussbaum, demanding primary allegiance to the community of humankind at the expense of all smaller allegiances. On the full side, the large and growing field of what Hollinger called new cosmopolitans refused the absoluteness of Nussbaum's commitment to humanity as a whole and instead tried to fill cosmopolitanism with historical particulars, reconceiving it as a balance of sorts between the particular and the universal. Though differing from each other, as might be expected from Hollinger's inclusion of so many critics of cosmopolitanism who might have preferred to describe themselves as pronationalists, the new cosmopolitans were said to share the impulse "to bring cosmopolitanism down to earth, to indicate that cosmopolitanism can deliver some of the goods ostensibly provided by patriots, provincials, parochials, populists, tribalists, and above all nationalists." Those who had been qualifying cosmopolitanism with adjectives like vernacular, critical, local, rooted, discrepant, comparative, pop, and actually existing had done so, Hollinger argued, in order to load up the otherwise empty concept with "history, the masses of mankind, the realities of power, and the need for politically viable solidarities."[16]

This new cosmopolitanism, a movement in which Hollinger generously counts my own work, has never been uncontested.[17] As Hollinger says, it has also never spoken with a single voice. But many new cosmopolitans have found it convenient to identify themselves with the supple, persuasive voice of the philosopher Kwame Anthony Appiah, whom I discuss in chapter 1. Since Appiah's major theme is the compatibility of cosmopolitanism and patriotism, his authority has encouraged a devout, if paradoxical, identification between cosmopolitanism and its old national antithesis. In the United States today, whatever the case in Ghana, that's arguably not a consummation to be wished. It may be that, as the code word of choice for a moderate multiculturalism in the American mold that renounces separatist assertions of ethnic or racial identity, domestic cosmopolitanism disciplines citizens in much the same way that planetary-scale cosmopolitanism tries to discipline nations. Yet whatever the pros and cons domestically, its primary effect at the planetary scale is to congratulate Americans on being who they already are. It encourages America's belief that its conduct in the world has been and remains on the side of the angels. There is no need to trot out the list of American military interventions around the world since 1900 or even since 1945—a list that is still capable of seeming much longer than one would have thought, so adept are we all at forgetting past unpleasantness—in order to see what effects that belief can have. Being cosmopolitan in the domestic sense, happy to be culturally hybrid or unhappy with any sense of identity insistent enough to disturb the harmony of the group, does not seem to have done much to deter U.S. military aggression in Latin America or in Iraq, Afghanistan, or Pakistan, the militarism that the United States supports in its allies (like Israel's lethal commando raid on ships carrying humanitarian supplies to Gaza at the end of May 2010), its promiscuous and sometimes fatal labeling of nonallies as terrorists. Americans' patriotic cosmopolitanism does not seem to have subverted in any way their usual oblique versions of "I'm great, you stink," like "where have the American jobs gone?" or "you can't buy anything these days that isn't made in China" or "look how they treat their women."

This point does not apply to the United States alone. (Taking the United States as the sole origin of evil and injustice in the world would not, needless to say, be a properly cosmopolitan position.) High on everyone's list of new, nonelite cosmopolitans in the 1990s were the transnational subjects of the various immigrant diasporas: Salvadorans in the United States, Sikhs in Canada, Senegalese in France, Serbs in Australia, and so on. Thanks in part to improved technologies of communication and transportation, many migrants remained closely connected with their place of origin and could be said to experience multiple national belonging. Had they therefore acquired, as it was imagined they might, some degree of detachment from nationalism or at least some interesting enrichment or complication of it? Had they become cosmopolitans in the old sense of the word? What *was* their state of feeling or indifference, affiliation or disaffiliation, with regard to the nation? Looking at diasporic communities in Sri Lanka, Namibia, Punjab, and Quebec, Arjun Appadurai hesitated between categorizing their identities and aspirations as cosmopolitan or "nonnational" or, on the contrary, as "trojan nationalisms" (417).[18] For Benedict Anderson, what diasporas tended to produce was nationalism, more precisely nationalism of a new, more virulent type. Bringing hostility toward others into nationalism or inciting further a potential for hostility that already existed there, what he called "long-distance nationalism" was not cosmopolitanism-from-below but, on the contrary, a pathology of global inequality; its effect was to make domestic, preexisting nationalism, which he saw as basically benign and a matter of internal solidarity rather than hostility toward others, infinitely more dangerous. Long-distance nationalism was "a rapidly spreading phenomenon whereby well-off immigrants to the rich, advanced countries (and their children) are becoming key sources of money, guns, and extremist propaganda in their distant, putative countries of origin—in perfect safety and without any form of accountability" (150).[19] His instances included support for violent Hindu fundamentalism among South Asians living in North America, Irish-American support for the Irish Republican Army, and the Zionism of Jewish-American settlers doing God's work by occupying the West Bank. Writing in the same spirit, Craig Calhoun noted that "migrants whose visions of their home cultures were more conservative and ideological than their originals" figured prominently in the events of 11 September 2001.[20] For him, too, it was not obvious how much there was to prize, normatively speaking, in the cosmopolitan subjectivity of the new, nonelite cosmopolitans (if indeed they could properly count as nonelite, which Anderson clearly doubts) that was now being so eagerly retrieved. Busy answering the charge of elitism by demonstrating again and again the number of subaltern groups that can qualify for cosmopolitan status, theorists of cosmopolitanism seemed to have devoted much less energy to the question of whether and to what extent these solidarities are moving away from "I'm great, you stink"—whether and to what extent the multiplying of loyalties or belongings produces critical distance from all or any of these belongings.

These are my questions as well. But to pose them is not to pretend to have answered them. I try to explore them here in a spirit that remains cautiously optimistic about the project of the new cosmopolitanism. It is true that rubbing two national affiliations together will not inevitably produce a cool detachment from "I'm great, you stink." The outcome may indeed be ethnic hatred that heats up and bursts into flame. But the result may also be the cosmopolitan sensibility of an Edward Said or a Noam Chomsky, each arguably fashioned in and through multiple national affiliations, American-Palestinian and American-Jewish, respectively. All the votes are not yet in on emergent forms of flexible and multisite citizenship. If the paradox of cosmopolitanism as multiple and overlapping belonging has become familiar, it's because, paradoxical or not, there is more and more historical evidence that such attachment can and does generate forms of detachment. Detachment is not an illusion; it is a social fact visibly embodied in actual lives and commitments. My son's "I'm great, you stink" comment is a small but nontrivial sign of a countercurrent within common sense that might be called, borrowing from Antonio Gramsci's "national-popular," the international-popular. It surely takes some of its rhetorical power, as Chomsky does, from the universal availability of the Golden Rule, whose potential for the production of insidious analogies between what is done unto you and what is done unto others should never be underestimated. Cosmopolitanism is promiscuous in its sources of energy and inspiration, religious as well as secular.

Cosmopolitan detachment has also, no doubt, found champions among free market individualists, who are all too eager to declare themselves free of any and all belonging. To say so is not, however, to discredit it; it is merely to offer evidence that cosmopolitanism is powered by real historical forces. No one should expect all these forces either to be ideologically pure or to produce nothing but conservative, system-affirming effects. If you inspect the popular genre of the commodity history, you will see the Euro-American consumer treated as the innocent victim of tradition-minded, superstitious, and officiously misguided regulators who try, but always fail, to keep exotic new commodities out of her or his hands. This is capitalist propaganda, flattering the consumer as well as the commodity, and it will unfortunately help undermine necessary projects of regulation—for example, the effort to regulate financial markets. Yet it is also a refreshing and important departure from civilizational self-flattery. The supposed primitives whose lands send chocolate, tea, coffee, coca, and so on to the metropolis are shown to be basically right in their traditional valuing of those materials, and the prohibition-generating West is shown to be silly and wrong. Again and again the commodity histories offer occasions for an energetic and far-reaching self-anthropologization of Western civilization.[21] On these occasions, one need not hesitate to say that some of the wind in cosmopolitanism's sails comes from capitalism.

The point is general and important. The interests of the capitalist system may coincide for a time with the interests of a given nation, but the two sets of interests never remain identical for long, and the historical tendency for them to drift apart can be exploited. It seems entirely within the dialectical spirit of Karl Marx to try to fashion a left politics that would use the contradictions of capitalism against nationalism (where we need it now) as well as against capitalism itself. Let me try to rephrase this point, which is central to everything that follows. The demand for detachment from the nation may sound like an abstract moral imperative, a simple return to the normative Kantian conception of cosmopolitanism. My title alludes to Immanuel Kant's "Perpetual Peace"—an expression of graveyard humor on Kant's part, intended for "heads of state who can never get enough of war"— and I will not discourage anyone who is open to Kant's ethical plea for an alternative. After all, the wars go on, and we are counting the bodies every day. Julien Benda, whose *Treason of the Intellectuals* (1928) charged French intellectuals with caving in to the pressures of national belonging in a time of national crisis and thus betraying their vocation, would have had a field day with the liberal hawks who in 2003 flocked to the national project of invading Iraq. Assuming, as Benda does, that intellectuals indeed have a vocation and that their vocation is cosmopolitanism is no doubt self-flattering and elitist. But the risk of self-aggrandizement, real as it is, seems less worrisome than the risk of complicity in the daily, democratically supported bombing of civilian populations and its various nonmilitary equivalents.

That said, what I am arguing for would be more accurately described not as a Kantian but a Hegelian cosmopolitanism: an imperative that emerges in, is limited by, and takes support from the unrepeatable trajectory of history. As Hollinger says, the adjective historical is another way of describing the new cosmopolitanism, though I would like to turn it in the direction of a still newer cosmopolitanism. By *historical* I probably mean more things than can be explained satisfactorily in a brief introduction, but let me at least mention three linked points. (1) I assume, following Thomas Haskell's argument on the origins of humanitarianism, that ethical obligations to strangers are not atemporal and absolute but rather proportionate to historically developing technologies of communication and transportation, which is to say, social mechanisms that stretch solidarity and make larger versions of it seem imaginable and feasible.[22] (2) This assumption implies another: that it is impossible to know in advance how far cosmopolitanism's normative impulse can or should extend. Cosmopolitanism as I see it is not abstract universalism in disguise, a call for detachment from the nation that begins with the United States, but is in fact aimed at all nations equally, powerful or powerless, in whatever situation or stage of development they find themselves.[23] If it were, it would be susceptible to the charge that I elaborate apropos of Chomsky and the Golden Rule in chapter 2: in the act of applying, very properly, the same standard to our own nation that we apply to other nations, we might also be seen as arrogating to ourselves the right to set the standard and thus to choose one that can comfortably be applied to us as well as others because it favors us at the expense of others. (I make this argument about Walter Michaels, whose rhetoric is very Chomsky-like in this respect, though the charge would not, I think, properly pertain to Chomsky himself.) In other words, antinationalism is fine as a critique of the United States, but it would be dangerous if universalized, that is, extended to other, less powerful countries. In my view, the issue of how far antinationalism extends cannot be adjudicated once and for all. "Less powerful" is neither a fixed signifier nor a stand-in for virtue. Power cannot be expected to sit still. It was never so neatly and conveniently distributed as to justify either Americano-centrism or Americano-phobia. Thinking historically therefore means neither universalizing nor refusing to universalize. It means I need not and in fact do not root against nations which have been denied sovereignty when they try to achieve it, like the Palestinians or the world's three hundred million indigenous people; sometimes the proper cosmopolitan position is a demand for statehood, for without it certain options for transnational agency are nonstarters. As a matter of principle, cosmopolitanism's range of application simply cannot be decided a priori.

(3) It follows that cosmopolitanism at the planetary scale cannot properly be accused (the accusation goes back at least to Jean Jacques Rousseau) of evading domestic political responsibilities. Those responsibilities cannot be shielded from its normative glare, however harsh and unaccustomed. George Orwell notes in *The Road to Wigan Pier* that he first discovered class injustice in England because the English working class supplied an analogy for the Burmese, whom he had learned to see as victims of imperialism when he served the empire abroad. When he was growing up in England there was no scandal about class; it seemed like second nature. He needed Burma in order to defamiliarize it. A similar defamiliarization might work in America. Many Americans have learned that English has a grammar—grammar not being much taught in American schools—only by encounter-

ing the grammar of a foreign language. The same may hold for class, which in America largely remains untaught and indeed unspeakable. All analogies are imprecise, which was precisely my point about the nonalignment of different scales. Yet as such they are also the portals of discovery. Crucial to my argument here is Immanuel Wallerstein's notion of the modern capitalist system (discussed in chapter 3) as one structured so as to permit the global North to siphon off surplus from the global South. If this is the system under which we live, then the unsettling but inevitable result is that the meaning of class identity is transformed in both regions.[24] What it means to be a worker in the global North includes both being exploited and being the beneficiary of exploitation performed on your behalf. One cannot responsibly do class politics in the United States without knowing this. Understanding cosmopolitanism historically means understanding how, for better or worse, different scales do interfere with each other.

From the usual perspective of the new cosmopolitanism, the cosmopolitanism of Said and Chomsky and Nussbaum can look ahistorical or old, a matter of principles universally applied without special dispensation for allies, neighbors, or compatriots and hence in denial about its own historical belonging while also weakened by the lack of outreach to particular constituencies. Said himself saw his intellectual practice as cultivated in and by exile, a "secular criticism" defined against the theological partialities and dogmas imposed by all forms of social belonging and most damagingly by nationalism. Chomsky appears to see his cosmopolitanism as a simple, natural application at the level of the species of a species-wide capacity for rational thought. Neither of these self-perceptions satisfactorily accounts for the locations Said and Chomsky have occupied or the political clout they have wielded. But if political commitment can be conceived as another form of multiple and overlapping loyalty, that is, as a form of belonging in its own right, then Said and Chomsky too can be made to count as new cosmopolitans rather than representatives of an unsituated normative abstraction. (A version of this case could also be made about Nussbaum.)[25] And if so, then we can perhaps also use Said and Chomsky as a standard by which to judge their fellow new cosmopolitans. Like Said and Chomsky, in other words, they can be asked what they represent, how far their words carry, and above all what content those words will bear. Perhaps the new cosmopolitanism can be asked to do the same kind of political work as the old. Perhaps it can even be asked to fulfill promises that the old cosmopolitanism made but was itself unable to keep.

This talk of cosmopolitanisms old and new may seem to complicate the issue needlessly. For some readers there will seem to be a very simple problem here. Isn't this version of the new cosmopolitanism just detachment by another, fancier name? And isn't it therefore a political mistake? It would seem to encourage a political irresponsibility that is already too prevalent and is indeed a known deformation of intellectuals in our time. In his book *The Intellectuals and the Flag* (2006) Todd Gitlin takes this view. He sees Said and Chomsky as quintessential representatives of an empty and therefore hopeless cosmopolitanism (153). When Gitlin brings up the word *cosmopolitanism* (130), he does not in fact speak scornfully of it. On the contrary, he suggests that for the members of his 1960s generation the rejection of patriotism offered their "most powerful public emotion" (131). But whether because the strategies of the 1960s failed or because circumstances have changed, what Gitlin calls for now is a patriotic about-face. He does so in the name of political effectiveness. Cosmopolitans like Said and Chomsky, he says, make up a "fundamentalist left" whose mistake is to condemn "the American use of force" (153) as such. This takes them out of the political game: "Viewing US power as an indivisible evil, the fundamentalist left has logically foregone the possibility of any effective opposition beforehand. . . . It takes refuge in the margins, displaying its clean hands, and recuses itself" (153).[26]

I share Gitlin's suspicion of moral purity and complacent marginality. I will have a brief say in chapter 7 about the limits of a certain academic anti-imperialism in America. Many sins are committed daily in anti-imperialism's name. Critics of imperialism also have a responsibility to those against whom those sins are committed. The fact that bad governance is so often the explanation given by the global North for its gross disparity in resources with the global South is no excuse for the symmetrical lie that all evil comes from the metropolis. I agree with Gitlin as well about the need to enlist (American) national solidarity on behalf of the welfare state, an argument I've made elsewhere and return to below.[27] Though my target in this book is first and foremost American support for American militarism, I find it absurd to contend that there can be no such thing as meaningful reform at home as long as violence continues to be perpetrated abroad. To believe that all suffering is produced by a single, undifferentiated, all-seeing agency is to throw one's lot in with theology.

If I have so much more positive a view of Said and Chomsky, however, it's because I differ drastically on Gitlin's central argument, which comes in two steps: (1) that self-chosen marginality is the characteristic and inevitable fate of the cosmopolitan, who by nature is abstracted from real constituencies and real politics, and (2) that the only alternative to marginality is liberal patriotism. "The left helped force the United States out of Vietnam," Gitlin argues paradigmatically, "but did so at the cost of disconnecting itself from the nation" (135). For Gitlin, to disconnect yourself from the foreign policy of the United States is to disconnect yourself from the nation, and to disconnect yourself from the nation is to disconnect yourself from politics as such. Cosmopolitanism thus becomes the simple refusal of all belonging. It's as if Gitlin cannot imagine any form of political belonging for Americans that would connect them politically to others outside their nation or that, in doing so, could have any real effects.[28]

Imagining is always to be encouraged, but simple observation should suffice to raise some doubts about this position. The field of examples that my own presupposes is sketched out in considerable detail in a book called *Nongovernmental Politics* (2007) edited by Michel Feher, Gaëlle Krikorian, and Yates McKee.[29] This book assembles a number of reports by activists from various transnational organizations and movements, like the movements by and for European refugees and *sans papiers*, who have taken upon themselves political tasks in the transnational domain. It does so in order to argue that this is a domain of real political possibilities and responsibilities. In passing, it shows that this domain is neither politically irrelevant philanthropy, as someone like Gitlin might assume, nor a covert expression of the imperial will of the United States, as is often assumed by Gitlin's enemies. This is a case that should not need to be made. But there are people who seem to believe that when Human Rights Watch repeatedly condemns the human rights case by which the administration of George W. Bush justified its invasion of Iraq, or when the American Civil Liberties Union brings legal suits against the U.S. government over Abu Ghraib and Guantanamo, these NGOS are actually helping the United States exercise global power or simply being self-righteous and self-interested while doing nothing whatsoever of real political significance. Gitlin's view of cosmopolitanism's political emptiness is shared by any number of theorists with whom he otherwise shares very little. These theorists assume that the NGOs live and work in a supranational wasteland where no such thing as true politics is even conceivable. For Giorgio Agamben, for example, the humanitarian relief of refugees and the spread of human rights discourse belong to the same all-inclusive nightmare of "bare life" as the extermination camps of the Holocaust. Victims of total and incomprehensible disaster cannot be imagined, or imagine themselves, as political agents. From the perspective of the victims' political agency, efforts to help are indistinguishable from efforts to victimize. Thus *l'Europe des camps* can appear to blend into the extermination camps. For the writers of *Nongovernmental Politics*, on the other hand, refugees remain political agents. They are drawn to identification with the political systems they belonged to before they became refugees, and they are capable of highly varied identifications with other marginal groups; they are political subjects of a sort even in their dealings with NGOs. To pretend they are below the threshold of the political, Amy West argues, is almost to support their marginalization (410). Like Gitlin, though from an opposite perspective, she warns against the "romanticization of marginality" (412).

Any number of further instances might be given from this volume to illustrate the unromantic, everyday alternatives open to a cosmopolitan politics. One is the so-called planespotters who monitored obscure but publicly available data of the Federal Aviation Administration in order to figure out which civilian airlines were participating in the CIA's program of extraordinary rendition. Another is the project of the Israeli architect Eyal Weizman in collaboration with the human rights group B'Tselem to show that the apparently random pattern of new settlements in the Occupied Territories corresponds to a deliberate long-term plan to secure Israeli control of Palestine. A third is the work of the Council for Responsible Genetics, an NGO based in the United States, that tries to publicize how genetically engineered crops affect both agriculture in the global South and consumers in the global North. The political stakes articulated in this last example are pertinent to a number of other issues and organizations: the project of creating an as-yet-nonexistent political subject that would include both global South and global North and (as both cause and effect of such a subject) a discourse that would simultaneously address both the victims and the beneficiaries of global capital. This is no small thing, to say the least. It is no surprise, therefore, that the groups and movements reaching out for it remain fragmentary, far from that level of relative self-consciousness and cohesion achieved by, say, domestic political parties in the nineteenth century or the international Communist movement in the twentieth. Yet many of them are also trying to find a working synthesis of collectivities and struggles that previous internationalisms did not recognize or have to deal with, like the situation of North Africans in Europe and people with HIV/AIDS, who are sometimes the same people.[30]

People with HIV/AIDS provide one last illustration of what this transnational politics means in practice. The coeditor of *Nongovernmental Politics* Gaëlle Krikorian offers an account of the struggle against the big pharmaceutical companies for democratic access to generic antiretroviral drugs.[31] The struggle succeeded, at least partially and provisionally. It succeeded because, though spearheaded by international NGOs, it was also able to enlist (along with the good offices of Jacques Chirac and Bernard Kouchner, not every progressive's favorite political figures) the willingness and resources of state governments, especially those of India and Brazil, which bravely defied the regime of intellectual property and did what was necessary to produce and export inexpensive generics. Cosmopolitics and politics at the level of the state, as this experience shows, are not mutually exclusive. The movement required even the unintended assistance of Bush. After the attacks of 11 September 2001 and the anthrax scare that followed, the Bush administration discovered that Bayer, which held the patent on the antibiotic used to treat anthrax, was demanding a rather high price. In this time of emergency the U.S. government threatened to suspend Bayer's patent and produce its own drugs: "This announcement was heard around the world. The United States was preparing to do for anthrax what it was trying to prevent developing countries from doing for AIDS" (256). It was a propaganda godsend for the NGOs, and they knew how to use it. Within a year there was "an international consensus in favor of access to medication" (256).[32] However precarious this victory has proved, it marked a moment of practical transnational politics whose immediate effect was incontestably what Gitlin calls improvement. If the word *improvement* does not apply to the treatment and survival of large numbers of people who were otherwise condemned to horrible, lingering deaths, what does it apply to? Its long-term effects may also include a more general weakening of the regime of intellectual property. If there were any doubts that saving hundreds of thousands of lives should count as a systemic political victory, this should assuage them. In any event, it was not a victory that could have been won on the territory of any one nation or by the efforts of any one nationality. It was an example of real cosmopolitan politics.

I do not idealize the international NGOs, which, as has often been noted, are unelected and unaccountable and as shot through with conflicting values and interests as any other human enterprise. If there is no single norm on which all those who participate in these transnational groups and organizations have been able to agree, it's because there is as much variety among them as anywhere else. Those who see a continuity between U.S.-funded organizations fighting dictatorial regimes in Eastern Europe today, on the one hand, and on the other hand American policy, direct and covert, during the Cold War have a point. It is no wonder that many NGOs are staffed by recent alumni of the Western foreign policy establishment and seem intent on using humanitarian cover to pursue the same ends, like military intervention.[33] Properly considered, however, these facts simply make my case: if the Powers That Be have invested so heavily in fighting off the struggling constituencies and underfunded NGOs that challenge them, it seems clear that the transnational domain is, after all, a zone of real political struggle and real political belonging. It is not a mere excuse for self-chosen marginality or irresponsibility.

When I first wrote about cosmopolitanism in 1992, I tried to argue, though I did not manage as clearly as I would have wished, that the real problem lurking in the paradox of cosmopolitanism as a mode of belonging was not too old-fashioned a notion of cosmopolitanism but too narrow a notion of belonging. Cosmopolitanism, I said, is always situated, never a mere abstraction, never a matter of either belonging everywhere or belonging nowhere. On the other hand, what people meant when they spoke of the particular, the local, and the situated was always shot through with unacknowledged distances. It was never the warm and cuddly belonging they seemed to want, but always epistemologically uncertain and ethically strenuous. The consensus that "intellectuals are not detached but *situated*" (249) was no sooner put in place than it became a bit of a thought-stopper: "If our supposed distances are really localities, as we piously repeat, it is also true that there are distances *within* what we thought were *merely* localities" (250). Most important, cosmopolitanism was about those distant things that we belong to or that belong to us by the very fact of existing where and when we do. In the introduction to *Cosmopolitics*, where that essay is republished, I wrote, "Instead of an ideal of detachment, actually existing cosmopolitanism is a reality of (re)attachment, multiple attachment, or attachment at a distance. . . . We are connected to all sorts of places, causally if not always consciously, including many we have never traveled to, that we have perhaps seen only on television—including the place where the television itself was manufactured" (3). This is the source of our responsibilities. "It is frightening to think how little progress has been made in turning invisibly determining and often exploitative connections into conscious and self-critical ones, how far we remain from mastering the sorts of allegiance, ethics, and action that might go with our complex and multiple belonging" (3).

The chapters that follow were written over the past decade as efforts (that is, essays in the older as well as the present sense of the word) to make further progress in this same urgent but paradoxical zone. They are almost equally motivated by rage against the militarism of the United States, on the one hand, and by the complexities of belonging, on the other—belonging, first of all, for me and many, if not most, readers in and to the United States. The chapters call for detachment, and their inevitable subject is belonging. I argue throughout the book, but especially in the chapters on Appiah (chapter 1), Chomsky (chapter 2), and Wallerstein (chapter 3), that local belonging, peremptory though it may be, offers no escape from cosmopolitanism's normative or global justice dimension. The definition of the word *belonging* helps make this point. According to the *Oxford English Dictionary*, to belong means, among other things, to be appropriate to, to pertain, concern, refer, to be the proper accompaniment, to be the property of, or the rightful property of, to be connected with, as in a family, society, or nation, a native or inhabitant of a place, or, again, a proper or rightful inhabitant. The meaning vacillates between accompanying and properly accompanying, between merely inhabiting and rightfully inhabiting, between being the property of and being the rightful property of. That is, the word itself stops one from evading the normative question, the question of rightfulness that is posed over and over in its history, as it is in ours.

As I've also said, however, norms are relative to historical circumstances and socio-technological possibilities. I do not pretend that cosmopolitanism as I present it definitively solves the problem of how to negotiate between obligations that fall to us because of where we live and those that come to us from afar through a kind of belonging at a distance. "Distant belongings," a phrase which might have served as the title of this book, is a reminder of those obligations we incur merely by getting dressed or consuming our usual caffeinated morning beverage.[34] It is no easy thing either to acknowledge these obligations at all or, on the other hand, to do so without falling into a sense of infinite, unredeemable indebtedness that is theological as well as politically unprofitable. How radically are we—we in the more or less comfortable metropolis—obliged to change our lives? In chapter 4, "The Sweatshop Sublime," I try to work through a properly secular or nontheological sense of responsibility in the face of global injustice.[35]

Tricked out as the defense of democracy, a concern with global injustice has served to excuse unfortunate exercises in military strong-arming. In the United States and other powerful countries such concern is always in danger of luring cosmopolitanism away from the antimilitarism I want for it and sending it out on missions I would want it to refuse, and indeed that I would define it in opposition to. There is no surefire way of protecting it from these temptations. Pacifism, a solution for some, will not work for those who cannot condemn the fight against Nazism or to end slavery or, for that matter, against colonial occupation. My somewhat old-fashioned emphasis on detachment from the national interest is intended in part to do this work. To demand that a proposed intervention, say, to stop genocide, not be part of a nationally self-interested plan to take revenge on an old adversary or control supplies of petroleum or secure some other geopolitical advantage is at least to reduce the likelihood that a global justice cosmopolitanism will get one into trouble rather than out of it. Still, a certain amount of trouble seems to me inescapable, as inescapable as the exercise of power itself. In the chapters on Said (chapter 5) and on Stefan Collini and Slavoj Žižek (chapter 6) I suggest that if intellectuals see belonging as the threat of self-betrayal, it is perhaps less out of fear of partiality than so as to stave off the realization of their relative but real empoweredness. Power is a large, though ordinarily hidden, element of what it means to belong. If you see yourself as exilic or free-floating, then what is scariest about belonging is that you can no longer deny that you do possess power. Yet power is what cosmopolitan attachment requires if it is to stand up to military mobilization. In this sense, cosmopolitanism cannot afford either not to belong or, what follows from it, not to have any enemies. It is not a pure, disempowered virtue. After all, it has a somewhat intimate relation to nationalism's "I'm great, you stink."

These complications of belonging come to the fore in the last two chapters, which deal, respectively, with Louis Menand's history of pragmatism in *The Metaphysical Club* (chapter 7), a book that is provocatively organized around the Civil War as an instance of voluntary military intervention, and W. G. Sebald's lectures on the Allied bombardment of Germany in the Second World War (chapter 8). In the Menand chapter I worry over the sort of belonging that underlies domestic cosmopolitanism, with its ironic detachment from beliefs and identities, and can take the form of an apparently desirable anti-interventionism (where *The Metaphysical Club* starts) but equally well the form of military intervention (where the book ends). In the Sebald chapter I try to sharpen the paradox that while cosmopolitan detachment can be compromised by covert styles of national belonging, it can also require an intensification of national belonging, if only in the style (adopted by so many Germans after 1945) of national shame. The cosmopolitan project of making Americans see a relationship between the air attacks of 11 September 2001—which made good on the "how would you like it?" threat from *Three Kings*—and the decades of American foreign policy that preceded them, a crucial step in the pedagogy of national detachment, may require, I suggest, the nurturing of a kind of national belonging that American individualism has heretofore resisted.

When Raymond Williams set off the term *alignment* against the more familiar *commitment* and when Said developed the idiosyncratic terminology of *filiation* and *affiliation*, both were trying to square a circle: on the one hand, to see politics as free choice, irreducible to the prior givens of identity, and, on the other, to register the ways in which such a choice is in fact always determined in part by the situation in which one finds oneself. In renegotiating the balance between attachment and detachment, I'm trying both to redescribe the same dilemma and to give the paradox of cosmopolitanism and belonging an unusually aggressive spin. Here again I seek help in etymology. As it happens, the English word *attachment* is cognate with the Italian *attaccare* and the Spanish *atacar*, meaning "to attack." *Attachment* originally meant arrest, apprehension, and seizure; to attach was to lay hold of, as with hands, claws, or talons. In sixteenth-century England, *attach* had the explicit meaning of attack, as in laying siege to a castle. If we think of attachments first of all as connections by means of sympathy or affection, which is now the word's primary sense, we are likely to forget the residual element of violence in our attachments or belongings. This book was written to help recall it. By this I mean, first of all, the military and economic violence perpetrated by the United States. But in order to answer that violence, I also recall and call on the cold, hard, ethically stringent memory of *detachment*—itself a word with military resonance—that attachment cannot escape. What cosmopolitanism must seek to become in order to make wars harder to mobilize is what William James called a moral equivalent of war. Both the history of English words and the history of American wars suggest that this enterprise is a bit less farfetched than it may seem. (In a forthcoming book entitled *The Beneficiary*, a sort of companion volume to this one, I argue that encouragement about the possibility of a global redistribution of resources can be found in, of all places, the experience of wartime rationing.) The national sentiment of "I'm great, you stink" being as violent and massive as it is, so violent and massive as to appear, in bad moments, not merely national but fatally coterminous with the human itself, the project of changing it needs all the force and all the forces it can muster. Cosmopolitanism cannot afford to be bland, pious, or powerless.

# 1 COSMOPOLITANISM, NEW AND NEWER
Anthony Appiah

Anthony Appiah has been saying for some time that cosmopolitanism, properly conceived, does not contradict patriotism. He said it
with his characteristic eloquence and verve in a piece called "Cosmopolitan Patriots" in the *Boston Review* in 1994, protesting gently
against Nussbaum's call for a primary allegiance to humanity as a
whole. He made the same argument in the final chapter of *The
Ethics of Identity* (2005), entitled "Rooted Cosmopolitanism." And
he makes it again in *Cosmopolitanism: Ethics in a World of Strangers*
(2006).[1] It seems reasonable to ask what might lie behind this
apparent compulsion to repeat. It's not because Appiah's vision
of cosmopolitanism is still struggling to overcome stout, well-
entrenched resistance. On the contrary. In the circles where Appiah
is a familiar and trusted figure, the older, singular cosmopolitanism
in the mode of Nussbaum is now regularly dismissed as other-
worldly, elitist, Eurocentric universalism in disguise. It has not been
refuted, but it does seem to have been overwhelmed by the pluralizing tide of smaller, subuniversal cosmopolitanisms. Each of these is
qualified by a boldly paradoxical adjective like *rooted* or *indigenous*.
Each freely concedes, to use Appiah's preferred word, its partiality.
Rather than making trouble for patriots, these vernacular, discrepant, local, and actually existing cosmopolitanisms are often seen,
as I've said, as versions of patriotism. In many, if not quite all,

instances the sharp knife of antinationalist critique has been sheathed. The hypothesis presents itself, therefore, that cosmopolitanism in this newer, humbler rewording is so repetitiously invoked, by Appiah and by others, because it has become a comfortable piety: an ideal whose periodic reiteration helps us evade the actual, pressing complexities of the case, a credo that can be easily affirmed because it makes no unpleasant weekday demands. Readers who discovered a portion of Appiah's *Cosmopolitanism* excerpted in the *New York Times Magazine* on New Year's Day 2006 may have felt that the term, which always seemed to teeter on the brink of a fatal complacency, had finally gone over the edge.

The danger that cosmopolitanism may have become a piety or is on its way to becoming one seems real enough to warrant further investigation.[2] Still, it would be irresponsible not to leave open the possibility that what will be uncovered is not conventional piety but, after all, some sort of genuine virtue. Virtue on a global scale may sound like a conceptual nonstarter likely to produce only embarrassment, but it is the theoretical possibility of which cosmopolitanism is in effect offered as a provisional instance. A concept that would stand for the proper ethical attitude toward global connectedness and would do so no matter what particular cultural vantage point one viewed the global connectedness from—such a concept is conceivable but is not an obvious match with any presently flourishing position, at least one that can withstand critical scrutiny. The phrase *world citizenship*, for example, invites dismissal as an oxymoron or worse, a free pass offered to the mighty on the condition (a not very onerous one) that they reframe their militaristic adventures as humanitarian interventions and nation building. Yet we can't help but go on asking what it would take to build an international sense of right and wrong powerful enough to put some perceptible restraint on such militarism, or for that matter what it would take to get something done about the economic disparities that militarism feeds on. While such questions remain insistent, so will inquiries into cosmopolitanism. This is a site where important thinking has to be done. And enough is at stake in it to justify an impulse to return to the scene of the original argument, repeating and perhaps repenting.

In the past two decades, as noted above, the updated, amended, conciliatory version of cosmopolitanism has emerged as a wildly popular term of approval. This is partly because of the term's classical pedigree and partly because in its new versions it is felt, rightly or wrongly, to resolve some of the more troublesome antitheses that currently plague cultural interpretation at a planetary scale: local/global, tradition/modernity, ordinary culture/high culture. At the same time, it is also attractive because it takes attention away from other, still more unwieldy contradictions, like that between cultural inequality and economic inequality. Cosmopolitanism posits the option that fidelity to a particular place and tradition can be understood, like Aymara-speaking Bolivian rappers, as simultaneously and successfully participating in the global, the modern, and the innovative. However limited the rappers' caloric intake may be, therefore, however modest their living conditions and life chances (surely improved with the political ascension of Evo Morales), their indigenously inflected rapping is taken as grounds for rejoicing, or for what Appiah has called "celebration of cultural variety" ("Cosmopolitan Patriots," 29). Today it is hard to find a place where the celebration is not at full blast. I offer a couple of book-length examples: Jacqueline Loss's *Cosmopolitanisms and Latin America: Against the Destiny of Place* (2005) undertakes to show that what has often been taken as local is "frequently more cosmopolitan—interactive, porous, and translational" (3);[3] *New Cosmopolitanisms: South Asians in the US* announces the discovery of a new subject, not adequately covered by "traditional diasporas": "We define new cosmopolitans as people who blur the edges of home and abroad by continuously moving physically, culturally, and socially, and by selectively using globalized forms of travel, communication, languages, and technology to position themselves in motion between at least two homes, sometimes even through dual forms of citizenship, but always in multiple locations. . . . It is these new forms of shifting choices and complex relationships that emerge from what were earlier 'knowable' as diasporas that we call new cosmopolitanism" (2–3).[4]

Note the accumulation here of value-positive terms: "new," of course, but also "choice," an indicator of freedom, as well as "complex." Unlike ordinary diasporas, these are enriched by a spicy hint of unknowability. "Selectively" suggests the not otherwise obvious assumption that the cosmopolitan status of most South Asians in the United States should be understood as primarily intentional, a form of self-fashioning. The result is that "occupying in-between spaces of identity, culture, and communication" (3) becomes a familiar badge of privilege: a claim to fly free of the labels assigned to others by nature or tradition, or at least to have achieved mastery over them.[5] James Clifford proposed years ago that cosmopolitanism might be a welcome replacement for the overtasked term *culture*. Now cosmopolitanism is praised because it is perceived, however subliminally, to resolve the contradiction *within* culture between the anthropological sense (ordinary culture) and the high or aesthetically valued sense. Cosmopolitanism is lived, like diasporic identity, at the level of the everyday, yet it allows everyday culture to display the signs (freedom, selectivity, imaginative blurring of accepted categories) that are usually associated with a higher, more rarified, more praiseworthy artistic creativity.[6]

Is all this praise for the new cosmopolitanism a good thing? By definition, the new version seems more accessible than the old, closer to a hybridity we already possess and merely need to acknowledge than to an ideal we might have to step outside and fight for. One review of Appiah wondered, "Aren't most of us already the 'partial cosmopolitans' Appiah wants us to be?"[7] In order to make cosmopolitanism seem rare, strenuous, and praiseworthy, the new cosmopolitans sometimes seem obliged to confuse the new with the old, the descriptive with the normative sense of the term. However fleeting and fragmentary, the new sense (cosmopolitanism as a description of the actually existing, ineluctably mixed-up state of modern identity) is perceived as reflecting the moral glory of the old, normative sense (cosmopolitanism as an unfulfilled task or ideal of planetary justice), even as the latter seems less and less visibly active. I myself am on record as having wagered on the new: on cosmopolitanism reconceived as something more weighty, positive, and socially grounded than detachment from one's nation, as a mode of attachment which cannot therefore claim to stand for a universal ethical ideal but also, as multiple or distanced attachment, seems unlikely merely to reconfirm the givenness or singleness of nationalism. The results are not yet in on this wager. I still have hopes. But since I have raised the question of self-revision and even repentance, let me admit that, having praised or at least withheld judgment in the hope that the actual would turn out to be a vehicle for the normative, I have come to feel that, in many cases at least, the actual has stalled out en route. Perhaps it needs a jump-start. To switch metaphors: celebrations of cosmopolitan diversity have largely been uninterrupted by issues of militarism, economic equality, and geopolitical justice, issues which are more readily taken up by the cleaner or older cosmopolitanism. Hence the impulse to check up on the now-aging category of the new and ask what work is and isn't getting done.

Given how much agency the nation-state still enjoys and the active militarism in which it has so often expressed itself, especially though not exclusively in the United States, my own curiosity fixes first of all on the problem of cosmopolitanism's relation to patriotism. Appiah, who is cited as an inspiration by Hollinger, is confident that the two do not contradict each other. Can we accept his confidence? Many critics seem to have no trouble with it. Jessica Berman, whose *Modernist Fiction, Cosmopolitanism, and the Politics of Community* finds an Appiah-style cosmopolitanism in the experimental modernism of Henry James and Gertrude Stein, is particularly taken with the idea of noncontradiction between nomadic cosmopolitanism and Americanness.[8] Berman credits Appiah with the phrase "rooted cosmopolitanism" (27), which seems to have begun the contemporary habit of waving off the contradiction as illusory. It may be of trivial importance, but the phrase seems to have been used slightly earlier and perhaps indeed coined by Mitchell Cohen in the pages of *Dissent*.[9] In *Dissent*, as elsewhere, the paradoxical alliance of patriotism and cosmopolitanism (once a slur directed at the Jews, among others) often seems intended to reconcile a self-image of modernist detachment with practical loyalty to one form of patriotism in particular: Zionism.[10] I would hope that Israeli patriotism will appear controversial enough, in light of the bloody invasions of Lebanon in 2006 and of Gaza in 2008, among other long-standing and everyday outrages, to suggest that if and when cosmopolitanism declares itself constitutionally unable or unwilling to oppose patriotism, a warning signal should sound. American nationalism should set off the same alarm. Here, then, is one plausible criterion for the evaluation of new or adjectivally modified cosmopolitanism: to what extent does it prepare us to bow down before patriotisms like these?

The patriotism Appiah seems to have in mind when he talks about cosmopolitanism is not his own but his father's. The first line of the essay "Cosmopolitan Patriots" reads, "My father was a Ghanaian patriot." The first line of "Rooted Cosmopolitanism" is also about his father, this time about his father's dying injunction to his children to be "citizens of the world" (213). (When I began this book with a reference to my son, it seems likely that some part of my mind was remembering these father–son scenes.) His father,

Appiah says, "never saw a conflict between his cosmopolitan credo and his patriotism" (223). Meaning no disrespect, I note that this statement falls somewhat short of demonstrating either that there *was* no such conflict in his father's case or that, as Appiah allows it to imply, there need never be such a conflict in anyone else's. Appiah's father is also quoted as saying, "No one in Ghana is silly enough not to believe in God" (270). I hope we are not supposed to infer that the tricky old existence-of-God problem has been disposed of by the same means. Filial loyalty is an admirable sentiment, but there is something a bit suspicious about professing it publicly as if it could settle philosophical issues and as if we readers had the same motives as a son for reining in our skeptical, intellectually disobedient impulses.

The usual argument against Nussbaum's, Chomsky's, or Peter Singer's versions of cosmopolitanism is that we cannot possibly be expected to care about those far away as intensely as we care about our families. In his response to Nussbaum, the political theorist Benjamin Barber writes, "We live in this particular neighborhood of the world, that block, this valley, that seashore, this family" (34). "Above all," the historian Gertrude Himmelfarb declares in her response, "what cosmopolitanism obscures, even denies, are the givens of life: parents, ancestors, family, race, religion, heritage, history, culture, tradition, community—and nationality" (77). The dash at the end of this list acknowledges the decisive leap by which, starting out with a natural and inevitable love for one's parents, one finds oneself suddenly and just as naturally committed to one's nation and perhaps therefore also committed to the aggressions undertaken by one's government. Appiah himself writes that what a rootless cosmopolitanism, "taken as a sort of rigorous abjuration of partiality, the discarding of all local loyalties" (221), doesn't have, a family does: a "grip upon our hearts" (221). To insert Joseph Appiah into this argument as statesman and cosmopolitan as well as father is to suggest that there is no general conflict of interest or moral claim between the levels of family, nation, and world.[11] This lays upon Joseph Appiah a heavy burden of exemplarity. If Appiah's father is going to represent a programmatically asserted compatibility between the interests of humanity and the interests of a particular state, readers have to be told something about what he actually did on behalf of the state he served, how he managed the feat of avoiding any collision between national and transnational interests. A footnote (329n11) presents him as a figure of the permanent opposition. We are told about his honorable jail time, but not about actions devoted to defending any particular government. In his foreword to Joseph Appiah's autobiography, Henry Louis Gates Jr. speaks of a "phase of diplomacy on behalf of his country" that involved Appiah in explaining, in Gates's words, the rationale for the "bloody coup" by which the military deposed Kwame Nkrumah (xvii–xviii).[12] This is not the place to enter into the rights and wrongs of Nkrumah (about whom Anthony Appiah writes very lucidly in *In My Father's House*) or of the coup that sent him into exile. It ought to be enough, for the purposes of the present argument, to remind ourselves that any political career put forward in this rhetorically forceful way can and must be examined objectively and nonreverentially.[13]

Rereading the essay "Rooted Cosmopolitanism," which begins with the words, "When my father died," I recalled the experience of being in a large audience some years ago when Anthony Appiah asked us all whether we recognized another first sentence: "I was not sorry when my brother died." (I did—it's from Tsitsi Dangarembga's *Nervous Conditions*—and I was duly congratulated on it.) Improper familial feelings of the sort that Danga-rembga's female narrator expresses are not represented in Appiah's writing, at least thus far.[14] (The piece from 2007 in the *New York Times Magazine* about the fact that his Ghanaian family possessed slaves may mark a change in that.)[15] He is magnanimous to his family, and he typically extends this magnanimity to others who may be less deserving of it. He is silent about the support of British imperialism shown by John Stuart Mill, an intellectual hero of his. When presented with an opportunity to vent postcolonial anger, he generally passes. Indeed, he uses the word *empire* in a seemingly nonjudgmental sense, often modifying it with the casual adjective *great*. In "Rooted Cosmopolitanism" Marcus Aurelius is referred to as "one of the last of the great emperors of the greatest empire of the classical West" (218). The phrase has every reason to catch the eye, as Marcus Aurelius combined, via stoicism, cosmopolitanism with active empire building. A few pages earlier, on the same page where he notes that "cosmopolitan values" are often seen as "really imperial ones" (214), Appiah refers to the "great Asante empire that had dominated our region before its conquest by the British" (214). It looks as though conquests both by the British and by the Asante have abruptly fallen under the protection of that distanced, resentment-free historical forgiveness in which, many centuries later, we are now accustomed to drape the supposed greatness of classical antiquity's con-querors, whether philosophers or not. Perhaps at this point the British empire builders have to be forgiven so that the Asante aristocracy too can be forgiven. Those who have less greatness in their family backgrounds may want to go slowly here. I am willing to grant that certain grudges of the past, even the quite recent past, may have outlived their sell-by date. Recalibra-tion of targets and priorities is essential to politics, and the ability to forget is as crucial to political recalibration as the ability to remember. But the obvious risk of this particular magnanimity—a sort of temporal cosmopoli-tanism, not always easy to detect when it follows in the wake of the more ostentatious spatial variety—is depoliticization.

Liberalism tends to minimize the past's hold over political decision mak-ing in the present. It wants to accelerate the perhaps inevitable process by which the passing of time diminishes that hold. Liberal cosmopolitans like Hollinger, Waldron, and Posnock mobilize this presentist impulse against identity claims, like those based on race or indigeneity, that pull the separa-tist claimant away from the nation-state as a whole. It's in this sense that their cosmopolitanism always speaks for the nation-state, implicitly en-couraging patriotism in the present, even if nothing explicit is said on the subject and if there is no veneration expressed for founding fathers. Though he is quite respectful of the state, Appiah is also more appreciative of local identities than many of his liberal allies, more resistant to moral pressures urging global uniformity.[16] That he manages this upholding of difference while fighting off relativism (for him, a consequence of positivism) and indeed while subtly arguing in the name of moral universality, is perhaps Appiah's most distinctive philosophical contribution. This careful argu-ment comes closest to specialized philosophy talk in an otherwise deliber-ately nondisciplinary and reader-friendly book. For some readers it will be the book's center. For others, the means by which Appiah arrives at his difference-affirming cosmopolitanism will be less important than the fact that similar positions, though often less elegantly argued, take shelter be-neath it and propagate themselves, often with ethically mixed results. These readers will want to ask questions about, for example, the temporal enlarge-ment that seems to follow unnoticed in the wake of this cosmopolitanism's more obvious spatial expansiveness and about the politics thereof.

In Ghana, Appiah writes, "respect was precisely not something that belonged to everybody. . . . But just as *dignitas*, which was once, by definition, the property of an elite, has grown into human dignity, which is the property of every man and woman, so *animuonyam* can be the basis of the respect for all others that lies at the heart of a commitment to human rights" ("Rooted," 265). Time, which allowed formerly aristocratic prerogatives like *dignitas* to grow gradually into rights felt to be democratically shared, can be expected to have the same effect in Africa, Appiah argues, that it has had in Europe. It is an excellent point and entirely characteristic of Appiah's continuing pursuit of partial, provisional, or nonlogical resolutions to collisions of value that seem beyond the reach of rational mediation. The formidable requirement that we understand difference, Appiah suggests, can sometimes translate into the less disheartening process of merely "getting used to" it (*Cosmopolitanism*, 84–85). But the charm of this vernacular temporality demands a second look. Note the continuity between "getting used to" and the more general liberal presentism. The continuity suggests how much accommodation to the status quo this temporality may involve, how effectively a liberal mobilization of time may work to reinforce the power of the actual and the actuality of power.

The standard communitarian argument against a strong sense of obligation to distant persons is that one must begin where one lives and only gradually work outward to more distant solidarities. When Appiah quotes Edmund Burke on the need to love "the little platoon we belong to in society" ("Rooted," 241), he repeats Burke—"It is the first link in the series by which we proceed towards a love to our country and to mankind"— without asking what force it is that Burke thinks will eventually propel us from the first link to the last and whether that force seems to be working. Looking around, one might say that so far there has been a markedly insufficient movement toward love of humankind, while there has been a dangerous surplus of love of our own country at the expense of others, a love often expressed, as it is today, in the form of nonmetaphorical platoons sent on patrol in a number of occupied countries. There has continued to be too much "I'm great, you stink." Neither Burke nor Appiah has anything to say about how the sentimental journey outward might have gotten arrested or about how to adjudicate, when and if adjudication is called for, between love of humanity and love of country. In general, Appiah does not imagine that collisions will happen between local rooting and translocal justice. The local can be safely left alone, sacred and autonomous. "What is a virtue in a referee," Appiah writes, "is not a virtue in a prizefighter's wife" ("Rooted," 230). Well, okay. But what about those cases, which are not rare, in which prizefighters' wives are also victims of their husbands' pugilistic skills? This is a quick and dirty rephrasing of the question that has been put on the table by several decades of feminists. Appiah's defense of local ethical autonomy chooses to look away from it. The answer, it seems to me, is that the referee has to learn from the prizefighter's wife an additional lesson: not only that universal ethical reasoning must be informed and qualified by loyalties that properly remain local, as Appiah implies, but also that local loyalties cannot themselves be taken for granted as if they constituted an inviolable realm of privacy, as if their understanding of virtue remains out of bounds to referees even when husbands routinely beat up their wives.

In *Cosmopolitanism* the same temporality that quietly urges us to go easy on the imperial horrors of the past is credited with almost supernatural ability to resolve the contradictions of the present and future or at least to get us used to them. For Appiah, as for many champions of cosmopolitanism new and old, the abstraction time seems to imply one very concrete historical reality: the reality of commerce. The power of the actual, which both allows for eventual accommodation and defines the state of affairs one is expected to accommodate oneself to, tends to be lodged in what Appiah calls the "single web of trade" (xii).[17] It's as if time-as-trade, which is to say, time-as-capitalism, was at work both preserving differences and, miraculously, resolving the social contradictions that underlie those differences.

The linking up of time with Adam Smith's invisible hand seems equally implicit in the cosmopolitanism of Jeremy Waldron. Waldron has been discussing "indigenous communities in countries like the United States, Canada, Australia, and New Zealand" (103) and how, like an individualist in a state of nature, "they may yearn for the days of their own self-sufficiency" (104). Now, however, they find themselves both threatened and protected by larger political structures on which they are dependent, structures whose relation to them they must actively manage. Waldron writes, "Yet here we all are. Our lives or practices, whether individual or communal, are in fact no longer self-sufficient" (104).[18] "Yet here we all are": rather than the undeniable differences in where we have come from, what matters is a shared condition of interdependency here and now. One effect of this not-unattractive pragmatic disqualification of long-past injustice is an equally pragmatic disqualification of present economic inequality. In his own argument for cosmopolitanism and against artificially protecting cultures from the forces of change, Waldron proposes, rightly I think, that people do not in fact need a culture of the sort that Will Kymlicka imagines when he talks of belonging to a culture, in other words, culture seen as a bordered, integral whole. What people really need is cultural materials (107). And these cultural materials can come to us from any number of diverse and distant sources; indeed, like the other goods we use every day, they can and do come from around the world. As Waldron puts it, "The materials are simply *available*, from all corners of the world, as more or less meaningful fragments, images, and snatches of stories" (108). This is empirically true, and for the purposes of his argument about cultural need, the point is well taken. But the argument also has a hidden normative dimension. The model of cultural transmission it relies upon is that of the world capitalist system, which not only provides cultural materials "from all corners of the world," but does so in precisely the cosmopolitan spirit of "yet here we all are." How and where these materials are produced and what inequalities and injustices may have been involved in their production are judged to be irrelevant. What matters simply is that here these materials are, conveniently transformed into commodities, available on the market. One might say that cosmopolitanism has entered into the business of laundering culture, washing the commodity clean of whatever sweatshop-style indignities may have clung to its emergence and distribution, and allowing or enjoining us to look upon it here and now as conveniently fresh and ready for us to use.

When Appiah, like Waldron, confronts the question of cultural patrimony, a topic that occupies much of the latter part of *Cosmopolitanism*, he too strenuously rejects arguments in favor of the repatriation of indigenous artifacts. The indigenous groups who press such claims are presented as no more deserving, ethically speaking, than multinational corporations: "The vision is of a cultural landscape consisting of Disney Inc. and the Coca-Cola Company, for sure; but also of Ashanti Inc., Navajo Inc., Maori Inc." (130). Nothing could be more characteristic of liberalism's blindness to history than the assumption that the various contracting parties are free and equal and can be addressed as such. Disparities of power disappear. Yes, the world's indigenous peoples desire to get some benefit from their collective cultural production, of which corporations have persistently robbed them. But to conclude from this that indigenous peoples exist on the same plane as the world's corporations is to fall into a dangerous liberal formalism.

Other topical urgencies are not much discussed. The index has no entries on Zionism or Afghanistan or Iraq. HIV/AIDS comes up, but not the issue of how to speak to or about the South African government's attitude to its origins and treatment. Appiah is clearly aware of the consequences of "policies carried out by governments in our name." "Together," he writes, "we can ruin poor farmers by dumping our subsidized grain into their markets, cripple industries by punitive tariffs, deliver weapons that will kill thousands upon thousands. Together, we can raise standards of living by adopting new policies on trade and aid, prevent or treat diseases with vaccines and pharmaceuticals, take measures against global climate change" (xiii). This is well worth saying. But by lining these lists up next to each other, Appiah avoids having to face squarely the question of whether the choice of one over the other has been dictated by greater loyalty to the fatherland over humanity—the question of when, if ever, cosmopolitanism and patriotism might indeed find themselves in unavoidable conflict.

Conflict comes to the fore only in the final chapter, which deals with the moral obligation to help the distant poor. It does so at the level of individual charity rather than, say, the level of politics. "Each person you know about and can affect is someone to whom you have responsibilities," Appiah has declared earlier (xiii). So what are those responsibilities? On reflection, it turns out that they are rather minimal: "If you are the person in the best position to prevent something really awful, and if it won't cost you much to do so, do it" (161). Minimizing distant obligations seems to be one major reason for switching from rootless to rooted cosmopolitanism: "I have defended going to the opera when children are dying, children who could be saved with the price of admission" (166). Appiah is willing to shock in order to make a very necessary point: that individuals in the global North do not become moral monsters if they fail to abandon their possessions, careers, and opera-going habits in order to devote their lives to humanitarian missions. His critique of the short-term humanitarian model rightly lifts much of cosmopolitanism's ethical and psychological burden off the shoulders of the conscientious individual. Yet Appiah exploits the deliberate timelessness of the genre of the philosophical example—here, Peter Singer's example of whether I should save a drowning child even if it means ruining my suit—by keeping such mininarratives carefully isolated from his timely historical observations on, say, the falling price of cocoa in Ghana. No mention is made of the idea that, figuratively speaking, this child may be drowning because of the falling price of cocoa or what its causes might be, or because of arms sales to Africa by the five permanent members of the Security Council (two UN officials blurbed the book), or because of the world trade that is also producing so much aesthetically enjoyable cultural mixing. Nor does he take the conversation about conflicting interests beyond the charitable individual in order to place it at a more appropriate level of agency: the state.[19]

The weakness of our obligations to those at a distance, as Appiah sees them, is probably one reason cosmopolitanism as he sees it does not seem to thrust itself into more blatant or inevitable contradiction with our obligations to the nation. But many taxpayers feel quite distant even from their neighbors and fellow citizens. There is less difference between the two distances than there used to be. Thus there has been a certain leveling-out and intertwining of the two scales of responsibility. Of course the uncomfortable possibility also remains that you may at some point—for example, in wartime—be asked to choose one set of obligations over the other. If war played a larger role in Appiah's set of examples, the prospect of contradiction between cosmopolitanism and patriotism would loom larger as well. Still, I think Appiah is right that the abjuring of partiality must itself be abjured. And if so, then it's partiality for your state, and not just partiality for your family, your tribe, or even your nation, that you have to find a new, potentially more friendly attitude toward. Since it's the state that makes wars, this is more of a leap.

In 1994 I was one of the enthusiastic early readers of Appiah's "Cosmopolitan Patriots" essay, which responded to Nussbaum, and indeed was one of those who eventually reprinted it. Though I felt much closer to Nussbaum than to the piece to which she herself was responding, Richard Rorty's Op-Ed "The Unpatriotic Academy," like Appiah I felt the need for the grounding of cosmopolitanism. And however disorienting this turn might be, I too felt a need for political commitment to the state—in this case, a specific, limited commitment to those state institutions, remnants of past democratic struggles, that continued to provide for the welfare of those fellow citizens and fellow residents most in need. In a time of shameless deregulation, privatization, "welfare reform," reductions of food inspectors and clean air inspectors and financial inspectors, and so on, it seemed clear that the left had no choice but to struggle schizophrenically on two levels at once: for less national solidarity, if national solidarity means, as it so often seems to, military aggression and the displacing of capitalism's worst costs onto nonvoters, but also for more national solidarity, to the extent that solidarity means defense of regulatory institutions and the welfare state.

The defense of the welfare state offers one context in which cosmopolitanism and patriotism can be nudged closer together. A potential point of overlap between liberalism and the left, between Clifford's anti-elitist cosmopolitanism and Hollinger's patriotic cosmopolitanism, it is also a useful context in which to sketch out for cosmopolitanism, which is forever accused of being too vague and abstract, some concrete political goals.[20] "Until we have an international welfare system," Alan Ryan notes in a review of Appiah, "it will be hard to persuade even generous people to take fairness seriously."[21] This is already part of the program of the regulation branch of the counterglobalization movement. It could also be heard in *The Nation*'s call for a "Green Deal: an environmentally based New Deal" as an approach to long-standing ecological crisis.[22] At the point where idealistic projects for the future intersect, however messily, with what is already happening on the ground, there is perhaps also something to say about the role that the delivery of social services has played in the rise of political parties like Hizbollah in Lebanon and Hamas in Palestine.

The concerns I have stressed about Appiah's new cosmopolitanism are largely those of the old, clean, normative cosmopolitans: concerns about militarism and concerns for economic redistribution (as contrasted with recognition, in Nancy Fraser's useful distinction). But I am not appealing for a return to the old rootlessness. What I am trying to illustrate here is the new, dirty cosmopolitanism. What could be dirtier than support for the welfare state, which blatantly favors citizens at the expense of noncitizens, thereby risking an exacerbation of global inequality, and which depends on the notoriously alienating powers of a bureaucracy that often treats applicants as presumptive criminals?[23] Even a dual program of defending the welfare state at home while extending its protections as far as possible to noncitizens is far from a satisfactory synthesis of political obligations at different scales. I am talking about a straining toward global justice that knows from the outset it is partial at best, limited and distorted by national self-interest. Still, for those who see the need for a still newer cosmopolitanism, one that demands more than the new cosmopolitanism's celebration of our hyphenated heterogeneity, here is one project to begin with.

# 2 NOAM CHOMSKY'S GOLDEN RULE

Noam Chomsky, arguably the most cosmopolitan of American intellectuals, is also a conspicuous practitioner of comparison. This is natural enough, for comparison is often associated with cosmopolitanism and indeed is sometimes taken as its signature operation. For some critics this is a decisive argument against both. In demanding an ever-increasing inclusiveness, cosmopolitanism is held to produce the illusory spectacle of the-world-as-a-whole. This spectacle was and is a product of imperialist violence, so the argument goes, and that violence is repeated in the everyday act of comparison. Comparison presupposes common norms; common norms, which by definition impose sameness on difference, presuppose a view from outside or above; the view from outside or above presupposes that the viewer is a holder of power. Thus both comparison and cosmopolitanism can be assimilated to capitalist globalization, which is understood to rule by reducing difference to homogeneity.[1]

It is no surprise to find this line of argument popular within literary studies, where it repeats the discipline's self-defining reverence for the unique, the particular, and the incomparable while making it seem that the discipline itself is anti-imperialist by its very nature. By the same token, however, there is a certain interest in following out the relations between cosmopolitanism and comparison in Chomsky, who is second to none (not even the literary left) in his denunciations of imperialism, yet who could not be less literary either in his writing or in his philosophical premises.

"The average life expectancy of a species," Chomsky writes on the first page of his book *Hegemony or Survival*, "is about 100,000 years." With the help of evolutionary biology, which routinely counts in units of hundreds of thousands of years, Chomsky sets himself up to take a very long view of "America's quest for global dominance"—that's the book's subtitle—and of everything else.[2] One page later, as if the biologist's perspective were not distant enough, Chomsky evokes humanity's capacity for self-destruction by adopting an even more distant viewpoint: that of "a hypothetical extraterrestrial observer" (2).

It does not seem accidental that Chomsky should appeal in this way to a "hypothetical extraterrestrial observer." In a sense, the extraterrestrial observer is his tutelary spirit. Chomsky has arguably become the most famous and most cosmopolitan public intellectual in the United States in large part because his viewpoint so successfully mimics that of a visitor to Earth from outer space. When we read him, whether we are Americans or not, we feel at least momentarily as if we ourselves were aliens, spectators looking down from a great height on the bad behavior of our fellow earthlings. This alienness gives a distinctive kind of rhetorical pleasure, and it has a distinctive kind of political force. The pleasure and the force come together to define Chomsky's distinctive version of cosmopolitanism, which allows readers not only to take a giant step backward from the assumptions of the United States about the essential rightness of its habitual ways of thinking, but also to enjoy the experience. I insist on the enjoyment because cosmopolitanism is so often represented as aridly intellectual, abstract, and detached, empty of such potentially compromising creaturely delights. And I insist on the rhetoric because, as I will propose, it is his rhetoric that allows us to see where, politically speaking, Chomsky belongs.

I stress that the hypothetical extraterrestrial observer is indeed a rhetorical figure. Such figures are not easy to spot in Chomsky. His writing is unusually bare of metaphor, wordplay, tonal variety. If he has a rhetorical signature, it is perhaps the refusal of any and all rhetorical eccentricity or creativity. He seems to compose as if expecting at any minute to be interrupted in order to be translated and as if any stylistic embellishment on his part could only be expected to get in the way of that process. Both expectations are entirely reasonable. As Franco Moretti has noted, the narrator's voice is the element of literary structure that is most anchored in its locality. As opposed to plots and character types, which are readily borrowed, voice has much more trouble crossing national and linguistic borders.[3] Chomsky's prose, on the other hand, is remarkably efficient at crossing borders. *Hegemony or Survival* has already been translated into forty-six languages. In this sense, too, Chomsky must be considered a cosmopolitan. By offering a minimum of resistance to translation, his prose makes a visible effort to approach as closely as possible to extraterrestrial universality, to be as little marked as possible by the accidents of his birth in a particular nation and his being raised in a particular language.

If Chomsky is trying to be transparent and universal, it follows that in attributing rhetoric to him, I will appear to be arguing with him, arguing at least with his implicit claim to be a universalist or cosmopolitan in the strongest sense. Rhetoric, as I understand it, is an inevitable sign of partiality or belonging. To be shown to be using rhetoric undercuts the cosmopolitan's claim to exist in a state of pure extraterrestriality or detachment. This argument does not count as a crippling critique, however, if one believes, as I do, that there is no such thing as cosmopolitanism in the strongest sense— that, as I've said, all cosmopolitanism involves some mode or degree of belonging, however minimal or reluctant. But if the critique is not damning, neither is it trivial. If no cosmopolitanism is pure, this doesn't mean that all cosmopolitanisms are equal. My purpose here is the delicate one of beginning to distinguish among unequal cosmopolitanisms, searching for significant differences in their ways of inhabiting the paradoxical condition of detachment and belonging and ways of judging those differences.

Rhetorically speaking, the key component in Chomsky's cosmopolitan voice is the act of comparing or, more precisely, an unrestricted, uninhibited practice of comparing. Chomsky draws comparisons without concern for anyone's tender sensibilities, especially not those of his compatriots. To make one's country and countrymen freely available for comparison seems to be his fundamental moral gesture. Though the following is, as he says, a "moral truism," it is nonetheless a useful one: "The standards we apply to others we must apply to ourselves" (605).[4] The slogan sounds a lot like the Golden Rule, and that is no doubt one reason it travels so well. At any rate, Chomsky has gotten a lot of mileage out of it. Consider how often he makes the exact same move in his comments in January 2009 about the Israeli invasion of Gaza that was then in process and the heavy civilian casualties it was inflicting. When an Israeli journalist speaks of "the price the inhabitants [of Gaza] will have to pay" in order for Israel to achieve order and security, Chomsky sarcastically inserts the statement into an unpleasant series of analogies: "The problem has been familiar to Americans in South Vietnam, Russians in Afghanistan, Germans in occupied Europe, and other aggressors." (Sarcasm is one rhetorical mode that, perhaps because it is relatively unambiguous, seems to translate pretty well.) Again: "*Times* columnist Thomas Friedman explained that Israel's tactics both in the current attack and in its invasion of Lebanon in 2006 are based on the sound principle of 'trying to "educate" Hamas, by inflicting a heavy death toll on Hamas militants and heavy pain on the Gaza population.' That makes sense on pragmatic grounds," Chomsky notes drily. "And by similar logic, bin Laden's effort to 'educate' Americans on 9/11 was highly praiseworthy, as were the Nazi attacks on Lidice and Oradour, Putin's destruction of Grozny, and other notable attempts at 'education.'"[5] That which we criticize in others we must also remember to criticize in ourselves and our allies. If we disapprove of the attacks of 9/11 or of the Nazi massacre of civilians in retaliation for acts of resistance, we must also disapprove of the Israeli devastation of Gaza. We cannot assume that the United States and its most reliable ally are somehow magically protected from the judgments that are routinely brought to bear upon nonallies, for example, Russia bombing the population of Grozny, al-Qaeda flying planes into the World Trade Center, or whatever.

Friedman is an easy target, yet he takes for granted nothing more than what most of us take for granted most of the time: that it is as natural and normal to root for our country as to root for our team, that where national belonging is concerned, it is natural and normal to apply a double standard. It's this simple, shockingly pervasive assumption that Chomsky quietly rejects. And with that foundational premise disposed of, various ideological edifices crumble. Comparison liberated from this premise—an unshackled, free-range comparison that almost looks like a different species from the domesticated variety we thought we knew—is the hero of Chomsky's cosmopolitanism.

Following his vigorous version of the Golden Rule, Chomsky specializes in asking whether the United States has done unto others what it would like done unto it. He compares the actions of the United States with the actions of other countries, especially those of whom the U.S. government and media express their strongest disapproval, so as to make the point that the United States itself has been either as bad or worse. For example: "The US itself is a leading terrorist state."[6] Or: "The US, in fact, is one of the most extreme religious fundamentalist cultures in the world" (21). Apropos of the U.S. "drug war" in Colombia, he writes, "Imagine the reaction to a proposal that Colombia or China should undertake fumigation programs in North Carolina to destroy government-subsidized crops used for more lethal products" (60–61). Bush's policy of "anticipatory self-defense" in Iraq resembled the Japanese policy at Pearl Harbor (12).[7] And so on. These are all great lines. One would like to see more students trained to feel their force and sent out into the world prepared to deliver lines like them. Hearing calls to boycott the Beijing Olympics in the name of Tibet, I naturally asked myself what Chomsky would say. Why didn't the U.S. media see fit to add, I thought, that if the Olympics had been happening in an American city, the war in Iraq would offer much stronger moral grounds than Tibet for Americans to boycott a U.S.-based Olympics?

Chomsky goes well beyond the now-customary celebrations of cosmopolitanism-as-diversity. If some of the celebrants have forgotten to ask whether cosmopolitanism helps persuade Americans to adopt a relation to the rest of the world that would make them less likely to bomb, invade, occupy, or otherwise mistreat the rest of the world, Chomsky has not. His voice demonstrates the moral power of rising above loyalty to one's homeland, tearing free of its peculiar cultural assumptions, and looking at it with an alien's eye. At the same time, however, this is not cosmopolitanism in a pure or absolute sense. (Here my argument makes a turn.) It is not a view from nowhere. True, Chomsky blames the United States as if he did not belong in any way to the United States, and as if his readers didn't either. When we Americans read Chomsky, we feel at least momentarily as if we ourselves were extraterrestrials, looking down on the misconduct of others.

It's not *our* misconduct; we're from another solar system. Reading him is pleasurable the way certain works of science fiction are. It turns us into visitors from another world, taking in the bizarre customs. We are confident at every instant that they are not our customs. Yet on second thought it is strange that we are so confident, because if we are Americans, they *are* our customs, at least in a sense of *our* that remains to be specified.[8]

Chomsky's practice of comparison tries hard to escape the constraint of national belonging. But that constraint reasserts itself, so to speak, negatively. The United States is criticized in almost all of Chomsky's comparisons. But that makes it the one fixed point of those comparisons. In other words, Chomsky puts the United States at the center of virtually all his judgments. It occupies a negative, devalued, nonhonorific center, but a center nonetheless. This means that other things are marginalized or excluded. The one consistent principle that is followed in his commentaries is that what the United States has done or is doing is wrong. No other principle gets more than the briefest recognition. Though Chomsky sounds like a universalist, his practice of national self-blaming is not in fact universalistic, unless you are ready to count the presumptive guilt of the United States in every case under discussion as an example of universalism. Chomsky will compare an action by the United States—say, the claim to "humanitarian intervention" in the 1990s—with an action by another nation—say, the interventions of India in Bangladesh in 1971 or of Vietnam in Cambodia in 1978. He will ask, quite rightly, why the latter did not get described by the so-called international community as humanitarian interventions, though each might be said to have stopped a genocide. But Chomsky does not stop and ask whether the actions of the Indian and Vietnamese governments were actually worthy of approval or not. What were their motives? Were they acting in a more disinterested way than the United States? Does he approve the principle that intervention is acceptable if it does stop a genocide? If so, he might be obliged to praise the United States if and when (perhaps in the former Yugoslavia) it could be established that it did just that. But if not, then he would be obliged to be critical of the Indian and Vietnamese governments and *their* excuses for intervention. It would seem that he backs off from such criticisms on the grounds that he is not himself Indian or Vietnamese. In other words, here we seem to be in the presence of a double standard based on national identity or location—not universalism at all, but nationalism in reverse.[9]

As someone committed to universal rational principles and the rhetoric of the Golden Rule, Chomsky might be expected to reject any hint of a double standard. The fact that he doesn't do so, that he is so reluctant to consider, say, the opinion of an Indian citizen about the Indian government, or the opinion of a Vietnamese citizen about the Vietnamese government, or for that matter the opinion of a Cambodian citizen who was perhaps saved by the intervention of the Vietnamese government (you see how this could go on)—the fact that no perspectives matter except perspectives about America, as long as they are wholly critical, is the negative sign of a concealed, disavowed Americanness.[10] It indicates that Chomsky's cosmopolitanism is not, after all, extraterrestrial but very American.

What difference does it make if we recognize that Chomsky's cosmopolitanism is, in its way, an imperfect, local, Americano-centric cosmopolitanism? My own view could be predicted from the argument above: there are plenty of things for which one can properly condemn Chomsky, but one can't condemn him simply for being a partial or imperfect cosmopolitan. Partial, imperfect cosmopolitans are the only cosmopolitans. A full, absolute, genuinely extraterrestrial cosmopolitanism doesn't exist. There is no cosmopolitanism without some degree or mode of belonging, even if that belonging takes the negative form of shame rather than the positive form of pride. All cosmopolitanism is really local or rooted or discrepant, patriotic or vernacular or actually existing. Therefore all cosmopolitanism is more or less paradoxical. The question is, what follows?[11] What is the next step? If there is no clean escape from the cosmopolitan paradox, aren't there at least significantly different ways of inhabiting it?

In moving toward an answer to this question, it needs to be said first of all that Chomsky's negative but intensely possessive mode of belonging to America has certain political disadvantages. One disadvantage is that it makes the rest of the American left disappear. It's as if he were saying, There can be only one alien, and that alien is me.[12] Michael Bérubé has described this heroically self-isolating pose in a Melvillean phrase: "I only am escaped from America to tell thee."[13] This pose is not helpful, for example, for those interested in encouraging solidarity or building movements. A further, related disadvantage is the series of lapses of political judgment and instances of badly misplaced solidarity into which Chomsky's anti-Americanism has led him. One famous example is his defense of Pol Pot. When the official American discourse was calling Pol Pot a mass murderer, Chomsky compared the Khmer Rouge with French resistance to the Nazis. (It's this that he's trying to conceal, I think, with his faint praise of the Vietnamese intervention to stop the Cambodian genocide—he himself was very late in recognizing that a genocide had happened.) Another example is his de facto denial of the Serbian ethnic cleansing of Bosnia and Kosovo and his opposition to any supranational intervention to stop it. Slobodan Milosevic may have been a thug, but so was the United States. What could possibly legitimate the intervention of one thug against another? Well, it's a fair question, but it's not an unanswerable one. One answer is, when one of them is at the moment in the act of committing genocide. Attacking Milosevic's attackers at that moment had the practical effect of defending both Milosevic and genocide.

Chomsky's objection could have been raised against efforts to save the Jews of Europe from the Nazis, had the Allies made any such efforts. After all, the Allies were not saints, were they? This objection could also have been raised against efforts by the United Nations to stop the Rwandan genocide, had the Clinton administration permitted the United Nations to act or even to use the G-word. Political action is rarely carried out by the saintly. There is something both irresponsible and extraterrestrial, therefore, about Chomsky's suggestion that he has decided the issue when he declares to all that the United States is a sinner, and at least as great a sinner as any other nation. What the U.S. government thinks or does can't be enough to decide anyone's political judgments or solidarities, whether positively or negatively. This point also applies to those occasions when anyone is tempted to assert that colonialism necessarily remains the sole or prime causal factor in each and every instance of human suffering and injustice in the former colonies.[14] It is possible to recognize the living legacy of colonialism without being quite so provincial, so negatively narcissistic about "the West." Negative narcissism is still narcissism.

The moral to be drawn here might appear to be: do as Chomsky says, not what he does. Apply the same standards to every nation, whether the United

States happens to like or hate that nation. On second thought, however, it seems possible that this is not the proper moral after all. Do we believe it is in fact right to apply standards equally to all? The question arises in Walter Benn Michaels's book *The Trouble with Diversity*.[15] Strangely, though their political purposes could not be more opposed, Michaels adopts a rhetoric of comparison that closely resembles Chomsky's.

In his brief against identity politics, Michaels rather cleverly compares the American political theorist Samuel Huntington with the Aymara Indians of Bolivia. The demand of indigenous peoples that their endangered cultures be protected from the assimilatory pressures of modernization, Michaels says, is precisely the same demand Huntington makes when he opposes the cultural and linguistic influence of Hispanic immigrants in order to preserve and defend a distinct American, Anglophone identity. The comparison seems perfect: "What Huntington wants for Americans is what . . . the Aymara Indians want for themselves: to preserve their (and our) identities" (148–49). Here Michaels applies precisely the same standard to the United States as to the Aymara Indians. I have no problem with embarrassing Huntington by comparing his own cultural conservatism to the identity politics he despises. Why then do I feel that this rhetoric is less egalitarian than it seems?

The reason for unease becomes clearer when Michaels follows his argument up and away into the imaginative (and equally Chomskyean) domain of the counterfactual—a flight of imagination that is demanded by the Golden Rule itself. Let us "imagine ourselves," Michaels tells his fellow Americans, "on the losing side of globalization. Imagine the United States fifty years from now—we're so poor that China and India are outsourcing production to the desperate and hence very hard-working masses of Michigan and Ohio" (162). This fantasy turns into an argument against Americans hanging on to English: "If we don't learn Hindi, we won't even be able to get the call center jobs that would keep us out of the sweatshops, where all our friends who just speak English work twelve hours a day making athletic shoes to be worn by Asians. . . . So when the United States is going to become the place jobs are outsourced to, I want to be able to speak Hindi or at least make sure that my children do. In a world where economic opportunity depends on the ability to speak Hindi, why would I want them to keep on speaking English?" (164–65).

Michaels calls this the "final twist," but it is not where the argument actually ends up. As the counterfactual fades and we return to the world where Americans have spent most of their time on the winning rather than the losing side of globalization and where English is not threatened with imminent extinction, the point of the argument once again becomes the irrationality of globalization's losers, who really are faced with the loss of their language and culture and who insist, against the manifest imperative of "economic opportunity," on wanting to preserve both. All of this *jeu d'esprit* comes back to the aim of discrediting the Aymara Indians. And the discrediting is accomplished by none other than Chomsky's Golden Rule. Look, Michaels says, I'm applying the same standard to myself that I apply to others. I am willing to give up my language in exchange for further economic opportunity. So why shouldn't they? As a reward for my magnanimity, I win the right to say that the Third World in general and indigenous peoples in particular must accept whatever deal global capital offers them, even if it means surrendering their languages and cultures. That's what I would do if I were in their place. You've just seen me put myself in their place.

The problem here is not whether the standard is applied equally and reciprocally. The problem is the standard itself. Whose standard is it? For Michaels, the standard appears to be successful adaptation to global capitalism. This standard arguably assumes an American-style self that travels light, always remaining itself no matter what it has to jettison. This makes a certain sense (less than Michaels assumes, but that isn't the point here) from the perspective of those who have gotten a relatively good deal from global capitalism. It makes much less sense if, as for the Aymara, jettisoning things like culture and language means that one would no longer *be* oneself. It's not that economic well-being is irrelevant to the Aymara. On the contrary. No moderately interested observer of indigenous struggles to preserve their languages and cultures could miss the fact that language and culture are not merely tokens of identity to be preserved for their own sake; they are also means to an economic end. In the nations and situations where peoples like the Aymara live, securing the right to practice one's language and culture belongs to the larger economic and political enterprise, the effort to seize control over lands, territories, and resources that are at present controlled or severely threatened by foreigners, including multinational corporations. Michaels's solution for the Aymara and other indigenous peoples, conveyed by the call center analogy, is to submit to the multinationals, exchanging their native languages for economic opportunity. He does not seem capable of imagining that one might actually contest the claims of the multinationals rather than submitting to them. Nor does he notice that preserving native languages might be a strategy for contesting those claims.

The results of the comparison will depend on the standard applied. Michaels's standard of successful adaptation to global capitalism, along with the streamlined self it implies, manifestly pushes the comparison in a different direction than it might have gone had the standard been, say, economic well-being. Economic well-being might conceivably be embraced by the Aymara themselves. Economic opportunity probably would not. If the standard of comparison demands a free, presocial individual, imagined to remain itself no matter how much of its cultural and linguistic baggage it throws overboard, then the Aymara are clearly placed at a disadvantage from the outset. Applying that standard allows North Americans who are willing to give up their language to look better and ensures that the Aymara will look worse. Michaels is perfectly willing to apply the same standard to himself that he applies to the Aymara. But it's his standard, not theirs, and thus the comparison plays to his advantage. The same point might be made about Chomsky's Golden Rule. He wants the same standards applied to U.S. citizens that we apply to others. But he has no means of objecting to standards as long as they *are* applied to us as well, even if the standards themselves favor us, thus winning comparative advantage for us if and when we do apply them both to ourselves and to others.

The reader may already have been speculating about one inequality buried within Chomsky's version of the Golden Rule: the inequality of power between the parties compared. Indeed, it is that inequality, provisionally removed by means of Michaels's counterfactual, that proves decisive once it is brought back in. But this inequality seems to work in Chomsky's defense. If he has deviated from true universality by always putting the United States at the center, it might be argued that the United States belongs at the center, precisely because it has so much power. The United States is, after all, not merely a power but a superpower, and as such it tilts the playing field between nations in its favor. You cannot judge a small, relatively powerless country by the same standards. Chomsky's practice, which deviates from his Golden Rule, is ethically superior to the Golden Rule.

This comes very close to what Chomsky himself argues when accused of falling away from a universal standard, though he presents his position in terms of another moral universal. "The most elementary moral principles," he writes, "would lead to 'playing up' the crimes of domestic origin in comparison to those of official enemies, that is, 'playing up' the crimes that one can do something about."[16] Principles are relative to responsibility, which is itself relative to proximity. We have more responsibility to criticize that misconduct which lies closest to hand, which we are most causally involved in and which we can most easily have an effect on. In this sense pure universalism would be a moral and political error. Comparisons must, after all, be selective.[17] As Chomsky says, this does seem to be an elementary moral principle. It was the indispensable response, for example, during the recent massacre of civilians in Gaza, when Zionists demanded that American critics of Israel spend equal time criticizing Hamas. No doubt Hamas had things to answer for. But we Americans, and especially we American Jews, were ethically obliged to spend greater critical energy on the evils supported by our government and committed in our name.

Still, there is an issue here, that of the relation between cosmopolitanism and power. Chomsky's version of the Golden Rule—"the standards we apply to others we must apply to ourselves"—is so successfully cosmopolitan because it does not seem to represent any one nation at the expense of any other and seems to rise above the power alignments and power imbalances that otherwise structure the world of nations. As we have seen, however, it never completely separates itself from power; even Chomsky's self-defense (the need to "play up" the crimes of one's own nation) assumes a greater power to affect the crimes of one's own nation. It assumes, in other words, that the American cosmopolitan possesses a certain power.[18] But the point is not merely that Chomsky should confess to the powers he secretly possesses by virtue of being an American citizen. That could be said, and most often is said, as if the only proper position were to be powerless. It's that position, a position I associate, rightly or wrongly, with his anarchism and with the more pervasive antistatism of our historical moment, that I'm arguing against here.

I illustrate from the book *On Suicide Bombing* (2007) by the anthropologist Talal Asad. Asad notes that so-called "legitimate violence exercised in and by the modern progressive state—including the liberal democratic state

—possesses a peculiar character that is absent in terrorist violence (absent not because of the latter's virtue but because of the former's capability)."[19] The usual criteria of virtue have been suspended here and replaced by criteria of capability. It's not that terrorist violence is virtuous; it's merely that it has less capability to harm than the violence of the state. This is perfectly right. Yet the implication seems to be that the lack of the capability to harm becomes, if not virtue itself, then a new functional substitute for virtue, the basis for a new ethics. This new ethics is antinormative because it is assumed that ethical norms have been put in place by the powerful, those who do have the capability to harm. It is anticosmopolitan because the perception that your very survival is threatened—the ultimate degree of powerlessness—justifies, following the logic of Carl Schmitt, an absolute embrace of your nation in defiance of all cosmopolitan universals. And, by the same token, it dispenses you from making moral judgments.

Chomsky specializes in making moral judgments, yet there is a striking overlap between Chomsky and Asad nonetheless. They share a kind of extraterrestriality, an internationalism of the putatively powerless. I elaborate on this point in my conclusion.

Though Chomsky is best known in the humanities as a Golden Rule universalist, whether because of his belief in a biologically based human nature or his famous debate with Michel Foucault in 1971, he often insists on the contamination of supposedly universal standards by unequal power.[20] He has been extremely critical of the selectivity of human rights, so much so as to be taken by some as an outright opponent of human rights.[21] In *Hegemony or Survival* ethical norms are presented as merely the random ideology of the latest crop of thugs.[22] In the debate with Foucault, similarly, Chomsky notes that "international law is, in many respects, the instrument of the powerful; it is a creation of states and their representatives. . . . It's simply an instrument of the powerful to retain their power" (48). He adds, however, that "international law is not *solely* of that kind. And in fact there are interesting elements of international law, for example, embedded in the Nuremberg principles and the United Nations Charter, which permit, in fact, I believe, *require* the citizen to act against his own state in ways which the state will falsely regard as criminal" (48–49). His impulse is to suggest that while much international law, like all domestic law, is a creation of the state, some international law is not, and it's the part of the law that is not produced by the state that's valid. Here we see Chomsky's anarchism, his assumption that whatever is created by states is invalid and must be resisted. (The epigraph to Chomsky's *For Reasons of State* is from Mikhail Bakunin: "The State is the organized authority, domination, and power of the possessing classes over the masses.") It is this anarchist assumption that seems to underlie his rhetorical opportunism about humanitarian intervention to stop genocide.[23] He cannot come out and say that what the governments of Vietnam and India did to stop genocide should indeed count as humanitarian intervention because to admit this would be to endorse the action of a state. States are always bad guys, except perhaps when they are in the act of resisting the United States.[24]

Yet the state is precisely what Chomsky does partially endorse—what he can't keep himself from endorsing, I want to say—when he talks about the law. When he's talking about law in general, it's clear that domestic law too has ethical validity in his eyes: "To a very large extent existing law represents certain human values, which are decent human values: and existing law, correctly interpreted, permits much of what the state commands you not to do" (47). The same is true about the parts of international law that he likes: they too are largely, if not entirely, produced by "states and their representatives" (47). Chomsky cannot sustain his anarchism if he is also going to be a cosmopolitan, and he cannot be a cosmopolitan without the state and the state's power. That power is also his power.

Let me put this another way. Here Chomsky is accepting implicitly a series of principles he absolutely refuses to accept explicitly. First, the principle that cosmopolitan standards he considers valid are produced in part by the power of states, whose authority he rejects. Second, and by extension, the principle that the cosmopolitan standards he considers valid are invested in part with the power of states. Third and more simply, the principle that cosmopolitanism is invested with power. Finally and most simply, the principle that having power is a good thing: a good thing for cosmopolitanism and a good thing for anyone who wants not just to interpret the world but to change it.

These principles flesh out Chomsky's self-defense against the charge of selectivity in his comparisons. The states we inhabit are agents over which we can have a certain leverage. In that sense they are proper objects of selective or disproportionate criticism. But they do not merely deserve unequal treatment because they are near at hand, causes of an evil for which we are responsible. This criticism is also merited because they are agents on which we can have an effect. As an anarchist, Chomsky may only want to say that the state can be resisted. But once he opens the door to the possibility of successful resistance, he can't block the possibility of also pushing the state to do things he believes in, as indeed it has already done in passing the laws of which he expressly approves. He cannot consistently deny that the state has already done things he would have liked it to do. That might mean desegregating the schools in Alabama (in Alabama in the 1950s and 1960s the local meant racism, and the federal government was fighting racism). Or it might mean stopping a genocide, as Chomsky almost concedes the Indian and Vietnamese states did.

In a sense I am only illustrating here the abstract theoretical point already made. All cosmopolitanism is paradoxical or imperfect in the sense that it involves belonging as well as detachment. Cosmopolitanism and belonging to a nation-state are not always and everywhere antithetical to one another. Usable power is, as it were, the good side of the imperfectness of Chomsky's extraterrestrial detachment, the hidden benefit in a disavowed belonging, a disavowed partiality. The point seems worth insisting on because it undermines Chomsky's anarchism and because anarchism is such a large, if only implicit, impulse in contemporary celebrations of a supposedly postnational condition. We cosmopolitan humanists do not like to acknowledge that we belong, in the strong sense, to states, though states, when we push them, do the work of guaranteeing human rights and providing welfare as well as (when we don't stop them) making war and keeping out unwanted migrants. Anarchists like to think of themselves as free but powerless. They are neither as free as they think nor as powerless. Power is not something that belongs only to the bad guys; it's certainly not a way of telling who *is* a bad guy. A better way of inhabiting the cosmopolitan paradox would involve recognizing that we are invested with a certain power and that despite the threat it brings to our ideal impartiality, we wouldn't mind having more of it.[25]


I want to conclude by returning to the practice of comparison as seen against a troubling background of unequal power. It is true that the scale of power matters. Asad's point was made and remade during the Israeli invasion of Gaza. It is grotesque to assume that a few rockets aimed at Israeli civilians by Hamas, however wrongly, can be properly met with the wholesale slaughter inflicted on the Palestinian inhabitants.[26] Any norm that justifies such slaughter by equating or balancing the two, as mainstream American discourse has repeatedly done, deserves to be treated as worthless. But many of us in the humanities generalize this position (mistakenly, in my view), preferring, like Asad, to place ourselves outside norms, thereby evading the supposed arrogance of speaking for humanity.

In her book *Frames of War* Judith Butler counsels Asad to reject this move. She first makes the Foucauldian point that normativity is indeed interfered with by "the differential of power."[27] The category of the human, she warns, is already normative in a way that tilts the comparison in favor of some and against others. So, yes, speaking for humanity is a problem. Yet the refusal to do so is also a problem. When Asad offers an anthropological understanding of suicide bombing in place of and as opposed to any normative judgment, one might say he presents himself as a sort of extraterrestrial, looking on with complete detachment from the urgencies of judgment that mere humans feel obliged to respond to.[28] By this account scholarship itself would become a cosmopolitan space in the extraterrestrial sense: ethically speaking, it would be a space of perfect nonbelonging. Asad responds to Butler's call for explicit normative frameworks in *Is Critique Secular?* (2009). He rejects the evaluative, authoritative notion of critique, which he takes Butler to espouse, describing it as "no less violent than the law—and no more free" (14). His preferred alternative seems to be sensibility (47), which puts its emphasis "not on *doubt* but on a particular kind of cultivation of the self" (54). This attempt to hide behind the late Foucault reveals its fundamental evasiveness when Butler renews her question, asking Asad "what moral or political end" his efforts aim at. He replies that there can be no answer to this question. Why not? Because, he says, "it is precisely the implications of things said and done in different circumstances that one tries to understand" (138). In other words, all he is doing is trying to understand, and trying to understand is not an action in the world that itself has worldly implications and consequences. Again Asad claims to be above the fray, merely describing or analyzing but not judging, as if he enjoyed the peculiar privilege of operating outside of history and outside of politics. This is a traditional liberal position, even a caricature of it. It's a bit bizarre coming from someone who directs so much anger at liberalism.[29]

Asad's vanishing act is an acute danger for anyone who depends on a politics of comparison. One who criticizes another nation typically compares that nation with her own but leaves her own nation out of bounds, safely unscrutinized. It's this nationalist habit, particularly obnoxious in the United States, that Chomsky so vibrantly exposes and demolishes. He makes the unmarked term visible again. Yet the same thing can happen when one compares two other nations or situations, and in that case the risk is that the third term, the comparer himself, will become ethically invisible. It's this risk that I think Butler is revealing to Asad, and her warning seems relevant to Chomsky as well.

In the case of the Khmer Rouge, one of the statements that got Chomsky into trouble was an act of comparison between the outrage expressed in the West against Pol Pot and the relative silence that greeted the simultaneous, extremely bloody Indonesian invasion of East Timor in December 1975, which was backed by the United States. "In the case of Cambodia reported atrocities have not only been eagerly seized on by the Western media but also embellished by substantial fabrications," Chomsky wrote. "The case of Timor is radically different. The media have shown no interest in examining the atrocities of the Indonesian invaders, even though in absolute numbers they are on the same scale" (Rai, 28). Chomsky's defender Milan Rai comments that the focus in this piece is "on assessing the performance of the media—its handling of the evidence available at the time. The focus is not on judging the situation in Cambodia itself" (28). Rai finds it incomprehensible, then, that Chomsky and his cowriter Edward Herman "were harshly attacked for allegedly doubting the facts of the Khmer Rouge massacres" (29). A critic who accuses Chomsky of saying that the Cambodian "executions have numbered at most in the thousands" is reprimanded by Rai, who goes back to the original article. In that article we read, "Such journals as the *Far Eastern Economic Review*, the London *Economist*, the *Melbourne Journal of Politics*, and others elsewhere, have provided analyses by highly qualified specialists who have studied the full range of evidence available, and who concluded that the executions have numbered at most in the thousands" (29–30). Rai concludes, "Chomsky was not presenting *his* conclusion 'as based on the analysis of highly qualified specialists themselves'; he was presenting the conclusions of the specialists themselves, without comment" (30).

To pretend you can hide behind the authorities you cite is strange, especially strange for an anarchist who is so reluctant to attribute authority to experts or specialized knowledge. To hide behind the authorities is like hiding between the two objects of a comparison, such as Cambodia and East Timor: it assumes that the one who is making the comparison is not part of the events that are under analysis, that the speaker citing others need make "no comment" on what is going on. To present the analysis of qualified specialists without rebuttal and without comment is, in effect, to say those words oneself. In this case, it is to radically diminish the Cambodian genocide, even if only in order to prove the existence, in the Western media, of "an appalling double standard regarding Cambodia and East Timor" (31). Ethically speaking, Chomsky makes himself disappear—that is, he claims to be a "hypothetical extraterrestrial observer."[30]

Butler's point about Asad is that his extraterrestrial withdrawal from normative judgment is not wrong (there are good reasons to be wary of norms). Rather, it is weaker than it needs to be: "There is a *stronger* normative position here—a more consequential exploration of normativity—than its author explicitly allows." She repeats the comparative term "stronger." She insists that there is no stepping outside the practice of comparison. Asad's argument that terrorism cannot be considered apart from state violence depends implicitly on "a horizon of comparative judgment," she says, and when Asad is comparative he is also normative. He is normative despite his attempted refusal of normativity. This is what gives Asad's argument "its rhetorical force." Accepting that he is indeed speaking normatively, presumably even if this entailed making a moral judgment on suicide bombing, would make his argument stronger.

I read Butler's recourse to the vocabulary of force and strength as also, simultaneously, a way of making a theoretical point about power. I take her to be saying that, however reluctantly, Asad is participating in shared norms and thus in the social power that those norms embody. He seems to prefer imagining himself as outside such norms, hence as powerless. But that is not the case, either for him or for Chomsky, nor should it be what he and Chomsky desire. Both are right to condemn state violence. But they are wrong to condemn the state as sole possessor of power or, what seems to follow from it, to condemn the possession of power as such. State violence cannot be shielded from comparison with so-called terrorism, as it is by the prevailing discourse. But the comparison between the two, once launched, suggests that power can and must be fought with alternative power. A cosmopolitan theory of power must insist, with Foucault, that power is distributed more widely and unpredictably. Power is never absolute, and one can never reject it absolutely. Cosmopolitanism cannot go about acquiring more power unless it begins by admitting that it already has some power.

As I have established, the landscape of comparison is always distorted from below by differentials of power. Yet that should not stop anyone from practicing comparison, and practicing it both so as to expose the hidden normativity of certain comparisons and to find a normativity that will empower our own countercomparisons. Incomparability and incommensurability, which attempt to escape entirely from norms, cannot determine our goal. The aim, as Butler says, "is not to dispense with normativity, but to insist that normative inquiry take on a critical and comparative form." This measured embrace of comparison is what will make our cosmopolitan arguments stronger and our strength more cosmopolitan, at a time when we need both more cosmopolitanism and more strength.

## 3 BLAMING THE SYSTEM
Immanuel Wallerstein

I take the title "Blaming the System" from Luc Boltanski's book *Distant Suffering*.[1] Inspired, it would seem, by the relatively successful public opinion campaigns waged by NGOs like Doctors Without Borders, Boltanski turns his attention to a series of rhetorical tropes that were more and less effective in eliciting a large-scale public response. He runs these tropes through a body of thinking about compassion and philanthropy emanating mainly from the Anglo-Saxon tradition. Out of these materials he tries to build the supporting theory for a newly politicized humanitarianism. His point of departure is the situation in which suffering is observed by a nonsufferer, as in the story of the Good Samaritan. At least temporarily the nonsuffering observer is lucky, which is to say, circumstantially superior to the sufferer. The observer is therefore not the sufferer's natural political ally. There is no preexisting affiliation between the two, neither a common interest nor a common identity that would push the observer to come to the sufferer's aid. Hence a sense of solidarity or obligation must be created ex nihilo by the power of speech. For Boltanski, situations of detached, disinterested inequality like this, which seem to defy the categories of politics, pose a severe but unavoidable challenge to existing forms of rhetoric.

This challenge is at its most daunting in the case of speech across great distance, social as well as physical distance. An example would be someone (for Boltanski, it doesn't matter who) addressing a First World audience on the subject of Third World poverty. In the key chapter devoted to the rhetoric of denunciation, the act by which the spectator of suffering is moved from pity to indignation and accuses those responsible—that is, what I have been calling simply blaming—Boltanski writes, "The greater the distance between the persecutor and his victim," the longer the "causal chain between the unfortunate and the agent who causes his suffering," and the more rhetorical work has to be done to establish a connection (62). Consider "an unfortunate who dies of hunger in a shanty-town. His persecutor, who has never seen him, occupies an office in Paris or New York at the head office of a holding company from which he works on the financial markets. How can the connection between unfortunate and persecutor be made to stick?" (62). The ability to denounce successfully under these conditions, Boltanski says, requires the mediation of a "theory of power" (62). For only a theory of power will be able to distinguish such cases from cases of "suffering which, however distressing [they] may be, [are] inherent in the human condition" (62), that is, from suffering that cannot properly be described as political. This is an unconventional but useful frame in which to consider the account of global power that Immanuel Wallerstein's world-systems theory supplies.

Some kinds of suffering cannot be politicized, and their definition is neither obvious nor stable. Boltanski notes that the borderline between suffering that is and isn't held to be inherent in the human condition, hence between what can and cannot be denounced, is "constantly being drawn and redrawn" (63). The chapter ends by facing a related, even more sobering difficulty: the denunciation of system, or the question of how and whether accusation can be "shifted from *persons* on to larger de-individualized entities such as *systems* or *structures*" (73). Brought face to face, so to speak, with a faceless system, the rhetoric of denunciation becomes, if not paradoxical, at least "more fragile, because the extension of networks, the lengthening of connections, and the multiplication of mediations which have to be secured in order to make an accusation stick, increase the number of points on to which doubts and challenges can be hooked" (73). This confrontation with system seems to be replaying an origin story about the discipline of sociology, in which Boltanski, like Wallerstein, works. He notes that generalizing from particular unfortunates and their singular fates is what sociology has always done. Hence one would imagine that sociology had long ago figured out ways of dealing with the doubts and challenges provoked by distance and generalization. But perhaps, for Boltanski, sociology does not, after all, stand on firm foundations. At any rate, he does not seem to feel that the discipline's existence guarantees the feasibility of denouncing systematically produced suffering. Where denunciation is concerned, even the tiniest step away from his paradigm, for example, pity for a particular sufferer or indignation at a particular perpetrator, is presented as fraught with extreme rhetorical danger.[2] Whether an individual sufferer is made representative of some larger collectivity or a system rather than an individual is held responsible for the suffering, there is a lessening in the emotional intensity experienced by the listener. Where it is systems or structures rather than persons that must be blamed, the same theory of power that is needed to enforce the link between sufferer and accused would also seem to threaten the accuser's freedom to act otherwise, hence his or her responsibility. "Accusation cannot abandon all orientation towards responsibility without falling into self-contradiction," Boltanski writes. "It is the very possibility of things happening otherwise and, consequently, the existence of responsibility, which distinguishes the denunciation of suffering about which it seems reasonable to be *indignant* from the attitude of *resignation* which prevails in the case of sufferings about which nothing can be done" (75). The more powerful the system, the more resigned to it the listener will tend to be.

The chapter ends, a bit vaguely, on its own note of resignation. Regarding the possibilities for efficacious denunciation on the collective or systematic level, Boltanski suggests that perhaps after all the enterprise is doomed to failure. He quotes Paul Ricoeur on German war guilt to the effect that accusation is sound only if it is limited to the criminal accusation of individuals (76).[3] This citation helps undermine any confidence that humanitarianism can be raised to the level of a politics, as Boltanski wants—that is, any notion that mere words can create the sort of international solidarity that might make a significant difference to the shape of the world or the shape of world power. Though he is merely offering his judgment of what works, not of what he would like to work, Boltanski leaves readers feeling that they may have no choice but to resign themselves to the inevitable.

The moral of Boltanski's argument on denunciation, as I understand it, is that too much concern with or belief in an ultimate, distanced source of injustice will undermine solidarity with distant sufferers, along with the habit of denouncing and the faith that a spectator's words can make a difference. In order to keep the faith that words can make a difference, you would do better to give up on systemic theories of power and instead stay focused on individuals in pain, on individuals relaying that pain to us, and (in third place) on individuals immediately responsible for that pain, if such individuals are identifiable. In a sense, this would mean generalizing the media logic that has been observed over and over in cases of celebrity humanitarianism: publicity that is accorded to the celebrity (Bono, Angelina Jolie, Bernard-Henri Lévy) and to the individual sufferer who is discovered, pointed out, and emoted over by the celebrity is attention diverted away from the deep political causes that produced the suffering in the first place. In Boltanski's effort to politicize humanitarianism, there is a zero-sum relation between the power of words and a systemic theory of power. Political stupidity is built in.

It seems obvious enough that what is needed in such cases is, on the contrary, a mode of intelligence that is specifically political. After such disasters as the massive humanitarian aid to Rwandan refugees in 1994, aid which compensated psychologically for the international community's failure to stop the genocide but ironically helped sustain the power of its Hutu perpetrators, this point has become common sense among many humanitarian activists. As for humanists, the case is not so clear. Humanists tend to share both Boltanski's investment in words and his suspicion that to recognize power as systemic or structural is to undermine the power of speech. To humanists, blaming the system is likely to seem a mistake. In a forthcoming book called *Blaming the System*, Clifford Siskin argues in what I think is a representative way both that systems are a generic construct and that they are constructed in order to be blamed, that is, in order to help individuals evade their proper, that is, individual, responsibility.[4] Collective, structural, systemic responsibility is a problem for us. The question is whether belief in the constructive power of words, and other valuable disciplinary assumptions that extend into other cultural disciplines as well, can be reconciled with the best possible maps of systemic power. We need such maps. Without them, how can we separate suffering as such, to which the appropriate response may indeed be resignation, from suffering that can and should be an object of action? How can we know anything about the likely political effect of our words, however articulate and well intentioned they may be?

The mapmaker under consideration here, though he is by no means the only one to whom this argument might apply, is Immanuel Wallerstein. The humanities have been quick to address their responsibilities in the era of so-called globalization, but they have reacted to Wallerstein's world-systems theory with a strange mixture of attraction and repulsion. The repulsion is most often seen as the result of a fundamental difference of opinion about the value and significance of "culture," a term which I will here take as standing in, however crudely, for the object of knowledge of the humanities and will henceforth liberate from its quotation marks. The culture problem is real, but defenses of the cultural tend to be, one might say, defensive, that is, hasty, instinctive, and unedifying. Worse, they tend to ignore the rich uncertainties as to what culture is and does, uncertainties that we in the humanities would otherwise freely admit. For example, to what extent can culture be identified with the Kantian aesthetic and thus with the disinterestedness that Boltanski, Rawls-like, inscribes into the origin of his narrative of global ethics? Assuming, as I think most people in the humanities would, that culture provides necessary equipment with which to cross the planetary landscape Wallerstein has mapped, does aesthetic disinterestedness have the same depoliticizing effect on the humanities that it has, as I've just suggested, on humanitarianism?

The aesthetic coexists uneasily with terms like *blame* and *praise*, which belong to the instrumental, interested vocabulary of rhetoric.[5] Rhetoric, as I noted in discussing Chomsky, is a sign of belonging and thus something that both dirties cosmopolitanism and allows us to think of it as wielding a certain power. Whether rhetoric and aesthetics are taken as antithetical or not—within rhetoric, praise and blame are among the least functional, most nearly aesthetic forms—the issue is power. Words have it, but it's not enough to say so. There must be some way of avoiding a zero-sum game between belief in the power of words and belief in the power of the system, some way of overcoming in discourse humanitarianism's structural inattention to final causes and ethical ends.


In the introduction to his career-making book *The Modern World-System* (1974), Wallerstein describes his early intellectual trajectory as a quest for the "appropriate unit of analysis." This quest resulted, he says, in a rejection of both state and society on the grounds that each of these units is limited to the scale of the nation, hence incoherent: "I decided that neither one was a social system and that one could only speak of social change in social systems. The only social system in this scheme was the world-system" (7).[6]

The assumption that coherence, lacking at the level of the nation, is to be rediscovered at a global or transnational level is not an unfamiliar premise for humanities scholars. Thanks in part to the force of Wallerstein's arguments and his synthesis of historical scholarship, this premise has become one of the most appealed to and productive across a wide variety of disciplines and interdisciplinary areas. Sometimes the filiation to Wallerstein himself is explicit, as in the cultural criticism of Fredric Jameson and Edward Said and, more recently, in the intriguing theory of world literature proposed by Franco Moretti. But it is no less significant when it goes unacknowledged. The index to Paul Gilroy's pathbreaking book *The Black Atlantic* (1993) has no entry for Wallerstein, but when Gilroy proposes that cultural historians "take the Atlantic as one single, complex unit of analysis" (15), the borrowing seems unmistakable.[7] If scholarly justice were to be done, many of the copious footnotes in which recent writers on transoceanic diaspora and other versions of the transnational express their methodological debt to Gilroy would simultaneously be credited to Wallerstein's account.

Yet if Wallerstein stands among the founders of what is now very close to a scholarly consensus, the distinctness of his individual place in this distinguished company is less evident. Even many of those who cite him would probably not fully support his identification of system as the single mandatory unit of scholarly analysis. And a similar lack of clarity affects the consensus itself, which, like other collective enthusiasms, has been loath to slow down and ask where exactly it is heading or should be heading. I share the assumption that the transnational turn is desirable and in any case unavoidable. Yet it seems a good idea to ask how best to take this turn—where we are likely to end up, interpretively speaking, if we make use of any one of the intellectual vehicles available, each whipping us around the curve with various degrees of momentum and abandon. World-systems theory is one such vehicle, though to its critics not always the best-handling.[8] But the resistance to world-systems theory, of which there has been a great deal, especially in the humanities, is also a mode of conveyance. Whether or not it keeps us safe, it does not keep us in place; it takes us somewhere else. If we are going to choose between system and antisystem, it is better to know the alternative destinations.

My aim is to reflect critically both on Wallerstein's commitment to system as the privileged unit of analysis and on those habits of thinking in the humanities that appear to discourage such a commitment. One of those habits is reverence for our cultural objects, or the rhetorical practice of praise. (This is a practice that the most Wallersteinian of contemporary literary critics, Moretti, has characteristically and almost uniquely chosen to forego.) The practice of blaming has been less acknowledged, perhaps because the humanities have recently been accused of violating their very nature by doing too much of it. Yet blame is the inescapable counterpart of praise, and it is also a privileged link to the domain of the political. It's not for nothing that Chomsky is one of the great blamers of recent times. In search of greater lucidity about the conflicted nature of our commitments, as well as the promise or perhaps the threat of possible common ground between the humanities and Wallerstein, it seems worthwhile to pursue the difficulties and rewards of the practice of blaming when the object in question exists, as Wallerstein proposes, on the scale of the world-system.

In his essay "The Rise and Future Demise of the World Capitalist System: Concepts for Comparative Analysis," also published in 1974, Wallerstein defined *system* as follows: "We take the defining characteristic of a social system to be the existence within it of a division of labor, such that the various sectors or areas are dependent upon economic exchange with others for the smooth and continuous provisioning of the needs of the area. Such economic exchange can clearly exist without a common political structure and even more obviously without a common culture" (74–75).[9] Politics and culture exist within the system, but neither does anything to make it systematic. What defines it as a system, hence as the (one) unit of analysis that has to be studied, is a common division of labor. From the perspective of the humanities, whose object of knowledge is culture, this is an unacceptable privileging of the economic at the expense of the cultural. It has been unpopular, and understandably so.[10] The most obvious reason the humanities have not made more of Wallerstein's work is that while culture shows up from time to time, it is never allowed to play a very significant role. Here

Wallerstein differs from, say, Michel Foucault or Pierre Bourdieu. Each could be described as a systemic thinker, yet each has had a more visible individual impact on the cultural disciplines, and this despite the further fact that, unlike Wallerstein, each has had rather hostile things to say about culture. Indeed, both Foucault and Bourdieu could be said to attribute many of society's ills to the cultural-discursive realm. In so doing, however, each attributes great causal importance to culture, an importance that both assert is irreducible to noncultural or nondiscursive factors. This is more than enough reason for Foucault and Bourdieu to have been embraced. From the viewpoint of the cultural disciplines, blaming culture is a way of flattering culture.

Is flattery what the humanities require? I hope not. In taking culture's relative insignificance as a slap in the face, have the humanities overreacted? Perhaps. These questions offer an invitation to disciplinary self-consciousness that there is good reason to accept.

As a further motive for self-consciousness in the humanities, consider this further explanation for our resistance to Wallerstein. It's not just that Wallerstein's scheme doesn't give culture much of importance to do. From its very beginning, the concept of culture has also been deeply opposed, indeed constitutively opposed, to the very concept by which Wallerstein defines system, namely, the division of labor. As Raymond Williams tells the story in *Culture and Society* (1958), the division of labor names the characteristic disease of social and individual fragmentation that, in the decades following the Industrial Revolution, first calls into being the compensatory wholeness of the culture concept. As an antidote to society's modern divisiveness, culture is antisystem, at least in Wallerstein's sense, from its very origins in the romantic movement.[11] Thus almost all of the "Culture-and-Society" tradition, left as well as right, identifies system as its enemy. Matthew Arnold is "eternally dissatisfied with 'the men of a system,'" that is, "with men like Comte, or the late Mr Buckle, or Mr Mill."[12] On the whole, so are thinkers and writers like Charles Dickens and George Orwell, George Eliot and T. S. Eliot. This aspect of the tradition persists bizarrely into figures who might otherwise have seemed antithetical to it. Foucault was professor of the History of Systems of Thought, but he could take over from Arnold as the preeminent thinker for scholars in the humanities largely because, for him as well, system seemed to name society's prime antagonist.[13] Said, arguably Foucault's most important mediator in the United States, managed this mediation only by demanding a place for criticism that would be "between culture and system," a position that, despite its apparent symmetry, favors culture over system.[14] At any rate, since his death in 2003 Said has consistently been praised, in terms he himself sometimes invited, as a fundamentally antisystemic thinker, where *system* is a code word for the French theory builders. Thus Abdirahman Hussein suggests that Said troubled other people's wisdom instead of offering any systematic wisdom of his own, rejecting methodology in order to be open-ended (4).[15] If these are the standard terms of praise, then Wallerstein will not often be praised by the humanities, though he is in fact praised by Said himself.

Many readers will judge this suspiciousness about system to be no more than common sense. And to some extent it is, even if the humanistic common sense that values the particular over the general is no less ideological than the reverse. Doubts can and should be raised about the notion of system as pure economic necessity, unaffected in any decisive way by culture or politics. Wallerstein writes that his "concept of a grid of exchange relationships assumes a distinction between *essential* exchanges and what might be called 'luxury' exchanges. This is to be sure a distinction rooted in the perceptions of the actors and hence in both their social organization and their culture. These perceptions can change. But this distinction is crucial if we are not to fall into the trap of identifying *every* exchange as evidence of the existence of a system" (82–83).[16] In an "exchange of preciosities" between two systems, he goes on, "each can export to the other what in *its* system is socially defined as worth little in return for the import of what in its system is worth much" (83). Social perception, or what we might want to call culture, is allowed to define worth for the exchange of luxuries. But the exchange of luxuries does not define a system, for it entails only " 'reaping a windfall' and not obtaining a profit" (83). Or does it only entail, as Wallerstein then suggests, not obtaining a maximum profit? If *some* profit can indeed be reaped by an exchange of what might be called luxuries, as the word *maximum* suggests, then there can be no absolute, theoretical line between luxuries and necessities, between the purely economic logic of the division of labor and a messier logic that would have to factor in the effect of cultural perception, class struggle, and so on. In short, there would be no purely economic line between system and nonsystem.[17] This does not imply that there cannot be any such thing as system, but only that if there is—and in any given case it seems advisable not to assume in advance that system does in fact exist—then culture cannot ipso facto be excluded from what makes it systematic. In other words, all significant causal necessity cannot be denied to noneconomic factors like politics and culture.[18] Indeed, Wallerstein himself cannot flesh out the recent history of the world-system without making continual reference to these factors.[19]

To say this, however, is not necessarily to embrace the classic critique of world-systems theory (to many humanists, a conclusive critique) articulated by Marshall Sahlins. Indignant at the idea of culture as merely a passive reflection of economic relations, Sahlins insisted that in indigenizing Western economic and cultural exports, so-called peripheral peoples were shaping their own history, not allowing it to be shaped by a world-system. World-systems theory made "colonized and 'peripheral' peoples the passive objects of their own history and not its authors," thereby leaving nothing for anthropology—you could as easily substitute English or comparative literature here—to do "but the global ethnography of capitalism. Anthropology would be manifest destiny. For other societies were regarded as no longer possessing their own 'laws of motion'; nor was there any 'structure' or 'system' to them, except as given by Western-capitalist domination" (412–13).[20] The logic here takes for granted the absolute claims of the particular, not universally, as it were, but at the level of the discipline. If you are right, Sahlins in effect complains, then my discipline would be in trouble. Anthropology's disciplinary object would become insignificant. Therefore I can't allow the possibility that you might be right.

This is not strong logic. Disciplinary special pleading cannot settle the question. For the humanities, the fact that Wallerstein doesn't accept the premise that culture is causally decisive or relatively autonomous or otherwise especially significant ought, on the contrary, to be taken as a valuable aid to reflection. We can hardly ask anyone outside the humanities to accept the value of our work if we take our premises for granted, no matter how blatantly self-serving they may be, and never expose them to a hostile or merely skeptical scrutiny. Your true friends are not the ones who politely withhold that scrutiny. They are the one who force you to make the case.

A response that would look better in public, and to ourselves, would have to engage more directly with the motives and results of Wallerstein's work—

not necessarily in its own terms, but at least as translated into a cross-disciplinary ethical lingua franca. Such translation would not be difficult. As seen with nonspecialist eyes, Wallerstein's research seems to have had a relatively simple and compelling motivation: a desire to understand the sad state of the postcolonial world in the 1970s, the failure of seemingly victorious movements of national liberation to change the basic political and economic inequality between developed and underdeveloped countries. What was needed, it seemed to Wallerstein, was a deeper level of causality. In search of it, he went back to the acquisition of European political and economic superiority in the early modern period, the moment when a division was established, he argued, between core and periphery. The modern world-system he saw taking shape in that period worked to ensure the systematic transfer of surplus from the periphery to the core without military conquest and without the universalizing of wage labor but merely by means of market exchange. The result, in other words, was a theory of power at the global scale, a theory that was all the more persuasive because it accounted not only for how the present inequality of power and resources at the level of the planet came to exist, but also, and crucially, for how it managed to perpetuate itself despite seemingly dramatic rebellions and reversals, like the movements of national independence.

This theory puts social scientists on the spot, but not them alone. Anyone recognizing and wishing to change the present continuing state of global inequality, whatever her or his discipline, would seem to have an unavoidable interest in such a theory. This would include most humanists I know. If planetary injustice matters to us as much as we say it does, then we cannot in good conscience stand up for our particular zone of expertise without trying to show what effect phenomena within that zone and our expert way of interpreting such phenomena are capable of having on the fate of planetary injustice. This is a task that Sahlins, for all his outcry on behalf of the agency of non-Western people, simply does not undertake. In *Genealogies of Religion: Discipline and Reasons of Power in Christianity and Islam*, Talal Asad comments on Sahlins's "protest against the idea that the global expansion of capitalism, or the World System so-called, has made the colonized and 'peripheral' peoples the passive objects of their own history and not its authors" (3). As Asad says, "no one is ever entirely the author of her own life" (4).[21] "To the extent that what Sahlins calls the larger system determines the conditions within which things take on meaningful places, all peoples can be said to be the passive objects of their own history and not its authors" (5). "To take the extreme example: even the inmates of a concentration camp are able, in [Sahlins's] sense, to live by their own cultural logic. But one may be forgiven for doubting that they are *therefore* making their own history" (4). The system cannot be treated (here Asad's object is Sherry Ortner) as if it were an abstraction or "a mere fiction" (5). In fact, "some theoretical idea of world capitalism is necessary if its historical consequences are to be recognized" (5). Asad concludes, with powerful understatement, "If anthropology's distinctive contribution requires it to take a *ground level* view of things, it is difficult to see how confining oneself to that level is sufficient to determine in what degree and in what way other levels become relevant" (6).

That people make their own history should not be pious dogma, cut loose from all pragmatic concern about global injustice and how to work against it. It should be an open question: how far have people actually been able to make their own history in this case or that case, under these circumstances or those? Phrased as a genuine uncertainty, this proposition can guide research that will be genuinely valuable precisely because it will help us understand what can and can't be done about global injustice and thus how our interpretive puzzles do (or don't) contribute to that goal. To put this in a more popular register: you have to remain open to the possibility that the ship you are on might be the *Titanic* and what you are doing might be of no more consequence than rearranging the deck chairs.

The lack of clarity that results when scholars in the humanities, reacting against systematicity, refuse to ask Asad's question or Wallerstein's—the question of whether or how far culture really does make a difference to inequality at the world scale—can be illustrated by an article in PMLA called "Beyond Discipline? Globalization and the Future of English." The author, Paul Jay, declares that although the nation-state persists, "the rapid circulation of cultural commodities . . . has come at the expense of the nation-state's ability to control the formation of national subjectivities and ideologies. . . . Culture is now being defined in terms less of national interests than of a shared set of global ones" (32).[22] As a result, Jay declares, the prime task of English today is to wean itself away from its national and nationalist paradigm and adapt instead to the new global givens. But what does this mean? What version of the transnational turn is he describing? Initially, the answer is: Wallerstein's. But having laid out Wallerstein's theory of the world capitalist system, Jay immediately steps back from it, complaining that this notion of system is primarily economic. On this point Jay takes the side of what he calls "globalization theorists." Globalization theorists, from whom literary and cultural studies will properly take their cue, hold that "culture is not subordinated to the economy. Rather the two are interdependent" (35). Here the crucial figure is Arjun Appadurai (38ff), whose object is "'the social work of the imagination.'"[23] For Appadurai, "Globalization cannot be reduced to Westernization or Americanization" (39).

This sounds innocuous enough; indeed it sounds like a point that in many situations still very much needs to be made. But to say that culture and economics are interdependent (neither of them causally privileged at the expense of the other) is not quite accurate, at least where Appadurai is concerned. The title of Appadurai's position-defining essay was "Disjuncture and Difference in the Global Cultural Economy." The word *disjuncture* marked a crucial and very explicit insistence not on the interdependence of the cultural and the economic, but on the disjoining of culture from economics. In cutting the legs out from under the Americanization thesis by asserting (rightly) that indigenization often trumps homogenization and that flows of capital do not dictate the one true meaning of flows of culture, Appadurai went further: he asserted, in effect, that there is no system which links the two sorts of flows. There is no system, period.[24] That's why the global cultural economy is divided into a series of so-called scapes, each distinct and disconnected from the others. When Appadurai says that Wallerstein's theory has "failed to come to terms with what Lash and Urry have called disorganized capitalism" (275), disorganization is a synonym for disjuncture, which is the antithesis of system. The result, considered as a way of taking the transnational turn, is to conflate that turn with an emancipatory flowering of the cultural, but one in which culture is disjoined from other dimensions of the project of emancipation.

Like the humanities generally, Jay does not seem to take the full measure of his own hesitation in the face of system and what it entails. He is critical of Appadurai for not considering the "class differences" that "mark these cultural flows and transformations" (40). The criticism may not be unfair, but Jay has forfeited his right to make it. For in opting for the piety of interdependence and allowing that piety to replace any actual, necessarily less pious theory of what is in fact more or less dependent on what—in other words, in rejecting system as such—Jay has ruled out just the sort of explanation that he criticizes Appadurai for not proposing. Appadurai, having floated the slogan of disjuncture, is perfectly consistent in evading the weighty yoking of culture to class. For theories of class are theories of inequality, theories of systematic injustice—theories of the conjoining of culture to economics. To add class is to give up on disjuncture. Trying to add class as if it were a random constituency or as if the researcher had an obligation to ask how globality looks to the inhabitants of Sioux Falls or Fall River, Jay is asking for something he doesn't want: a systematic account of inequality. If we want class, then we want system, or want to be able to see real, if always provisional and imperfect, systematicity wherever it may exist. And we cannot be critical of Wallerstein for being committed to system in this sense.

In defense of Appadurai and Sahlins, one could retort that their arguments do not in fact ignore the question of global injustice, as they seem to, but rather imply an alternative view of what injustice and its remedy are. For Appadurai, disjuncture is not only the rule, but it is growing (280). If disjuncture is growing, then Appadurai seems committed, as I hinted above, to an undeclared metanarrative in which culture is gradually escaping from beneath the heavy heel of economics. This is an undeclared and perhaps undeclarable metanarrative of emancipation. It has its attractions, but it immediately gets Appadurai into epistemological hot water. For if the increasing independence of culture and imagination from economic determination is simply real, an empirical fact, then culture and imagination cannot have jurisdiction over the history of their own liberation. If they did have such jurisdiction, then that history could not be presented as empirical fact. Yet that is precisely how the narrative is presented. Whether the linear narrative is convincing or not, its telos hides, in a familiar diachronic camouflage, the author's interpretive priorities, his positive values.[25] Appadurai seems to be telling us, in other words, that history is moving toward greater global justice, and this precisely because more voices can now make themselves heard, because there is increasing emancipation at the level of cultural self-expression.[26] Cultural self-expression is the bandwagon we should be climbing aboard.

Do Wallerstein's critics really mean to imply this alternative view of injustice? It would seem that they must. But if they do, their view is rarely declared and defended explicitly. Perhaps this is because it has so little chance of satisfying anyone but those who, for disciplinary reasons or others, are already convinced. Who else would choose cultural silencing as our world's characteristic version of injustice while ignoring, say, political subjection or economic deprivation? This choice gets a well-deserved scolding in the account that fellow cultural anthropologist James Ferguson offers of the phrase "alternative modernities," a slogan that has had all the success in the transnational zone of the humanities that world-systems theory itself has not.[27] What is the effect of that success? Ferguson writes, "The deployment of the idea of alternative modernities in Africa has a rather different significance than it has in Asia. East and Southeast Asian versions of alternative modernity have mostly argued for the possibility of a parallel track, economically analogous to the West but culturally distinctive. Broadly, the idea has meant the possibility of achieving a first world standard of living, while retaining so-called Asian values, or maintaining a more restricted version of individual rights, or avoiding the West's perceived moral vices. But in Africa, where the idea of economic convergence has lately lost so much of its plausibility, pluralizing the concept of modernity has proven attractive for very different reasons" (173). All cultures are now modern, in the sense of being (1) historical rather than traditional and (2) not incompatible with the successful manipulation of today's high-tech habitat. As such, all cultures have won the right to equal respect. But this is not the modernity, Ferguson notes, that Africans want. The modernity they want, knowing perfectly well that they don't already have it, is "economic convergence." And that is something that all the cultural pride in the world cannot supply.

Perhaps out of fidelity to his African subjects and the bitterness they feel, Ferguson writes with a certain bitterness of his own about this academic effort to pass off a prescriptive, universal equality of cultural respect as a substitute for what Africans themselves might recognize as equality: equality of living standards, equal access to the goods and services of the earth. There is no excuse, he implies, for focusing on the "happy story about plurality and nonranked cultural difference" to the neglect of a second, much less happy story which results in "relatively fixed global statuses" in a "world socioeconomic hierarchy" (179). What Ferguson calls hierarchy is more or less what Wallerstein calls system. The slogan "alternative modernities" allows anthropologists to tell their happy story about culture without bringing that story into any confrontation with system in the zero-sum sense of global economic hierarchy. It is another way of suggesting that there *is* no system. But it is little short of obscene to talk about cultural liberation if diverse, imaginative cultures, once liberated, have so little effect on the hierarchical order of power and wealth in which those cultures are obliged to scratch out a living. This is not to say they cannot have an effect, but only that in any given case strong evidence is needed that they are indeed having one.

When Ferguson speaks of "relatively fixed global statuses," he seems to be both invoking and avoiding a global concept of class, a concept that would be something like "class-among-nations."[28] The neologism is not a bad way of describing Wallerstein's core–periphery vision of world-system. The absence Jay bemoans in Appadurai and could well have bemoaned in the discourse of alternative modernity as well can be filled in at the global level only by something like what Wallerstein offers.

I do not claim that what Wallerstein offers supplies anything and everything the humanities might need in order to turn their scholarship more effectually against global injustice. There is also a sense in which Wallerstein fits into and flatters a paradigm by which the already-existing humanities both lay claim to politics at a global scale, on the one hand, and evade the shifting contingencies of direct political commitment, on the other.

The world Ferguson presents is one in which Africa has not risen, but China has. China's rise, though it is not Ferguson's subject, would seem to make an immense difference to how and in whose interest the world-system is thought to be operating. Yet in Wallerstein's view, China's rise doesn't seem to make any difference at all. For Wallerstein, transfer of surplus from the periphery to the core would not be affected by sudden Chinese prosperity, since even if China were to become part of the core, the theory posits that there would be equal need for a periphery: in this case, to return to Ferguson's example, Africa. As Jan Pieterse puts it, "According to the theory, these shifts [earlier ones] are of no consequence as long as the system itself does not change; it does not matter whether Brazil or Britain occupies a particular world market niche, whether particular countries rise or decline in the system: 'since the system as a whole creates pressures to maintain a certain mix of core, semiperipheral, and peripheral activities'" (38).[29] Wallerstein writes, "We have had very large shifts of production from North America, western Europe, and even Japan to other parts of the world-system, which have consequently claimed that they were 'industrializing' and therefore developing. Another way of characterizing what happened is to say that these semiperipheral countries were the recipients of what were now less profitable industries" (51). Both "claimed" and the scare quotes around "industrializing" express a barely concealed reluctance to see any genuine shift here. The reason is evident. If his theory holds that there is something like class-between-nations, then the rise of a peripheral nation to become an economic superpower, especially a peripheral nation that holds as high a proportion of the earth's people as China, raises the possibility of a drastic change in the system and a possible need for more or less drastic adjustments to the theory.[30] The prospect of a country from the periphery becoming hegemonic is a very different thing from the usual musical chairs since the 1500s, a game restricted to the various core nations.[31] In this case, we are talking about a substantial proportion of the inhabitants of the world's periphery passing out of absolute poverty. Relative inequality has risen, yes, but the threshold has also risen, and this is not a negligible fact, whether from the perspective of China or from that of humanity as a whole. Is this a result that asks us to look at the system with new eyes? Was it accomplished by government intervention that is in some sense non- or even antisystemic? Faced with rising economic nationalism in the United States, whether over perceived lost jobs or the fear of lost economic preeminence, what is the proper cosmopolitan response? Wallerstein doesn't register the new and tricky political challenges that such a shift entails.

Longtime readers of Wallerstein will notice in his refusal to be impressed by the economic rise of East Asia a characteristic intellectual gesture. Events, actions, and movements tend not to register on Wallerstein's screen as more than the briefest of blips. According to "The Rise and Future Demise," the end of slavery (95), decolonization (98), and the rise of socialism (101) were all something less eventful than they seemed; indeed, each was more or less what the system wanted.[32] That's counting out quite a bit of what would otherwise appear to be significant history—for someone on the left, a history of praiseworthy achievements which, however tainted, we rely on to sustain our faith that further progress is possible. Wallerstein seems to do without this evidence. He often finds, plausibly enough, that wars end in "truce more or less at the starting point" (*Decline*, 37). This is said here about the Korean War, and it is said elsewhere of the Gulf War. But are there no wars about which this would not be true? How about the American Civil War, which ended slavery? (See my discussion of Louis Menand on the Civil War in chapter 7.) Another characteristic move is to claim that "the very success of the antisystemic movements has been the major cause of their undoing" (*Decline*, 39).[33] But the same thing is also asserted about hegemonic movements. For Wallerstein, it seems to be true of any movements, or any successful ones. But if there is so little difference in the end between the results of systemic movements and of antisystemic movements, then the real dividing line would seem to fall not between system and nonsystem. Everything is or threatens to become system. The real division is between movement itself and stasis, with stasis seemingly predestined to win out. Stasis would become the deep or functional truth of system as such. In a signature effect of his rhetoric, Wallerstein announces that the attacks of 11 September 2001 seemed "dramatic and shocking" (*Decline*, 1) but were actually much less significant than they at first appeared.[34]

Wallerstein notes somewhere that his notion of system was inspired by the solar system, which can be observed in its coherence but cannot be interfered with and which exists on a time scale utterly divorced from our own—a system that is functionally, if not absolutely, immortal.[35] Like Chomsky, Wallerstein here identifies himself as a kind of extraterrestrial. The difference is that if for Chomsky being an extraterrestrial means that the central political practice will be blaming, for Wallerstein it means a disabling both of blame and of praise, a general lowering of the rhetorical temperature, as if political changes for the better were always trivial or delusory and as if Wallerstein's political indignation (about which there has never been any doubt) had trouble fixing for long on any given object. Only one piece of real news enlivens his voice, and that is the end of the world capitalist system, an event that is endlessly prophesied and endlessly deferred. This secular messianism cannot be disproved—the economic crisis since 2008 surely quickened the pulses of many of Wallerstein's faithful readers—but, like all messianism, it drains the interest from days that are not the end days and leaves readers fighting off monotony.

The sort of change Wallerstein has no trouble acknowledging is change for the worse. Military aggression may tend to leave a country's borders where they started and will not, Wallerstein follows Adam Smith in assuring us, improve its economic fortunes, but it can certainly hasten a power's decline. This was the case for Germany in the twentieth century, he suggests, and it is again the case for the United States in the twenty-first. In both instances this may well be true, but it leaves a question mark hanging over imperialism and more generally over coercion—the very element of Wallerstein's most daring and successful revision of Marx—as a possible agent of historical change.[36] Does coercion matter, or not?

Only a programmatic commitment to change for the worse can explain Wallerstein's emphatic proposal of the unfashionable and, to me, untenable thesis that capitalism has produced absolute immiseration. In *Historical Capitalism*, Wallerstein writes, "I wish to defend the one Marxist proposition which even orthodox Marxists tend to bury in shame, the thesis of the absolute (not relative) immiseration of the proletariat. I hear the friendly whispers. Surely you can't be serious; surely you mean relative immiseration?" (100–101).[37] Adding the historically implausible idea that sexism and racism form "a new framework of oppressive humiliation which had never previously existed" (102), he arrives at the conclusion that "in both material and psychic terms (sexism and racism), there was absolute immiseration" (104). In other words, the civil rights and women's movements accomplished absolutely nothing. Both the content and the tone—a tone suggesting a position that is not the result of empirical assessment, but an a priori, arrived at early and from a great distance away, unavailable to further review—ought to be familiar to humanists.[38] Breaking with the dialectical Marx—"It is simply not true that capitalism as a historical system has represented progress over the various previous historical systems that it destroyed or transformed" (98)—Wallerstein carries the antiprogressive impulse he shares with the humanities even further than most humanists would be tempted to. Here he sounds very like those antiprogressive thinkers the humanities have most eagerly embraced, the odd couple Foucault and Arnold.

The thesis of absolute immiseration ought to provoke humanists to consider whether we too may not have come to a collective decision in advance, independent of actual evidence: a decision that our culture must be responsible, at least in large part, for whatever suffering happens to be under discussion. There must be an absolute sufferer, and the suffering can be debited to only one account, ours. This looks like system, but it might equally well be the sort of self-flattery that can hide in self-blame, a response to the disciplinary imperative to achieve self-importance, an unearned guarantee of a significance for culture that might otherwise be doubted. The humanities are making a case for the significance of culture. Wallerstein is making a case for the significance of the periphery. The overlap between the two cases comes at the point where culture and periphery coincide: that is, the significance of the cultures of the Third World. Here, agreement has been possible. But it does the Third World no favors to force its cultures to serve as the invisible evidence by which the study of culture in general is legitimated as significant, the foundation on which a First World program of intellectual examination is based.

The same doubts that could be raised about culture have already been raised about Wallerstein's implicit case for the decisive significance to world capitalism of the periphery. Robert DuPlessis writes, for example, "By inflating the small-scale, loosely articulated international trading networks of the mercantilist age into an integrated world-economy, and then investing that system with causal primacy, Wallerstein not only substantially overestimates the contribution of the periphery for growth in the core but overlooks forces for change and divergence internal to each of the three zones" (20).[39] If Sahlins accused Wallerstein of giving too little importance to the periphery, at the level of culture and agency, DuPlessis says the problem is that he gives too much importance to it. The absoluteness of the absolute immiseration thesis suggests that, beyond the actual suffering on the periphery, which is not in short supply, peripheral suffering also plays a systemic role, so to speak, at the level of the argument. Built into the logic, it must be protected from any shifting in the historical facts. How inconvenient it would be if the facts were suddenly to reconfigure themselves! In this sense, Wallerstein might be said to veer toward a fundamentally ethical position rather than an empirical or indeed a political one.

In the humanities, this constellation of features ought to be recognizable. Taking for granted that our vocation is to foster remembrance of what society wants to forget and not, as politics would demand, some contingent mixture of remembering and forgetting, we tend to jump to the conclusion that the more inclusive the temporal viewpoint, the better. The long, almost inhuman temporal perspectives that result are inimical to the urgencies of topical intervention. The aesthetic, as I have suggested elsewhere, is sometimes nothing more or less than a version of retrospect, that structural remove from political commitment that is presumed by making judgments about the past rather than the present. About the past, no commitment in the strongest sense is possible.[40] These hidden commonalities between Wallerstein and the humanities, commonalities in the chosen time scale (the long term) and the deferral or dilution of political agency (an anti-interventionist ethos that might also be called aesthetic), will, I hope, be somewhat disquieting to both pro- and antisystem readers.

Wallerstein's belief in system as definitive object to be blamed, sucking up all the blame in the vicinity, seems the very antithesis of the humanist's disbelief in system. For the humanist, what must be blamed is, precisely, thinking systematically. Yet as I've suggested, these apparent opposites have similar and disquieting political effects, specifically, quietist ones. And the counterintuitive symmetry goes further. I have tried to show that Wallerstein has more in common with the humanities than he appears to, but I hope I have also managed to suggest that the humanities need more of Wallerstein's sense of system than they admit. For if system makes blaming difficult, as Boltanski says, it is no less true that without system, blaming in Boltanski's sense is not really possible.[41] In order to blame well, one has to know that this is not just any random suffering, the result of nature or accident or perhaps even the fault of the sufferer. The recent fashion in the humanities has been to avoid such knowledge, to view the suffering body in close-ups that leave the potentially explanatory background out of focus or out of the frame. It's as if humanists could not bear the threat that, once allowed into the picture, the background would throw epistemological or ethical doubt on the fact of suffering, which is properly left autonomous and indisputable. Lacking or deliberately evading any theory of power, we find ourselves imitating the news media and the news-dependent humanitarian NGOs, which do not want the flow of sympathy and dollars checked by worry about wasted or badly bestowed efforts. (Along with the example I mentioned, international support for hungry, homeless Hutu refugees after the Rwandan genocide of 1994, which turned out, in effect, to be support for those who had committed genocide, one could also think of the Biafra crisis of the 1960s, which led to the splitting off of Doctors Without Borders from the Red Cross. The issue there was a loose and premature use of the term *genocide*, again leading to more loss of life than would have been the case without the humanitarian intervention.) Without system, you get celebrity humanitarians like Lévy pointing to themselves pointing to a sufferer and programmatically refusing any theoretical explanation that might link the lives of their entranced tele-spectators to those of their telegenic victims.

To put this in Boltanski's terms: perhaps we can come to act in imitation of the Good Samaritan only if we realize that we are not Good Samaritans, at least according to Boltanski's paradigm of the disinterested observer. His paradigm is fundamentally and unreconstructedly humanitarian; it suggests that there is no causal relation between the spectator and the sufferer, that the spectator is appealed to only on the basis of conscience and free will. This model has to be supplemented, at least, with a model of causal interconnection that acknowledges interests, both shared and colliding.


As Boltanski tells it, the story of the Good Samaritan goes like this: "Three passers-by traveling from Jerusalem to Jericho *see*, one after the other, an unfortunate who has been left half-dead by robbers. The first two carry on regardless. The third 'exercises charity' towards him" (8). It is because the so-called unfortunate is neither friend nor enemy, an unidentified figure without salient characteristics other than the need for assistance—anyone, "*n'importe qui*"—that the parable has been able to buttress legal attempts to define an obligation to assist someone in danger. Boltanski sets the Samaritan, as a non-Jew who would not be expected to feel solidarity, at the beginning of a tradition of disinterested solidarity that is contrasted with the more usual sense of obligation based on preexisting social bonds, like kinship or shared ethnic or class identity. The opposition between these two forms of solidarity, distanced and not, repeats questions familiar to the theory of cosmopolitanism in its classic Kantian version: the dilemma that a primary universalizing commitment to humanity as a whole, which would not favor those close to you over those far away from you, almost by definition has no political force, no particular constituency, no claim to constitute a genuine politics.

The encounter between Good Samaritan and unfortunate happens only because the Samaritan is on a journey between Jerusalem and Jericho, a long journey then, and now again a long journey, at least if you are Palestinian. Transport technology has improved, but there are a lot of checkpoints. As Boltanski does not say, the fable of the Good Samaritan has become a story of the Palestinian Occupied Territories. One of the largest of the so-called settlements in the Occupied Territories of the West Bank is located next to the very spot along the Jerusalem/Jericho road where this exemplary charity is said to have been exercised. When I visited Palestine for the first time in 2004 I did not see this spot, nor can I say that I knowingly saw any Samaritans, but my visit was the occasion of the first attention I have ever paid to the Samaritans, if only via my guidebook. Like me, the Good Samaritan seemed to be, after all, a sort of Jew. The very innocent guidebook I brought with me, following the advice of the alternative tour people not to bring any materials that might get me interrogated at the airport, talks about the Samaritans in a chapter entitled "Lands of the Bible." The story is that when most of the Jews were sent into exile after the Assyrian conquest around 720 BC, some were left behind. "Returning from exile in 538 BC, the Jews shunned the Samaritans for their intermarriage with the conquerors, although the Samaritans claimed strict adherence to the Mosaic Law" (283). The guidebook I did not bring with me, entitled *Palestine* (Bradt), puts the Samaritans in a section called "Sites in the Nablus Area." But it also gives more space to the Jewish view that the Samaritans were not originally Jews but Assyrians who were shipped in after many of the Jews were exiled, then intermarried and adopted the Jewish faith. In either case, however, there remains some question as to whether the Samaritans were simply enemies of the Jews or something more intimate and more confused, and thus whether the Good Samaritan can stand for something as simple as a disinterested spectator. Perhaps this charitable action was not simply charitable but closer to a form of solidarity or the overcoming of a specific hostility.

Starting at this slight remove from pure charity, we can go on to other impurities in the ideal of disinterestedness. Boltanski mentions the supposedly small set of cases in which the spectator is already complicit in the sufferer's suffering. Intervening becomes a fuller, weightier obligation, he adds, somewhat obscurely, when "the action of causing suffering and the action of giving assistance" can be placed in the "same framework." To translate: you have more of an obligation to fix it if you're the one who broke it. "You're the one who broke it" would have made a more realistic starting point than pure disinterested compassion in the case of Americans pondering whether to get involved in the Middle East suffering they see on their televisions. "The action of causing suffering and the action of giving assistance" can indeed be placed in the "same framework," since it's American military, economic, and political aid that sustains the intransigence and brutality of Israel's government. For us, there may be experiential distance—say, not having visited the West Bank—but there is no causal distance, and there is not enough knowledge distance to let us off the hook. In the age of the Internet and for that matter of a decent if beleaguered progressive element in the press, there is no excuse for not knowing. The same is true about the commodities on which our daily lives depend and which often come to us from far away. They are among our distant belongings, one might say, and they come to us bearing both distance and obligation.

But this is not to say that we can return to the traditional line between disinterested humanitarianism and genuine, that is, purely interested, politics. Even a theory of power that takes a further step and insists on the causal linkage not merely between perpetrator and victim, but between perpetrator and spectator—that takes off from a spectator who does have some sort of interest in the spectacle—would not entirely remove us from the terrain of disinterestedness. I will say more in the next two chapters about the aesthetic as a form of disinterest that demands a certain unlikely notice in the context of commodity exchanges between core and periphery and political efforts to interfere with them.

Here and now, however, I have a more urgent point to make. If every ethics presupposes a sociology, as Alasdair MacIntyre teaches, then the sociology behind Boltanski's dilemma—what do you say to get people in France or the United States to show compassion about things that happen far away?—would seem evident enough. In *The Road to Wigan Pier* Orwell writes, "Under the capitalist system, in order that England may live in comparative comfort, a hundred million Indians must live on the verge of starvation—an evil state of affairs, but you acquiesce in it every time you step into a taxi or eat a plate of strawberries and cream" (140). These may not be the right words, but surely we need words like them in order for Americans to see how far from disinterested they are. To put it crudely: every American except the very poorest has an objective and appreciable interest in the continuing exploitation of the rest of the world, the siphoning off of resources there so as to support a disproportionate level of comfort here. In spite of the dramatically unequal distribution inside America of the benefits brought to America by our government's traditional and hypocritical mixture of dogmatic free trade and actual protectionism, backed up by military as well as economic power, American hegemony has paid real across-the-board dividends. Even the poor in this country are, on the whole, much better off than the majority of the population of many other countries, and the majority of Americans are much better off. What this means is that for Americans and other beneficiaries of the system, politics at the global scale cannot be what politics has always been taken to be: the pursuit of self-interest. On the contrary. The American left is asking Americans not to throw off their chains but to surrender their privileges. It is because of this structural self-interest that disinterestedness cannot be rejected out of hand, whether in the form of humanitarianism or in the form of the aesthetic. A rhetoric that not only tries to be critical of the system but tries to be critical of the system *to those who are its beneficiaries*, is a rhetoric that cannot say a simple no to disinterestedness.

Addressing the system in this double sense, that is, speaking both of it and within it, means acknowledging that the speaker and the listener, however cosmopolitan, also belong to it. It means doing something with words that is rhetorically more complicated than constructing a convenient but arbitrary object, and it means doing something more politically complicated than opening up gaps and weaknesses in a supposedly absolute system so that words can appear to be correspondingly more significant and more efficacious. There is no guarantee that blaming the system in this complex sense will itself be efficacious. What this sort of multidirectional blaming offers is the prospect of some purchase on the system, a guarantee that on this site, words and system are inextricable with each other.

# 4  THE SWEATSHOP SUBLIME

There is a passage in David Lodge's novel *Nice Work* (1988) in which the heroine, Robyn Penrose, a Marxist-feminist critic who teaches English literature, looks out the window of an airplane and sees the division of labor:

> Factories, shops, offices, schools, beginning the working day. People crammed into rush-hour buses and trains, or sitting at the wheels of their cars in traffic jams, or washing up breakfast things in the kitchens of pebble-dashed semis. All inhabiting their own little worlds, oblivious of how they fitted into the total picture. The housewife, switching on her electric kettle to make another cup of tea, gave no thought to the immense complex of operations that made that simple action possible: the building and maintenance of the power station that produced the electricity, the mining of coal or pumping of oil to fuel the generators, the laying of miles of cable to carry the current to her house, the digging and smelting and milling of ore or bauxite into sheets of steel or aluminium, the cutting and pressing and welding of the metal into the kettle's shell, spout and handle, the assembling of these parts with scores of other components—coils, screws, nuts, bolts, washers, rivets, wires, springs, rubber insulation, plastic trimmings; then the packaging of the kettle, the advertising of the kettle, the marketing of

the kettle, to wholesale and retail outlets, the transportation of the kettle to warehouses and shops, the calculation of its price, and the distribution of its added value between all the myriad people and agencies concerned in its production and circulation. The housewife gave no thought to all this as she switched on her kettle.[1]

To contemplate one's kettle and suddenly realize, first, that one is the beneficiary of an unimaginably vast and complex social whole; and, second (a point further emphasized elsewhere in the novel), that this means benefiting from the daily labor of kettle- and electricity-producing workers, much of it unpleasant and under-remunerated—neither of these realizations is entirely outside the domain of everyday experience. What seems special about this passage is a third realization: that this moment of consciousness will not be converted into action. The passage concludes,

> What to do with the thought was another question. It was difficult to decide whether the system that produced the kettle was a miracle of human ingenuity and co-operation or a colossal waste of resources, human and natural. Would we all be better off boiling our own water in a pot hung over an open fire? Or was it the facility to do such things at the touch of a button that freed men, and more particularly women, from servile labour and made it possible for them to become literary critics? . . . She gave up on the conundrum, and accepted another cup of coffee from the stewardess.

Let me now juxtapose this passage with a *New Yorker* cartoon by Roz Chast. Its protagonist, "you," is an unshaven man in pajamas. He or "you" combines Lodge's tea-drinking housewife with his airborne intellectual; your feet are firmly on the ground, indeed you are not yet out of your own door, yet you do "give a thought" to the system that provides you with goods and services. And it is this thought that we follow. At the top of the cartoon are the words "One morning, while getting dressed." From that common point, lines branch off toward boxes containing different possible outcomes. One morning, while getting dressed, you either do or do not examine the label of your shirt. If you do, you either do or do not realize the conditions of life under which this shirt was, or perhaps was not, produced: the pitifully inadequate wages, not to speak of the locked fire exits, the arbitrary harassments and firings, the refusal of genuine union representation, and so on. But whether your thoughts linger or not, whether the shirt turns out to have been made in Mexico or Thailand or the United States, the result is the same, the same as if you had not examined the label. All lines converge in the end on the same box: you put on the shirt and forget about it.

In both cases there is a moment of insight accompanied by a surge of power. In thought, at least, you are launched on a one-click leap from the tender, drowsy privacy of early morning at home—the shirt not yet on your back, the first cup of tea just finished—to the outer reaches of a world economic system of notoriously inconceivable magnitude and interdependence, a system that brings goods from the ends of the earth (as Charles Baudelaire put it, with an accuracy that you suddenly recognize) in order to satisfy your slightest desire.[2] Yet at the same time this insight is also strangely powerless. Your sudden, heady access to the global scale is not access to a commensurate power of action upon the global scale. You have a cup of tea or coffee. You get dressed. Just as suddenly, just as shockingly, you are returned to yourself in all your everyday smallness.[3]

"That in comparison with which everything else is small" is one of Kant's descriptions of the sublime, also defined as "a feeling of the inadequacy of [the] imagination for presenting the ideas of a whole, wherein the imagination reaches its maximum, and, in striving to surpass it, sinks back into itself, by which, however, a kind of emotional satisfaction is produced."[4] Considering how Lodge and Chast play up and down the scales of the immensely large and infinitesimally small, how they combine pleasure with pain in contemplating the obscure infinity of the social whole, and above all the paradox by which they make us sense that we possess transcendent powers (albeit powers exercised on our behalf and in this case without our active will) and yet finally let us "sink back into ourselves," failing to express those powers in any potentially risky, disobedient action, I would suggest that we provisionally call this trope, with a certain inevitable discomfort, the sweatshop sublime.[5]

The sublime may not seem like the most obviously useful way to pose the question of our responsibilities as citizens faced with the reality of sweatshop labor. A certain usefulness will, I hope, become more apparent as I proceed. But the pairing of sweatshops and sublimity is also intended to raise issues of politics and aesthetics, scholarship and commitment, that have become irritatingly familiar of late to progressives working in and around the humanities. Rather than rehearse those issues here, let me simply assert, by way of setting an agenda, two propositions that the notion of a sweatshop sublime is meant to suggest. First, that literary critics in allegorical airplanes, looking down from above on putatively unconscious housewives—let's say, intellectuals contemplating nonintellectuals—are subject to the same dilemma of concern and confusion, action and apathy. To recognize that this *is* a dilemma means that we should not expect any simple solution to it. And to recognize that it is a shared dilemma rather than a dilemma resulting from the uniqueness of our work ought to help us calibrate more accurately the responsibilities that do and do not attach to that work.

At the same time (this is my second point), the idea that intellectuals do not escape this dilemma is not merely an argument in favor of modestly retracting some of the political expectations we attach to our work. It's also a fact of wider political importance. This is especially true for those of us searching, perhaps immodestly, for political answers that would operate on the same global or international scale as the causes of our ethical and political problems. If internationalism in the desirable sense is ever going to come into existence, if we are ever going to see some organized impulse toward the equalization of life chances between those who make shirts and those who wear them, this will clearly not happen by means of a sudden mass exercise of Kantian ethics. It is going to happen as an outgrowth of habitual desires, fears, and anxieties, embarrassed perceptions and guilty pleasures that, though pervaded by thought, do not belong on that level of rigorous conceptual rationality Kant elsewhere demanded. An example is the childhood experience of being told to eat an unappetizing food because children elsewhere are starving. The experience of sweatshop sublimity is another item in this illogical but peremptory series. Unpropitious as it may seem, this limited moment of ethically inspired consumer consciousness is just the sort of raw or semiprocessed phenomenological material in which private and public, domestic and international are fused, and it is out of such materials that an internationalist antiglobalization politics on a mass scale will have to emerge, if indeed it ever does emerge. To put the idea in other terms, this moment of awareness is a rough analogue to what Antonio Gramsci called the "national-popular": an imperfect and historically determined version of common sense, perhaps only emergent but significant enough to be worth tracking, that links the thoughts and feelings of ordinary people to the fate of others within a larger collectivity. To Gramsci this collectivity was the nation. But I see no reason why the process of collectivity-formation should somehow stop at the nation's borders, as if fellow-feeling found its natural and inevitable telos in nationality. The gradually increasing reservoir of everyday tropes and images that connect our sense of ourselves and our fate with the fates of those who are not our fellow citizens can be thought of, I propose, as the international-popular.

It is to be expected that the international-popular will fall well short of any ideal action-oriented solidarity. But it is also to be expected that, under present global conditions, solidarity and even action itself will fall similarly short, will be subject to the same sorts of quasi-sensory, all-too-human interference that we have come to associate with the aesthetic—the illegitimate but seemingly irremediable tyranny of the close over the distant, the analogous perspectivisms of the other senses, the vulnerability to shapeliness, decibel level, boredom, and so on. Thus sweatshop sublimity offers grounds for anyone interested in defending the significance to society at large of work performed in the domain of the aesthetic—a kind of case that can never rely on the language of the aesthetic alone, must always step outside that language in order to anchor itself in other interests and concerns.

Now there are things to be done about sweatshops. The literature of groups like the National Labor Committee, the Campaign for Labor Rights, and United Students Against Sweatshops abounds in invitations to sudden perception more or less like the cartoon's. For example, "When you purchase a shirt in Wal-Mart, do you ever imagine young women in Bangladesh forced to work from 7:30 a.m. to 8:00 p.m., seven days a week, paid just 9 cents to 20 cents an hour?" But this literature always follows with a section called something like "What We Can Do," urging readers to write to Walmart with specific and entirely reasonable demands. And it has real grounds to claim, as it does, "We do have an impact. We do have a voice."[6] It has helped rally supporters, and it has won a number of small but significant victories. The celebrity of the American television personality Kathie Lee Gifford was successfully used against her and against the brands she endorses to publicize sweatshop abuses in Honduras; many American universities have agreed to new standards concerning how school sweatshirts and other paraphernalia are to be manufactured. If little progress has been made on the crucial questions of wages and the right to unionize, where corporations have been most resistant, it is nonetheless a genuine accomplishment to have brought the beginnings of transparency, monitoring, and accountability to the murky domain of anonymous subcontracting in which the brand-name multinationals have so profitably been hiding out. The antisweatshop movement, increasingly active on campuses in the United States, was one of the most powerful constituents of the volatile protest mixture against the World Trade Organization in Seattle and, later, in other cities. Moves toward alliance between students and labor unions and between unions and environmental groups are two of the most promising features of recent international activism aimed against no-holds-barred globalization.

In short, to discover that the sales price of one Disney Pocahontas T-shirt, sold at Walmart for $10.97, amounts to five days' wages for the women who sewed that shirt is not necessarily to be struck down by paralysis and inertia, though it helps if some available mode of action is specified. Even the cartoon by Chast, which offers a description of lethargy, might also be interpreted as a provocation intended to shock us out of lethargy. Literary analogues are not hard to find in which economic epiphany leads toward rather than away from action. Consider the passage toward the end of George Eliot's *Middlemarch* in which Dorothea, who has just spent a miserable, sleepless night after finding Will in a compromising position with Rosamond, gets up at dawn and asks herself, "What should I do—how should I act now, this very day, if I could clutch my own pain, and compel it to silence, and think of those three?" (the third being Lydgate, the husband Rosamond seems in danger of betraying):

> It had taken long for her to come to that question, and there was light piercing into the room. She opened her curtains, and looked out towards the bit of road that lay in view, with fields beyond, outside the entrance-gates. On the road there was a man with a bundle on his back and a woman carrying her baby; in the field she could see figures moving—perhaps the shepherd with his dog. Far off in the bending sky was the pearly light; and she felt the largeness of the world and the manifold

wakings of men to labour and endurance. She was a part of that involuntary, palpitating life, and could neither look out on it from her luxurious shelter as a mere spectator, nor hide her eyes in selfish complaining.

What she would resolve to do that day did not yet seem quite clear, but something that she could achieve stirred her as with an approaching murmur which would soon gather distinctness.[7]

Dorothea follows through on her resolution to act. And though the sphere of her action is quite limited—it does not include, for example, the people she sees out her window or the system that sends them into the fields at that hour—it is rewarded with visible results. Like the antisweatshop movement, she feels with a jolt her place in the "involuntary, palpitating" world of labor around her, resolves to do something, and does. And with such an example in mind, it's tempting to conclude that the later texts by Lodge and Chast represent a moral step backward, a sophisticated evasion of the responsibility for action.

But the sweatshop sublime is not, I think, a simple or easily avoidable error. And error or not, I would argue that, appearances to the contrary, it is precisely the mode in which Eliot herself is writing. Dorothea's early-morning revelation, in which everyone else who is awake is going off to work and only she remains behind in her "luxurious shelter," has been anticipated some chapters earlier by what is surely the novel's most direct reference to the sublime, and perhaps also its most sublime moment. "If we had a keen vision and feeling of all ordinary human life," Eliot writes in a famous sentence, "it would be like hearing the grass grow and the squirrel's heart beat, and we should die of that roar which lies on the other side of silence."[8]

In the later scene Dorothea is hearing the grass grow. She suddenly takes in the daily "labor and endurance" that put the bread on her table but that do not ordinarily attract any notice. And she draws from that extraordinary perception stern, not to say self-punishing conclusions. The problem is the self-punishment, which is just what is predicted by the metaphor of "hearing the grass grow." Going to see Rosamond is action, but action that displays an altruistic self-effacement so radical as to leave behind almost no self, or no self-interest. To hear the "roar which lies on the other side of silence" is indeed, from the point of view of an ordinary self, to die. The purely disinterested, selfless self that remains to Dorothea is only too well suited to the metaphor, for it is incapable of forceful action that would change the rules or terms of ordinariness, and forceful, extraordinary action of this sort is just what is rendered irrelevant, if not precluded, by the notion of "hearing the grass grow." Asking us to hear the grass grow is not asking us to interfere with it. The only imperative here is to be conscious of what is already happening, to respect what exists. And respect for what exists is a better argument against change than for it. If the division of labor in the early morning passage is like the grass in the "hearing the grass grow" passage, and I think it is, then the same moral applies: the only scandal is unconsciousness of the division of labor, not failure to change the division of labor. As Steven Marcus puts it in an essay on Eliot's social theory, "Society, however errant and unfair some of its arrangements may be, is never a scandal in this way of conceiving things. To say so would be tantamount to saying that human existence itself is a scandal."[9]

The larger story in which Dorothea is obliged to abandon her heroic St. Theresa–like ideal of action, to which this hesitation belongs, can perhaps be explained in part by Eliot's intermittent attraction to the values of the landholding gentry, which owned a good deal of grassland and had famously mixed feelings about plans for modernizing interference with it. It is most neatly described in Raymond Williams's account of Eliot's organic view of social interdependence: "Her favorite metaphor for society is a network: a 'tangled skein'; a 'tangled web' . . . 'One fears,' she remarked, 'to pull the wrong thread, in the tangled scheme of things.' The caution is reasonable, but the total effect of the image false. For in fact every element in the complicated system is active: the relationships are changing, constantly, and any action—even abstention . . .—affects, even if only slightly . . . the very nature of the complication." Eliot fails in her depiction of working people, Williams concludes, because to her "there seems 'no right thread to pull.' Almost any kind of social action is ruled out."[10]

Lodge's moment of sublimity produces more or less the same effect. In the name of realism, he too chastises and paralyzes his would-be activist heroine. For both novelists, to glimpse even for a moment the unimaginable face of society-as-a-whole is to go through a near-death experience in which the activist self dissolves. Forced to ask, "Are My Hands Clean?" to quote a sweatshop poem by the African American writer Bernice Johnson Reagon, each loses the moral leverage that has helped her challenge the status quo and sinks back into the private.[11] Sublimity is not the end of action itself—Robyn, like Dorothea, is successful in her personal mission—but, to repeat Williams's judgment, "any kind of social action is ruled out."

Yet "social action" sets a very high standard, both for the novel and for academic discourse. To say that Eliot rules it out is to imply that it would otherwise be available. Is it available even to so severe a critic of Eliot as Williams himself, available, that is, while he is in the act of writing criticism? Francis Mulhern, in a book entitled *Culture/Metaculture*, suggests that Williams's judgment of Eliot can be extended to most if not all of the "Culture and Society" tradition Williams so influentially assembled, a tradition that has joined Marxists with romantic reactionaries on the common ground of visions like those of Eliot and Lodge, visions of "organic interdependence."[12] For Mulhern, Williams's identification of culture as ordinary, which inaugurates the era of cultural studies, has much the same effect as Eliot's hear-the-grass-grow openness to the ordinary. In Williams's own words, "The arguments which can be grouped under [the heading of culture] do not point to any inevitable action or affiliation."[13] Williams stands at the juncture between the older Kulturkritik tradition of Thomas Mann, T. S. Eliot, F. R. Leavis, and company, for which culture was extraordinary, a standard cutting against "mass society," and cultural studies, for which culture is ordinary, not readily separable from the status quo. But this is less of a break than it appears, Mulhern suggests, for both senses of culture are antipolitical. The cultural studies formula "everything is political" leaves nothing political in a usefully specifiable sense, and thus has the same practical effect as Mann's explicit ideal of the "unpolitical man," inspired by culture to reject with disgust both mass democracy and political instrumentality as such. In other words, Dorothea looking out her window in the morning, hearing the grass grow, sensing the organic interdependency of the division of labor, is a figure for the academic study of culture *tout court*, whether in the older or the present generation. Both versions of literary criticism represent the individual's relation to an obscure, infinite whole that is at once politically compelling and yet seemingly deterred by its premises from resulting in a proper political subject or proper political action.[14]

I will not pursue this parallel here, though there is more to be said, for example, about how Dorothea is eventually rewarded for her visit to Rosamond to deliver the news that Will does love her after all, and we humanists too are rewarded for our apparent altruism, with employment that is not very high paying but relatively stable, unusually autonomous, and unusually gratifying—desirable enough, in short, to make others wonder whether we are quite as disinterested as we pretend to be. For us, too, an apparent exteriority to the division of labor helps secure a place within the division of labor. And for this reason inaction should not be seen as a lapse that humanists tumble into in a moment of moral inattention and that can be corrected by resonant calls to stand up and grasp once again our designated responsibilities. Inaction or hesitation when action seems called for is built into the conceptual structure we inhabit. And so too, therefore, are calls to responsibility, which must be perpetually repeated and must remain perpetually unanswered. One of the strangest things about words like *action* and *activism*, at least as they are currently used in the humanities, is their functional equivalence to apparently distant words like *culture*, *intellectual*, and *art*, each of which is accorded the privilege of transcending the division of labor. Even when what is meant is not revolutionary action, action is the latest in a series of terms that, for reasons that go back to our own disciplinary formation or deformation, we have asked to stand for the magical resolution of social contradictions, the ideal unities, the antidotes to the state of division, fragmentation, reification, and so on that we imagine reigning outside, thereby justifying our disciplinary existence. But if we actually look outside, it is immediately clear that action is no such thing, possesses no such impossible powers, has less to do with art than with politics, politics in the deidealized, messy sense.

Mulhern accuses the Kulturkritik tradition of covert nationalism, and he accuses cultural studies of incoherent populism. Both charges are reasonable and important, but neither can be pinned to the concept of culture. For the antisweatshop movement, which does not share our academic dependence on that concept, is saturated with both nationalism and populism. How could it not be, given the movement's need to juggle or reconcile the interests of constituencies as different as organized labor, with its history of protectionism, and the ethical universalism of the so-called constituencies of conscience? This is what politics does. It brings groups together in a common action that will not, cannot perfectly represent the interests of any of them, that will oppose an antagonist each of them will find scandalous for a slightly different reason—will oppose, in effect, a slightly different antagonist.

At the bottom of the *New Yorker* cartoon, three boxes offer three possible facts about the people who made your shirt. In the middle there is an exaggerated clarity: they "earned three cents an hour." To the left, however, there is ambiguity: they "probably have dysentery or diphtheria or worse." This could be another sign of their misery but could also be a reason for our anxiety and disgust (yuck, germs on my shirt). And to the right is more ambiguity: they "hate your stupid Yankee guts." To which the likely American response is, "In that case, too bad for them." In one box we have fear of foreign infection in the AIDS or Ebola style; in the other we have a national circling of the wagons in the presence of hostility judged ("*stupid* Yankee guts") to be childish. In other words, two of the three confirm the strong hint of American nationalism suggested above when the cartoon assumes, or assumes its readers will assume, against all the evidence, that a label reading "Made in USA" guarantees union wages and decent working conditions—in effect, that there are no sweatshops in the United States (which gets no illustration). Pushing these nationalist buttons no doubt helps Chast prepare for her anti-anti-sweatshop climax. But they are not just her buttons. They are also the antisweatshop movement's buttons.

The history of checking for a "Made in USA" label has recently been recounted in Dana Frank's book *Buy American: The Untold Story of Economic Nationalism*. Frank opens the book by describing what she calls an "import panic attack" (ix): "Ms Consumer's epiphany" that "all the goods she had examined" at the local mall "were made in China, Japan, or Korea . . . she peered at label after label and discovered to her horror that she couldn't find a TV or a VCR or a toaster made in the U.S.A." (ix). What follows is the conclusion that "because people like herself were buying imports, American workers were losing their jobs" (ix).[15] The power of the "epiphany," in Frank's analysis, is in direct proportion to the weakness of the logic, or rather its failure to impose an appropriate conclusion, either about the causes of this phenomenon or what to do about it. The general reaction in the United States has been to want to buy American, and anti-immigrant racism has never been far away. Epiphanies like these have often led to action, in other words, but action of a sublimely confused and nationalist kind, including bashing a Toyota with a sledgehammer and the no less confused act of lobbying the U.S. Congress to deny normal trade relations to China, thereby claiming a presumptive national virtue for the U.S. government in the very act of refusing it to another government.[16] Once you are attuned to the motif of nationalism, examples are all too easy to come by. Randy Shaw, the activist and historian of activism, entitles his account of the antisweatshop movement *Reclaiming America: Nike, Clean Air, and the New National Activism.*[17] The America Shaw sees the movement trying to reclaim is one that, as recently as the 1970s, was supposedly "moving toward the equitable society envisioned in the ideals of its founders" (1). If you can believe that, then you will have no trouble referring, with ambiguous restrictiveness, to the "new *national* activism."

Yet if we drop the requirement that this activism be genuinely internationalist, then Shaw's patriotism has a certain specifically political astuteness. A Disney spokesman, responding to accusations about conditions in a Haitian factory that produces Disney clothes, turned the question back at the newspaper reporter: "With the newsprint you use, do you have any idea of the labor conditions involved to produce it?" (198).[18] I have little sympathy for Disney or its spokesmen, but the point, however disingenuous, is not irrelevant or uninteresting. How special a case are foreign sweatshops? When Lodge omits the international dimension, talking about the kettle but saying nothing about the tea and treating bauxite as if it were a product of the Home Counties, is he making a significant omission? What precisely is added by the realization that those who work and suffer on Asian tea plantations and in Mexican maquiladoras are not fellow nationals? If the foreignness of the Disney factory in Haiti offers political leverage that is not offered by the production of newsprint, it's in part because of national shame. And there is no national shame without national pride. Can national pride be turned into an ally of internationalism?

Many others have suggested before me that it can and must, and, more generally, that global commitments can emerge only in a more or less organic and continuous way from local, personal, familial commitments. This is a point where agreement is suspiciously easy, yet getting to the next step of the argument—agreeing, say, on a tipping point where continuity will switch over into opposition—is much more challenging. Consider, for example, the somewhat risky role in antisweatshop discourse of disease and disgust. People are not worried about the "moral losses" occasioned by their reliance on paid household help, Barbara Ehrenreich speculates in one of her undercover essays on menial labor, because "almost everything we buy, after all, is the product of some other person's suffering and miserably underpaid labor. I clean my own house . . . but I can hardly claim purity in any other area of consumption. I buy my jeans at The Gap, which is reputed to subcontract to sweatshops."[19] "We can try," Ehrenreich continues, "to minimize the pain that goes into feeding, clothing, and otherwise provi-sioning ourselves—by observing boycotts, checking for a union label, etc.—but there is no way to avoid it altogether without living in the wilderness on berries. So why should housework, among all the goods and services we consume, arouse any special angst?" But having paid workers clean one's home does arouse angst, she says, and the reason is that one's home is felt to be different: "Someone who has no qualms about purchasing rugs woven by child slaves in India or coffee picked by impoverished peasants in Guate-mala might still hesitate to tell dinner guests that, surprisingly enough, his or her lovely home doubles as a sweatshop during the day."[20] It is not the simple existence of sweatshops, but seeing your home as a sweatshop that offers a political hold. The Orwellian disgust that makes something seem actionably political in the household is akin to the disgust that makes us squeamish about something foreign suffusing our shirts, our breakfasts, our most intimate space. Fine if I know it's happening, just so long as it's not happening right here. This is the slogan of the NIMBY movements: not in my backyard. Once you think about it, the disgust is itself a bit disgusting. And yet one asks oneself whether there can be any politics without it, in other words, without provisionally reinforcing borders and hierarchies, privileges and property lines that we know to be more or less illegitimate.

The "moral challenge," Ehrenreich concludes, "is to make work visible again: not only the scrubbing and vacuuming but all the hoeing, stacking, hammering, drilling, bending, and lifting that goes into creating and main-taining a livable habitat. In an ever more economically unequal culture, where so many of the affluent devote their lives to such ghostly pursuits as stock-trading, image-making, and opinion-polling, real work—in the old-fashioned sense of labor that engages the hand as well as the eye, that tires the body and directly alters the physical world—tends to vanish from sight"

(70). Hoeing, stacking, and hammering, like Lodge's list of labors in *Nice Work*, belong to the argument that a "livable habitat" depends on a great many kinds of work that are normally invisible. But as the culmination of an argument about who cleans the toilets and mops the floors at home, the seemingly innocuous demand to make work visible also makes a riskier suggestion, a suggestion that might paradoxically work against this perception of interdependence. To refuse the division of labor at a point of intimacy is to flirt with refusing the division of labor as such. When Ehrenreich contrasts "real" work at home with such "ghostly" sorts of nonmanual labor as "opinion-polling," it seems to me she is inadvertently doing just what the ideology of the work ethic does: assuming a criterion of individual self-reliance and self-sufficiency. If it is disgusting to have someone do manual labor in your house, if within our own four walls at least we should be sturdily independent of the work of others, then how can we keep the desire for sturdy independence from spilling over and generalizing itself? Are we prepared to deny our dependence, for example, on such ghostly forms of nonmanual labor as the planning of rational traffic patterns or collecting opinions on behalf of national health care or teaching at public universities? The work ethic protects and legitimates the system of individual rewards: it suggests to people, falsely, that they've earned what they receive, that they receive what they receive because of their individual labors alone. In other words, it blots out the existence of society and the interdependence without which no individual effort could lead to any results, let alone any reward. Whatever else it does, the sweatshop sublime rightly forces upon us this knowledge of social interdependence. Ehrenreich, perhaps because she feels the pain of this knowledge more acutely than most, tries to escape it by imagining the home as an enclave of hard-working self-sufficiency. If the home is a pattern—and the essay's arc from housework to manual labor as such suggests exactly that—then the appreciation of real work can easily become, as it so often has in recent public discourse, an argument against the hard-won sense of interdependence, and the ethical conclusions drawn from that interdependence that have made possible voter support for the little we have left of the social welfare state.

In other words, disgust with dependence on the work of other people in the home risks passing over into disgust with dependence on the work of other people in general—a disgust with being part of a highly elaborated division of labor. Yet learning to be part of a highly elaborated division of labor seems a precondition for almost any progressive politics, both nationally and internationally. And it would seem to demand—on the as-yet-counterfactual and very urgent condition that everyone would receive proper wages and benefits—that we unlearn our desire that other people get out of our most intimate space: our shirt, our morning coffee. The social division of labor serves to naturalize and disguise social inequality. But that is not all it does. It was not so long ago that being poor was seen as an individual moral failing. Still more recently, it seemed unnatural and unethical for mothers who had any choice in the matter to put their children in the paid care of state-sponsored day care centers. To the extent that this is no longer true and to the extent to which our society has begun to act on the welfare state's no-fault poverty assumption, it's because we have taken some deep ethical lessons from the division of labor. It's at least worth speculating that ceasing to be scandalized by paid work in our homes may eventually have to be one of those lessons.

What exactly *is* the scandal about sweatshops? Naomi Klein, the author of the best-selling book on the antisweatshop movement *No Logo: Taking Aim at the Brand Bullies*, argues that the key to contemporary injustice is brand names: "The astronomical growth in the wealth and cultural influence of multinational corporations over the last fifteen years can arguably be traced back to a single, seemingly innocuous idea developed by management theorists in the mid-1980s: that successful corporations must primarily produce brands, as opposed to products" (3). It is this not-unfamiliar but really quite questionable premise that allows her to intensify the sense of scandal around the all-too-substantial sweatshop labor that goes into these, after all, so strangely insubstantial commodities. And this intensity has been a major political resource of the movement; the outrage against transnational corporations is special when they can be presented as a "global logo web," when there is "high name-brand recognition" (xviii). Note what assumptions this argument involves. Capitalists are "abandoning," Klein writes, "their traditional role as direct, secure employers to pursue their branding dreams" (441). "Direct, secure employers"? It would be news to workers who had been laid off or feared layoffs long before the logo takeoff of the 1980s that the "traditional role" of capitalists was to offer security of employment. It's as if what Friedrich Engels found in Manchester in 1844 was the good old days.

Klein's insistence that the real problem is brands means she has to overvalue the "old-fashioned idea that a manufacturer is responsible for its own work-force" (197).

This is indeed a very old-fashioned idea. It is old enough to reproduce that "organic conception, stressing interrelation and interdependence," whose opposition to crude laissez faire Williams termed "one of the most important facts about English social thinking in the nineteenth century." It's a bit surprising to find something so close to George Eliot's ethic of service and top-down solicitude, to the forthright paternalism of Elizabeth Gaskell's *North and South* (Lodge's model in *Nice Work*), reappearing now in the most up-to-date antisweatshop discourse. But it is not, I think, an absolute mistake. "As frustrating and irrational as it is," Shaw writes, "the stance that 'all corporations are evil so there's nothing to be done' has been a remarkably effective rationalization for inaction in the face of injustice." This is the commonsense version of "everything is political," and it too leaves people thinking, "in that case, nothing is political, so why bother?" In other words, a relative, compromised criterion will have to be posited according to which some corporations are less evil than others or else inaction will triumph. The willingness to accept, for rhetorical purposes, the somewhat mythic figure of the responsible employer offering secure employment makes sense as a way of opening up the landscape to action.

This is a backhanded case for the continued political relevance of the "Culture and Society" tradition, which turns up unexpectedly in the very middle of today's timeliest discourse of political action. It is also a case to understand action itself in a less theological sense, a sense that is not irreconcilable with the humble acknowledgment that, as novelists like Lodge and Eliot have suggested, those who want to understand the world are not thereby privileged to stand outside and against the division of labor. If action is just as politically confused and promiscuous as Mulhern says culture is, then action cannot serve scholars and critics of culture as a repository and arbiter of virtue. And the attempt to make it so serve is politically counterproductive for academics in that it can appear to potential allies only as a claim to moral superiority. To call on ourselves to aim our work at action or activism is to imply that we can have the singular good fortune to live, even potentially, a fusion of high moral principles with the universal need to make a living, a fusion that ordinary people could hardly dare to dream of. Listening in on this call to responsibility, the general population is likely to hear only another form of elitism. And when we need allies—and we do need allies, for example, in order to defend the dignity of our work against its reduction to the logic of the bottom line—we will have reason to expect more resentment than solidarity. If action is what we want, then action! is not the motto we want.

I have been arguing against the sort of self-aggrandizement that often hides out in calls to activist responsibility. I hope it's clear that I'm not arguing against responsibility itself. In pointing out that moments of insight like ours into the distant workings of the world are more ordinary than we like to think and that the weight of confusions, ambiguities, and other responsibilities that keeps ordinary people from acting on such moments is more characteristic of *us* than we like to think, I've been trying to give a more modest, more accurate sense of what our responsibilities are, but not a less binding one. The fact that even action against sweatshops must take place in a muddled zone where it's difficult at best to distinguish principled internationalism from scary nationalism can stand as one piece of evidence, among others, of the need for scholars and critics not to step out of character, but on the contrary to take up our responsibilities in the workplace and to exercise our most rigorous academically trained powers of analytic discrimination. And as far as action is concerned, there is always the imperative to do some institutional housecleaning—that is, to do what we can to ensure that we do not work in universities, libraries, museums, and other cultural institutions that for many of our colleagues will function, as they are under more and more pressure to do, like intellectual sweatshops.[21]

I began this essay by speaking about the division of labor and suggesting that the effort to perceive one's place in it offers a contemporary experience of the sublime. The critic who is most associated with this suggestion is Fredric Jameson. Indeed, Jameson is criticized on just this point by Gayatri Chakravorty Spivak in her *A Critique of Postcolonial Reason*. "It should . . . be clear," Spivak says, "that Jameson's fable about unrepresentable technology leading to a (generally unsatisfactory) paranoid social practice, a (satisfactory if correctly understood) schizophrenic aesthetic practice, and cognitive (not 'moral') political practice, is not a complete rupture with Kant's

Analytic of the Sublime" (325).[22] To put this more crudely: in the face of global capital, Jameson fails to imagine any satisfactory politics and offers instead the compensatory satisfactions, such as they are, of cognitive and, above all, aesthetic practice.

If this is true, there are extenuating circumstances. Among them is the difficulty of arriving at anything like a satisfactory politics under present global conditions—a shared difficulty. When heavy industry moves from Manchester and Milwaukee to Mexico and Malaysia, the map of political possibilities becomes more complicated for Mexicans and Malaysians as well. The complications are different, but they share the challenge of seeing, speaking, and acting transnationally. And it is at this point that expertise in cognitive and aesthetic practice can properly claim to be of use and even of significance.

In the final chapter of *Postmodernism, or, The Cultural Logic of Late Capitalism*, Jameson concedes that the word *reification*, understood as "the transformation of social relations into things," "probably directs attention in the wrong direction for us today." He sees more relevance, however, in a second definition of the word, " 'the effacement of the traces of production' from the object itself, from the commodity thereby produced. This sees the matter from the standpoint of the consumer: it suggests the kind of guilt people are freed from if they are able to not remember the work that went into their toys and furnishings. Indeed, the point of having your own object world, and walls and muffled distance or relative silence all around you, is to forget about all those innumerable others for a while; you don't want to have to think about Third World women every time you pull yourself up to your word processor, or all the other lower-class people with their lower-class lives when you decide to use or consume your other luxury products: it would be like having voices inside your head."[23]

The paragraph that immediately follows, however, makes the opposite point and makes it about art: "The reification of culture itself is evidently a somewhat different matter, since those products are 'signed'; nor, in consuming culture, do we particularly want, let alone need, to forget the human producer" (315). This frank admission changes everything. If in the case of art we don't need to forget the human producer, if we actively desire to remember the human producer, if we want to see traces of production, indeed will pay good money in order to have those voices echoing in our heads, then why mightn't we go on to want the same thing with other products as well, products that are not classified as art? The Lodge and Chast texts I've been discussing, taken together with the successes of anti-sweatshop campaigns based unapologetically in the psychology and ethics of the consumer, offer evidence that consumers don't come in two entirely distinct types, one artistic and the other unartistic—that there exists, in other words, a certain desire to live with voices inside our heads, not just among intellectuals and not just when contemplating works of art. This desire seems to mark a certain political possibility in the humanities. There are certainly less feasible and less consequential goals for humanistic education than the cultivating, augmenting, and channeling of the desire to have voices inside our heads. There are also worse ways of thinking about political action in the narrow sense.

Curiously, sublimity and sweatshops turn up together again on the back cover of Spivak's *A Critique of Postcolonial Reason.* The cover tells readers that the book "ranges from Kant's analytic of the sublime to child labor in Bangladesh." This is not quite so wide a range as Harvard University Press appears to think, for the discussion of the sublime in chapter 1 and the discussion of child labor in the conclusion are versions of the same argument. Questioning the "interested use of 'child labor' as a way of blocking export from developing countries" (416), Spivak accuses antisweatshop activists who call for boycotts against the Bangladesh garment industry of blindly helping to protect northern jobs and markets (415); "The transnationally illiterate benevolent feminist of the North supports this wholeheartedly, with 'ignorant goodwill'" (416).[24] The ignorant goodwill of northern progressives is also the theme of the philosophy chapter, which treats the figure of the aboriginal in Kant. So-called New Hollanders and "inhabitants of Tierra del Fuego . . . bubble up in the cauldron of Kant's contempt," as Spivak nicely puts it, because Kant needs examples of "man in the raw," man lacking in culture and therefore unable to appreciate the sublime (26, 28n). Only those lacking in culture will allow him to define the process by which culture is capable of manufacturing a rational subject, which offers in turn "a justification for Europe to be the global legislator" (32–33). Kant's "global project for the subject . . . of reason" is "the project of transforming [the New Hollander and the Fuegan] from the raw to the philosophical" (36).

According to Spivak, Kant's analytic of the sublime does precisely the same thing that Western human rights discourse does when addressed to Bangladeshi sweatshops: it flattens out the complexity and difference of Third World society to suit a First World standard of ethical rationality. But it is unclear that Kant was always and everywhere committed to that standard. He turns to the aesthetic in his *Critique of Judgment*, as I suggested hastily above, not because he wants to defend rationality but precisely because he can see that the rational community he desires will never come about by means of submission to rationality. People must be induced or cajoled by other means to bind themselves together. They are more likely to do so, he speculated, by means of their uncoerced and individual yet also universalizing act of appreciating the beautiful than by means of their rational obedience to the good. In other words, Kant's aesthetics can be read as his political theory, a theory rendered necessary by the political insufficiencies of Reason. According to this view, Kant would be saying that political action has to take on the limits and confusions of the aesthetic. For if it does not, if it attempts to embody and enact Reason itself, it risks producing effects which are rationally and ethically undesirable.

What this alternative account of Kantian sublimity seeks to accomplish is to support Spivak's argument concerning political action against Asian sweatshops, and to do so by showing how broadly she agrees with Jameson. What Spivak complains about, in northern antisweatshop campaigns, is the simplification of action whereby "the only imperative—'What You Can Do in India'—is boycotts and sanctions" (418n). In calling for resistance to sweatshops that would be accompanied by long-term "infrastructural followup" (420), Spivak is trying, one might say, to theorize a politics in which northerners would have to forgo the illusory satisfactions of immediate action in a domain of ostensible political transparency and ethical universality. Like Jameson, she writes in or near the mode of the Kantian sublime. She insists that constraints, obscurities, hesitations, and self-questionings, the inevitable by-products of capitalism in its global mode, must be factored back into the tempting simplicity of action, a simplicity that, as she points out, has not become less treacherous in the epoch of humanitarian intervention and human rights. For this "sinking back into ourselves" is what politics itself requires, even and especially at a global scale. Such sinking back also serves to confirm the emotional satisfaction we derive from intellectual work in all its lonely specificity, the slow and patient labor of filling in the steps, both analytically and politically, between the perceptual and emotional jolt and the outlet in action that may or may not be found to suit it. But if the public intellectual is to pursue something higher than publicity, this continuing communion with privacy is an inescapable part of her task.

# 5 EDWARD SAID AND EFFORT

Edward Said was my teacher before the publication of *Orientalism*, when he was best known as a critical advocate of so-called French theory.[1] Some years later he became a friend and mentor who, it is not too much to say, saved my life, professionally speaking and perhaps more than professionally speaking. I owe him a personal debt, therefore, and a debt that is probably larger than anyone should ideally owe anyone else. As a result of this debt, there were complications to our friendship. I do not intend to discuss them. But I do want to speak on the assumption that, to some extent at least, these complications can be generalized—in other words, that for all of us who share a collective debt to Edward Said, as a heroic example and a sort of ideal, this debt is not a simple thing to service or sustain, to live up to or know what to do with.

Among the many tributes paid to Said since his death in 2003, one of the most moving was the moment at his funeral in New York when his son Wadie spoke bravely and humorously about the difficulty of belonging to the next generation, about what a hard act his father is to follow. This was a confession, yet it allowed for movement from the personal to the general—for example, in Wadie's afterword to his father's book *From Oslo to Iraq and the Road Map*. "The amazing memory that I am left with," Wadie writes, "is his dedication to the idea of speaking out and staying informed, no matter how sick or infirm he was" (302). Beyond everything that can be said about the genius Said brought to the acts of reading and writing, there is the simple fact of effort, effort under circumstances of illness so oppressive that even so everyday an action as staying informed or staying informed enough to speak out with authority was indeed a piece of amazing heroism. Unlike genius, effort can in principle be successfully emulated. When we admire an effort, we accept a responsibility to try to emulate it. Yet there is a sense in which admiration, as it rises to ever-greater intensities of praise, seems designed, on the contrary, to leave lesser creatures much too satisfied with our failure to emulate, a failure that the magnitude of the praise suggests may be inevitable. I cannot imagine that Said would be pleased with this legacy: too much admiration, not enough effort.

Still, some part of me wants to blame Said for this dilemma. After all, it was in part his modesty that prevented him from theorizing his own achievement in such a way that other people might be able to assess the possibility or practicality of following even a short distance in his footsteps. In his book *Representations of the Intellectual* he holds fast to the tradition of Julien Benda, a tradition according to which the intellectual is, as Said described himself in his memoir, "out of place," an isolated, unaffiliated speaker of truth to power. In this tradition, the successful enactment of an intellectual vocation is obliged to present itself as an unsolved mystery, indeed, an insoluble one. For explanation of where any given intellectual comes from and why power would ever listen to her or him could emerge only via scrutiny of actions and affiliations—for example, Said's achievements in the academy and his affiliations with the Palestinian people—that take their meaning from the given context. By Said's account, however, the particular context by which his achievements were ratified, namely, scholarly institutions, and the partiality implied by his own affiliations, for example, some special degree of loyalty to the project of Palestinian nationhood, must be allowed no part whatsoever in the definition of the intellectual, which demands an ideal spiritual purity. If to be an intellectual is to enter into a sort of absolute, almost monastic exile, then belonging of any kind is grounds for instant loss of accreditation. As Stefan Collini points out, "For Said the preoccupying dialectic is that between 'purity' and 'contamination'" (432).[2] Like Benda, that is, Said defines intellectuals in such a way that the charge of *trahison* will be applicable always and everywhere. For all intellectuals can do, when seen as participants in the actual institutions of their time and place, is appear to betray their impossibly pure ideal or else threaten to disappear as a category. Disappearance and betrayal were what Said himself most often saw around him. The two words sum up many of his often harsh observations concerning intellectuals and their willingness to accept their professionalization or domestication.[3]

Those of us who admire Said and seek after our fashion to emulate him need more encouragement than this. For most of us most of the time, even in the absence of illness, merely staying informed seems strenuous and almost prohibitively exhausting. The lonely exilic hero speaking truth to power is only with difficulty imagined doing the everyday things that exhaust and preoccupy us: feeding the baby or taking out the trash or, for that matter, grading a stack of papers. Intellectuals have been so persistently imagined as masculine precisely because they have been imagined as instances of a more generally valued autonomy: ideal versions of the so-called liberal humanist subject.[4] But we cannot rest content with the assumption that someone else, probably female, is doing all the work necessary to the maintenance of biological and familial life, that intellectuals ought to have no children (a highly charged theme in Said's *Beginnings*) or will enjoy the financial means to hire servants for child rearing. Nor can we flatter ourselves that if we speak up, we will have done our part and satisfied all ethical obligations, whether or not the world and its powers, which we have no obligation to inspect too closely, decide to recognize that anything significant has been said or done. Whatever the risk of demystification or decathexis, then, a proper theory of the intellectual would seem to require more detail about the social field from which intellectual activity emerges and where it has or does not have its effects. Fewer portraits of the intellectual, more landscapes around the intellectual. Which is to say, less imagining of the intellectual as constitutively homeless, as cosmopolitan in the sense of absolutely detached.

Given the conceptual framework Said sets up around the intellectual, there has been an irresistible temptation to raise the charge of betrayal—that is, of unconscious social attachment and belonging—about Said himself. One recent and emphatic example is Gil Anidjar's essay "Secularism."[5]

Anidjar's indictment, which first avoids naming Said (there is no colon, no subtitle) then makes him personally and perfectly representative of its titular concept.

As I've noted, Said offers the homeless intellectual as a model for the normative subject. Homeless is what he teaches us to want to be. The putative advantages of homelessness can fit into different vocabularies: for example, hybridity, the perspective gained from multiple affiliations with no single center; or humanism, critical distance and impartiality; or cosmopolitanism. But, as I've said, Said's preferred personal term of self-description, perhaps the one that best indicates what his avowed humanism means to him, is *secular*. The introductory chapter of *The World, the Text, and the Critic* lays out a brief for what Said calls "Secular Criticism" (Said 1983). In case the point has been missed, the book's conclusion, summing up its values throughout, is entitled "Religious Criticism." There, Said observes "a dramatic increase in the number of appeals to the extrahuman, the vague abstraction, the divine, the esoteric, and secret" (291). Religion has returned, he suggests, as a result of "exhaustion, consolation, disappointment" among intellectuals. It appears in the form of a "Manichean theologizing of 'the Other'" as well as a cult of "unthinkability, undecidability, and paradox" (291). Against all this, much of it targeting the explicit antihumanism of French theory, he marshals a secularism derived from Giambattista Vico: "What human beings can know is only what they have made" (291). Such secularism contains quite diverse components—a preference for empirical particulars over abstract generalizations, for example, is by no means the same thing as "a healthy skepticism about the various official idols venerated by culture and by system" (290). But the key to Said's secularism, as I have argued elsewhere (Robbins 1994), is the conjoined refusals of "the need for certainty," on the one hand, and of "group solidarity, and a sense of communal belonging" (290), on the other. Though he assumes it is still available as pejorative metaphor (something that in today's climate has become even more questionable), Said does not take religion itself as his prime target. His target seems to be social membership. Any surrender to sociality, he suggests, will undermine the proper independence of critical knowledge. Belonging as such implies dogmatism. Religiosity, in Said's lexicon, is a compound of both. Criticism can be secular only if it takes nothing as sacred, submits to no certainties. And it can reject certainties only if it also rejects "group solidarity" and "a sense of communal belonging." This credo restates in the vocabulary of the sacred and the secular what Said elsewhere puts into a geographical figure: the sacred is being at home, the secular is being in exile.

Anidjar's main argument is that Said's secularism, on the contrary, makes him all too much at home, at home in Western culture. Secularism for Anidjar is not just a Western ideology but the particular ideology that sponsors the West's constitutive aggression toward the non-West. When Said participates in "the general movement of opposition to religion carried by the terms *secular* and *secularism*," he appears "simply to have forgotten the lesson taught by this most important of books, namely, *Orientalism*. For if *Orientalism* teaches us anything, it is that Orientalism *is* secularism" (56). To Anidjar, Said's espousal of secularism makes him not a critic of the West, but one of its most insidious propagandists. Thus, despite Said's scathing opinion of V. S. Naipaul (Said 2000, 98–104), he becomes fair game for satiric descriptions like Rob Nixon's of that other self-proclaimed exile: "Secure, esteemed, and integrated into the high culture of the metropolis, asserting his homelessness, while considerable numbers of genuinely disowned people battle to be acknowledged as legitimate members of the society he is at liberty to reject rhetorically though he depends on it in every way" (32).[6] Anidjar denies accordingly that Said's commitment to secularism is oppositional. On the contrary,

> Said was oppositional to the extent that he was only attacking victorious causes. And—is this really news?—secularism *is* a victorious cause. It participates in a set of devices that make religion (the religion of the others, that is, or their nationalism, primitivism, militarism, and terrorism) more of an ominous danger than, say, the dealings of the ruling and no-longer welfare states, the practices of giant corporations and their national and international backing, to say nothing of homeland security and its consequences. . . . Secularism continues to be fostered by the same institutions and structurally identical elites, who work out of the same centers of power that earlier spread their "civilization" and continue to expand their mission, be it economic, military, cultural, humanitarian even. It still has the bigger bombs—it *is* the history of bombing. (64–65)

As a champion of secularism, Said becomes for Anidjar not just a westerner but an Orientalist, and not just an Orientalist but (if the somewhat hysterical tone here allows the words to be taken as meaning what they say) a state terrorist actively supporting aerial bombardment.

It is tempting to read this accusation as simply another symptom of the irrationalism that Said called religious criticism. The passage could almost be said to act out an abandonment of secular rationality. For as it gathers momentum it flings away reason's tools—self-reflection, qualification, access to a spectrum of differentiated categories, and causal relations—and resolves itself into a single, brutally assertive act of predication. The finger points, jabbing for emphasis: x *is* y. Anidjar needs the repeated italicized *is* because, like the Orwellian assertion that war is peace, his argument has a great deal of rational skepticism to overthrow. An ordinary reader, even a sympathetic one, is likely to think that the relations between x (Said's secularism) and y (the history of bombing) are somewhat more complicated than simple equivalence. The drastic simplification, implying that responsibility for all the ills of the world can be located in one collective subject, even a subject as vast and easy to malign as the West, seems a good example of the "impossibly huge generalizations" (Said 1983, 291) that Said offers as instances of "uncritical religiosity" (292).

Yet if so, then Said's account of secularism might also be accused of uncritical religiosity. For in its strongest self-description, as I have noted, it refuses to admit that it, too, constitutes a worldly form of belonging and suffers necessarily from the imperfection appertaining thereto. To claim for the intellectual an absolute and mysterious separation from all human belonging is to claim a spiritual state that is truly not of this world. Why would we not think of it as a version of the sacred? I don't remember anyone pointing out, though I may simply have missed it, that spirituality is an essential assumption behind the famous words that Said repeatedly quotes as a critical and cosmopolitan manifesto: "The man who finds his homeland sweet is still a tender beginner; he to whom every soil is as his native one is already strong; but he is perfect to whom the entire world is as a foreign land" (Said 2000, 185). Hugh of St. Victor, the author of these sentences, was a monk living in the Catholic Europe of the twelfth century. Could he have embraced this absolute homelessness if he were not silently sustained by a sense of belonging on another level, by faith in a higher, otherworldly home? It seems plausible that Said's cosmopolitanism, though defiantly worldly, is similarly sustained by sources of authority that go unmentioned. Taken abstractly, Anidjar's argument is that while Said thinks he is in exile, he is actually a member, and that his membership empowers him. The all-powerful entities to which Anidjar thinks Said belongs, secularism, Christianity, and the West, may not offer the most precise explanation of the particular power Said came to wield, but the abstract point about Said's belonging and its authority seems right. Like all cosmopolitans, Said is attached as well as detached. It is only on these terms, that is, taking secularism not as exile but as a form of affiliation, that Said can be defended as a secular critic. Such a defense would involve qualifying some of secularism's claims as Said articulates them. It could be described as a secularizing of secularism, an expression that positions the secular as both a conceptual object in need of improvement and the conceptual subject called upon to perform that improvement, that is, seen as worthy of performing it.

Having made this concession, is it still acceptable to pronounce the term *theological* about a style of argument of which one disapproves? I think it is. Consider the account of secularism Anidjar provides. Where does secularism come from? As Anidjar tells the story, it comes from "one particular religion" (59), namely, Christianity. Christianity invents both religion (as a category) and nonreligion, or secularism. Christianity's powers of invention are all but miraculous. It does not seem too much to say that, in its overwhelming superiority to all other historical actors (there are none in Anidjar's story), it behaves like a monotheistic god. It is the source of everything and its opposite. The structure of the sentences leaves room for no other subject, whether grammatically or historically. Christianity "actively disenchanted its own world by dividing itself into private and public, politics and economics, indeed, religious and secular. And Christianity turned against itself in a complex and ambivalent series of parallel movements, continuous gestures and rituals, . . . slowly coming to name that to which it ultimately claimed to oppose itself: religion. Munchausen-like, it attempted to liberate itself, to extricate itself from its own conditions; it *judged* itself no longer Christian, no longer religious. Christianity . . . *reincarnated* itself as secular" (59–60). These are the actions of a Subject so transcendental that no other appellation will do: in Anidjar's account, it acts like a deity. No actions are mentioned that could be the work of any other subject whatsoever. Anidjar does not pause to mention the Greeks, for example, though for both Nietz-sche and Foucault Greece added to the mix of Western ideas something that remained significantly, if not completely, alien to Christianity. And the Jews and the Muslims, who are mentioned—in whose name, indeed, Anidjar seems to write—appear only as victimized objects, not as subjects: "Religion *is* the Orient, the imperial realm to be governed and dominated, bombed, reformed, and civilized" (66). Again, italics are brought in to enforce the otherwise implausible notion that any one actor can fill all the available space, leaving everyone else no choice but to be acted upon. Christianity does have a human side: it does Adam's job of the naming of species.[7] But its power to maintain itself in its essential identity as Christianity even while transforming itself into its opposite, secularism, can hardly be described as anything less than divine: "Secularism is a name Christianity gave itself when it invented religion, when it named its other or others as religions" (62). Secularism then became "the means by which Christianity *forgot and forgave* itself" (63).

For this style of argument, too, Said himself could be held accountable, at least in the eyes of his critics. This model of ambitious spatial and temporal totalizing could never have attained its present pervasiveness without the help of *Orientalism*. As Aijaz Ahmad puts it, Said visibly surpasses even his master Foucault in the scale of his temporal generalization: "The idea that there could be *a* discourse—that is to say, an epistemic construction—tra-versing the whole breadth of 'Western' history and textualities, spanning not only the modern capitalist period but all the preceding pre-capitalist periods as well, is not only an un-Marxist but also a radically un-Foucauldian idea" (166).[8] This is why, Ahmad goes on, "the only voices we encounter in the book are precisely those of the very Western canonicity which, as Said complains, has always silenced the Orient" (172). And it is why the book could suggest, going far beyond the mere historical record, that "Europeans were *ontologically* incapable of producing any true knowledge about non-Europe" (178). In short, it is why Said can be accused of "his own essentializ-ing of 'the West'" (183). Even readers who are largely sympathetic to the argument of *Orientalism* sometimes complain that in Said's account the Third World itself has no agency, while the West is a well-nigh omnipotent cause, responsible for all visible effects. In this sense, the argument of *Orientalism* can itself be called theological. Anidjar, unembarrassed to march under the banner of theology, can appropriate both *Orientalism* and Orientalism as his own: on the one hand, Said's critique of generalizing, on the other, the practice of generalizing itself, this time about the West. The strategy of enlisting Said, the author of *Orientalism*, against Said, the champion of secularism, seizes upon a genuine vulnerability.

More might be said about *Orientalism* and the degree to which it has quietly protected itself against such hostile takeovers. But I am more concerned here with Said's secularist credo as such, without regard for whether or not it is embodied in his most famous book. If aspects of *Orientalism* have to be jettisoned in order to mount a proper defense of Said's efforts on behalf of secularism, so be it.

In a perceptive review-essay about the book *Occidentalism* by Ian Buruma and Avishai Margalit, Akeel Bilgrami argues that so-called Occidentalism, that is, the set of critiques that generalize about the West as freely and disparagingly as Orientalism generalizes about the non-West, is not truly symmetrical and does not deserve the same dismissal. The key reason is power. The three defining features of Orientalism, civilizational condescension, stereotyping, and exoticism, "owed their influence in more or less subtle ways to the proximity of such writing . . . to metropolitan sites of political and economic power" (389).[9] A fourth feature, the fact that the first three are phenomena of the canonical mainstream rather than some eccentric fringe, likewise expresses "the deep links that writing has to *power*" (389). The "absolutely crucial" difference between Orientalism and Occidentalism is that in the latter the discourse's link to power is absent: "The enemies of the West who are presented in this book, far from being close to power, are motivated by their powerlessness and helplessness against Western power and domination" (390). In short, the presence or absence of power is decisive.

As a practical political judgment, this is a helpful reminder. The same ideas should not be acted on in the same way when they are spoken by the powerful and when they are spoken by the powerless. Nationalism, to give the obvious example, is not the same idea in the mouth of a Palestinian who has been denied a state and an American whose state has a well-recorded habit of trying to bomb foreigners into submission. But there is a danger in allowing power to divide the world in two. This clear-cut division does not help the reader figure out where she or he stands in the much murkier zone where most political actions are taken, a zone in which it is necessary to talk not about power's simple absence or presence but about kinds and degrees of power. The power-based distinction between Orientalism and Occidentalism does not invite us to think of ourselves as political actors, which is to say, as possessors and potential users of power. To possess and use power is what it means to act politically. Before one can decide what is to be done to redistribute power, one must know what power one possesses. To imagine that one has no power and—a special temptation in the humanities—that one's virtue depends on being careful at all costs not to obtain any is not only self-serving self-blindness; it is also a convenient means of taking oneself outside the sphere of politics completely.

Said's secularism, as I've noted, sometimes trips over this point, implicitly claiming a virtuous powerlessness as an unspoken corollary of the claim to homelessness.[10] The secularizing of secularism entails abandoning this claim. What I will suggest here is that this secularizing can be shown to happen in Said's own writing. The key to this argument is the term with which I began: *effort*.

The term *effort* is associated with Said's humanist impulse. His early writings suggested that French antihumanism gave too little importance to matters of intention, will, awareness, and free choice. When he speaks of Foucault, Said sets effort, which implies a certain freedom, against power, which sometimes seems to be no freedom, all constraint. As it turns out, however, the terms have both a genealogical and a conceptual intimacy. The first definition of *effort* given in the *Oxford English Dictionary* is simply "power." This definition is described as obsolete, but the current meaning is contiguous with it: "a strenuous putting forth of power." *Efforce*, from the Old French *esforcer*, meant to force open, to compel, to use violent means, and, as with the historical link between *attachment* and *attack*, the apparent innocence of modern usages cannot rid themselves of a residuum of force or violence. Effort, in other words, is the display of a power within that is in some way comparable or commensurate to the power without that it confronts. Said often seems to present himself as lacking or exterior to power, especially in his critiques of poststructuralism. But his repeated, insistent use of the word *effort* testifies to a half-recognized participation in power.

Somewhat surprisingly, Said's commitment to effort takes him away from those who align him in an uncomplicated way with humanism. Well before his death one could detect a tendency to lament his forays into literary theory as misguided and finally inessential to his project, a project for which humanism was the one genuinely necessary resource.[11] Tariq Ali, speaking of the influence of Foucault on *Orientalism*, adds "alas" (8).[12] When Said says that "history does not get made without work, intention, resistance, effort, or conflict," he is indeed suggesting that the freedom of the critic or intellectual to resist, to formulate an intention, to make an effort is a freedom for which there is no room in, say, Foucault's "micronetworks of power" (Said 1983, 245). In the same work religious criticism is described as "shutting off human investigation, criticism, *and effort* in deference to the authority of the more-than-human, the supernatural, the other-worldly" (290, emphasis added). Those who notice his use of the word *effort* tend to praise Said, in terms he himself invited, as a fundamentally antisystemic thinker, where *system* is a codeword for the French theory builders. Abdirahman Hussein suggests that Said troubled other people's wisdom instead of offering any systematic wisdom of his own, rejecting methodology in order to be "open-ended" (4).[13] I will not insist here on how far his work is from the banal, toothless liberalism for which such accounts seem to be preparing him. Nor will I do more than mention the prosystemic side of Said's work, which is obvious enough in its influence on Anidjar and elsewhere. In dialogue with Ali in 1994, Said described the genesis of *Orientalism* as a discovery that "distortions and misrepresentations [of the Arabs in Western discourse] were systematic, part of a much larger system of thought that was endemic to the West's whole enterprise of dealing with the Arab world" (Ali 62). *Orientalism* may not have allowed enough room for exceptions and discriminations, but this fundamental insight is surely correct. My question is whether Said in fact imagines system on a theological model, whether his sense of what sort of enemy we are up against permits any simple distinction between system and antisystem, humanism and antihumanism. His use of the word *effort* seems to resist such classification.

Talking about the popular impression of symmetry between the two sides in the Middle East, "as if each side *had* a side, a piece of land, a territory from which to face the other" (Said 1999, 9), an impression of symmetry that persisted even into the Second Intifada, Said described this "skewed picture" as "kept in place as a result of human effort" (9). Said's readers will recognize here one of his characteristically and wonderfully counterintuitive phrasings. The idea of valued accomplishment that we usually attach to great works of art, which are normally esteemed as the result of a successful expenditure of "human effort," is here presented instead as an attribute of the evils against which we struggle. The language of effort, which cannot be subtracted from our praise of Edward Said, is especially characteristic of his writing when he refuses to decide whether or not he wants to praise, or whether the moment is right for either praise or blame. In his contribution to an anthology called *The Landscape of Palestine*, he speaks of a "nationalist *effort* premised on the need to construct a desirable loyalty to and insider's knowledge of one's country, tradition, and faith" (Said 1999, 4, emphasis added). The examples here happen to come from the United States and Israel, so his refusal to join the "nationalist effort" makes political sense. And yet the same studied neutrality reappears later in the essay when he turns to the Palestinians. The language of effort seems to be a common denominator, shared by both sides, and in itself offering no clues as to which side one should take. Arriving at the Palestinians, he speaks of their collective memory in neutral, processual, constructionist terms that might apply equally well to Orientalism: as "a field of activity in which past events are selected, reconstructed, maintained, modified, and endowed with political meaning" (13). What he calls the "dialectic of memory over territory" (9) seems to work equally well for nationalism, on the one hand, and for imperialism, on the other. All the force of his intelligence seems concentrated on the goal of not dividing those -isms from each other easily or prematurely.

Said assumes, Hussein writes, that "what has been labeled as 'normal,' 'ideal,' 'natural' or 'commonsensical' in a given cultural or historical conjuncture has achieved that privileged status in virtue of the vast amount of concerted effort invested in its behalf by individuals, institutions, and indeed entire societies" (7). But note how Said's phrasing differs distinctively from the constructionist commonplace that what has been made by people can be changed by people. Said is saying this, too. But to use the term *effort* as repeatedly as Said does is to put extra stress on the common ground between Hussein's list—a list of things that are all assumed to need changing —and the positive terms that Hussein does not mention, including projects of change themselves. They too are products of effort. To use the same word about both, as Said so pointedly does, is to step outside of humanism, at least to the extent that humanism is always tempted by a scholarly open-mindedness that leaves the impact of its knowledge out of account and in so doing subtly or not so subtly rules out the choosing of political sides. If the identification of secularism with exile threatens to take Said out of politics, his habit of speaking in terms of effort acknowledges an inevitable participation in power and takes him back into the domain of the political.

I am not suggesting that there was ever any doubt about Said's commitment to the cause of Palestinian self-determination or to a liberatory politics generally. Among the many intellectuals who speak in the name of politics, Said has become a landmark, unique in his generation, standing out from all by virtue of his unfailing courage, energy, vision, and scrupulousness. Nor am I pretending that an everyday term like *effort* offers a definitive reconciliation of the conceptual strains that animated so much of his work. There was always an obvious tension between Said's credo of intellectual detachment and the political struggle to retrieve a Palestinian homeland. Was exile a desirable condition, necessary to the most rigorous intellectual endeavor? Or was it the regrettable result of a particular dispossession, something that could and should be made right by a return to a literal or metaphorical homeland—that should and would disappear with, say, the creation of a viable Palestinian state?[14] Part of the secret of Said's charismatic presence is that he seemed to solve in his own being a paradox or contradiction for which there is perhaps no purely intellectual resolution. But there was also a degree of coherence between his contradictions and those that beset the Palestinians as a group. In *The Question of Palestine*, as I noted in a review, Said suggests with a mixture of boldness and resignation that "the Palestinian experience has been one of homelessness, and in a sense it will remain one of homelessness, the homelessness that Said offers as the proper condition of criticism. As he says, 'the conservative version of the Palestinian quest is both historically and morally intolerable: the idea that we can all go back to 1948, to our property, to an Arab country' [Said 1979, 167]. When it comes, the Palestinian state will be a new construction on a new site" (Robbins 1983, 70–71). When the PLO, then the Palestinian Authority, accepted the principle of a state to be located on the West Bank and Gaza, that is, they were asking the Palestinians "to start thinking not in terms of the homes and property they had lost irrevocably to Israel, but in terms of new political gains" (Said 1979, 224). Whether what is pushed for in Israel/Palestine is one secular democratic state or two, what is demanded of both the Palestinians and the Israelis will be to give up some of what they feel is theirs, what they feel they are owed. Here once again the word *secular* can be understood neither as a disguise for imperialist Christianity nor as the literal antithesis of religion as such. To speak of a secular democratic state, as Said did, is to use the word *secular* so as to reactivate its impulse of detachment—from the land, from the past, from belief in the strong sense, from belonging in the strong sense—not just as part of an ideal of critical writing, but as essential to a pragmatic engagement with politics, an attachment whose stakes and substance are precisely the land, the past, belief, and belonging.

Said's persistent use of the word *effort* itself represents an effort on his part: an effort to win recognition for accomplishments that do not achieve perfection or closure, including his own; and an effort to recognize power as something possessed and used rather than something whose lack can serve as a mark of virtue. This latter point is one that scholars, who tend to pride themselves on their marginality, may need to be informed about more than nonscholars. How should we scholars take it, then, when the literary critic Giles Gunn describes Said as "the conscience of our profession" (71)?[15] On one level, this is perhaps no more than the truth. But if so, it is a very intriguing truth. What does it suggest about the relations between virtue, effort, and power?

Said's own view of the academic profession is often unsparing. Orientalism and Eurocentrism, as Said describes them, often seem too deeply entrenched in the assumptions and practices of the American academy for that academy to be imagined as ever taking the author of *Orientalism* as its conscience, let alone doing so within a decade or two of the publication of that book. Why should our profession have accepted his rebuke to its Eurocentrism and narrow nationalism? If criticism is, as Said wrote in 1983, "an academic thing, located for the most part far away from the questions that trouble the reader of a daily newspaper," if it is "an institution for publicly affirming the values of our, that is, European dominant elite culture," then why should it have embraced Said's unsparing judgment of it?[16] The question is crucial. If we do not ask it, our praise of his accomplishment risks sounding empty at the core, for we will have refused to consider exactly what he was and was not up against as well as what we ourselves are and are not up against.

The answer does not lie with what one might call Said's incidental humanism—his willingness to extend a magnanimous, somewhat unfocused respect to classic texts and favorite critics, pretending their value utterly transcended their time and place, refusing to blame them for the complicity with Eurocentrism or imperialism in which he nonetheless took some pains to catch and expose them. The sportsmanlike gesture might have reassured some scholars, but it would not have caught and held their attention in the first place. The professional conscience could have been activated, I think, only by the blame itself. According to Gunn, Said knew "that there is nothing strictly speaking innocent either about the act of writing or the act of reading" (71). There is an extra level to these words. When Said accused literature, our professional object of knowledge, of guilty complicity in imperialism, he seemed to threaten the value of professional attention to literature. But one might also say that this accusation paradoxically increased literature's social meaningfulness, a meaningfulness that has been exposed to ever-increasing doubt. Even if literature or discourse is serving the devil, or especially because it is serving the devil, it becomes important. It makes things happen. It needs to be taken into consideration. Hence the charge might be greeted by the more perceptive of his fellow professionals as a sort of gift. In accepting Said's accusation and thereby accepting him as their conscience, the humanities were also accepting an enormous and lucrative contract for further work. And not merely work, but work recognized to be socially meaningful. In other words, Said was embraced by the institutions about which he had so little good to say because when he said bad things about them he was implying that they possessed a kind of power. The success of *Orientalism* can be explained only by the fact that the book attributed so much power to writing, to knowledge, to discourse, in short, to the stock in trade of academics. Said argued that this power was serving the worst possible ends. But set against the alternative of powerless irrelevance, the option of blameworthy significance looks quite attractive: especially if one can simultaneously occupy the position of the (self-)blamer, that is, the critic. Said's success *in* the academy disproves his argument *about* the academy.

But this does not leave us with an idealization of the academy any more than with a simple repudiation of it. When critics in the Arnoldian humanist line claim for themselves an ideal disinterestedness, they invite the charge that such a claim, like that of humanitarianism, is also to some extent self-interested. What is one to make, then, of Said's emendation of the humanist position? Is it entirely self-interested to repudiate disinterestedness (detachment, exile) and to acknowledge one's self-interest? Perhaps not. At any rate, the question indicates an indispensable moral messiness that is part of the payoff for Said's insistence that the academy is a channel of power. Surrender our ostensible moral purity, he enjoins us, and we can win some purchase on the world. If the secular has threatened to propose an other-worldly model of exilic innocence, this would count as a secularization of the secular. Nubar Hovsepian nicely describes Zionism as "encumbered with Palestinians" (11).[17] In this sense, Said forces us to think of secularism too as properly "encumbered"—encumbered by the power it possesses as well as by the powers it is up against.

What power should we then attribute to the secular? For Anidjar, as cited above, secularism is a "victorious cause," fully, even divinely empowered. For Eve Kosofsky Sedgwick, on the other hand, the willingness of scholars to believe secularism has triumphed is itself as mysterious as popular adherence to the most groundless of superstitions:

> "The modern liberal subject": by now it seems, or ought to seem, anything but an obvious choice as the unique terminus ad quem of historical narrative. Where *are* all these supposed modern liberal subjects? I daily encounter graduate students who are dab hands at unveiling the hidden historical violences that underlie a secular, universalist liberal humanism. Yet these students' sentient years, unlike the formative years of their teachers, have been spent entirely in a xenophobic Reagan-Bush-Clinton-Bush America where "liberal" is, if anything, a taboo category and where "secular humanism" is routinely treated as a marginal religious sect, while a vast majority of the population claims to engage in direct intercourse with multiple invisible entities such as angels, Satan, and God.[18]

I recognize Sedgwick's world much more readily than I do Anidjar's. And my understanding of what Said called worldliness suggests that in this time and place some of our most urgent intellectual tasks must be guided by observations like Sedgwick's of the actual state of the electorate. Yet Said was not a narrow-minded pragmatist who thought only in the short term—if he had been, the disappointments of Middle Eastern politics might well have destroyed him well before his untimely death. Nor did he allow his intellectual agenda to be dumbed down to suit the crude demystificatory needs, important as these are, of a radically incomplete Enlightenment project.

Once upon a time, Said's qualified but unflinching commitment to the Enlightenment was more representative than not of anticolonial intellectuals in the Third World. That may in fact still be true. But many metropolitan intellectuals speaking in the name of the Third World have disputed this part of Said's legacy, tying critiques of his secularism or secularism generally to a rejection or radical revision of cosmopolitanism. For example, in his introduction to a group of essays entitled "Romanticism, Secularism, and Cosmopolitanism" Colin Jager lays claim to cosmopolitanism as a positive value, but only after first dissociating it from the Enlightenment virtue of detachment.[19] Cosmopolitanism, he assumes, is defined by taking up a planetary rather than a local perspective. But the planet is inhabited by more believers than secularists, and the number of the believers is increasing by the day. Whatever you may think about their beliefs, they make up the great majority of the world's population. Doesn't this non-European majority think of secularism as an alien, hostile European intervention? And if so, isn't it necessarily correct? Who are we to dispute the data? Jager concludes therefore that cosmopolitanism, properly conceived, is on the side of religion.

There is an acute irony in the fact that this line of argument can be formulated thanks only to the cosmopolitan critique of Eurocentrism, a critique which was carried out (most famously in *Orientalism*) in secularism's name. It was not so long ago that missionary Christianity, both Catholic and Protestant, would be counted as a self-evident agent of empire. No one doubted for an instant that the priests fitted snugly among the soldiers and traders who had seized and exploited the globe to serve European interests and beliefs. Now Jager invokes what he calls "the globalization of Christianity" as if it represented not the successful result of European imperialism but, on the contrary, a challenge to it. As he tells the story, all the violence of conversion drops out, whether non-Europeans were converted at gunpoint or, more recently, under pressure to adapt to capitalist modernity. As long as there is belief, it doesn't really matter which belief or how much force was applied to move the colonized from an old belief to a new one. The only real enemy is unbelief, if indeed such a thing as unbelief exists at all. The assumption underlying this bid to redefine common sense is often something like "everything is belief" or "everything is faith." From this perspective, unbelief is not itself an existing, substantial, historically grounded ethos but merely a false, arrogant claim to a privileged unlocatedness.

As I've said, Said was indeed ready to claim unlocatedness for himself and to urge it on intellectuals as a prerequisite of their vocation. But this does not mean that his strenuous cosmopolitanism has to be surrendered to a lazy, undiscriminating platitude like "everything is faith." Said's detachment was as real as his attachments, and as necessary. Like Chomsky, he defined universality so that it entailed an unstinting effort of self-detachment that could neither embrace norms nor do without them: "looking for and trying to uphold a single standard for human behavior when it comes to such matters as foreign and social policy. Thus if we condemn an unprovoked act of aggression by an enemy we should also be able to do the same when our government invades a weaker party. There are no rules by which intellectuals can know what to say or do; nor for the true secular intellectual are there any gods to be worshipped and looked to for unwavering guidance" (xiv).[20] If this sounds a bit paradoxical, it stands for a paradox we have no choice but to inhabit. The state of the world does not permit us to walk away as if the contest between descriptive and normative versions of cosmopolitanism had been decided once and for all—that is, as if description had carried the day.

However you describe Christianity, its globalization does not ipso facto confer honor or credibility upon Christianity any more than the globalization of capitalism obliges us to honor capitalism. (Yes, in both cases some quantity of respect does follow—but respect of the same limited and amoral sort.) One of the questions raised by Jager's jujitsu move on cosmopolitan anti-Eurocentrism concerns the respect he accords to numbers—to the numbers of the faithful, but one might also say to actuality as such. What is this numbers game? Assuming that appeals to providential history have been successfully banished from the repertoire of secular progressivism, surely the same ban must apply to the religious thought from which progressives once unconsciously and incautiously borrowed. After what we have learned of history's unending swerves, false trails, and dead ends, it seems foolish for anyone to take the latest headlines or what Jager calls "demographic trends" as decisive evidence of which way history is heading. It seems late in the day to seize upon any (perhaps evanescent) constellation of facts on the ground as if it made a strong case that the endpoint those facts, writ large, might seem to gesture toward is desirable.

It is by playing this game with "demographic trends" that Jager defines his position on cosmopolitanism. When he expresses his ambivalent approval of the brand of cosmopolitanism articulated by the journal *Public Culture*, which he judges more likely to make room for the multitudes of new Christians, it's on the grounds that this is cosmopolitanism as large numbers of people actually live it—cosmopolitanism as "lived process." It's worth pausing over the bland, almost redundant word *lived* in this phrase. If this word has been saved from the copyeditor's redlining or "Track Changes," there must be some term to which it is implicitly contrasted. What is it? The only answer I can find in the text is *self-consciousness*. What must be rejected, Jager implies, is a cosmopolitanism that rewards and demands self-recognition. And what can be embraced, he therefore implies, is life without self-recognition. Jager's "lived process" assumes that life is as it appears to the demographer. The demographer's trends do not rely on anyone's self-conscious identity. To live, in this tendentious sense, means never having to say who you are. This is bare or naked life, one might say, life that has sunk below the threshold of reflection or ethical action. Or you might call it uncritical life, life without alienation, immune from all normative demands. Normative demands are presumed to be unlived or unlivable, at least by the many. Cosmopolitanism is desirable only if it can be lived by the majority of the world's population, and it can be lived by the majority of the world's population only if it refuses to look at itself from without— refuses, that is, what Jager calls secularism.

To put this issue so starkly may seem like bad faith on my part, since all critical enthusiasm for the so-called new cosmopolitanism, my own as much as Jager's, has involved some unbending toward the actual at the expense of the normative. In principle, however, this project has always tried to maintain a tension between the actual and the normative; it has not recommended that the normative dimension be allowed simply to dissolve into the actually existing. In many critics who joyfully celebrate the discovery of each new diasporic cosmopolitanism as an achievement of cultural self-expression, uncomfortable demands have simply been dropped, demands, for example, that this and every mode of life be inspected and sometimes found wanting. Religion, of all things, would seem miscatalogued in this particular nonnormative slot. From this angle, it is not religion but secularism that can be abruptly labeled otherworldly. Global Christianity must be accepted as cosmopolitanism, it is implied, because, unlike other versions, it demands of its believers nothing but practice. This is religion not just without theology but without even a pause for self-recognition. That's pretty counterintuitive, to say the least. As if trapped in the old equation of religion with the eternal sleep of tradition, Jager seems almost prepared to keep the equation while reversing its values, that is, to mobilize religion as a way of defending unselfconsciousness itself. I can't imagine that this desperately defensive understanding of faith will satisfy even those who identify themselves as postsecular.

Here I am self-consciously reading against the grain. Jager explicitly presents religion as part of modernity; he aligns himself not with tradition but, on the contrary, with "alternative modernities." But the phrase "alternative modernities" sustains the concept of modernity as a desideratum. It's unclear to me that Jager can both claim alternative modernity and endorse, as he seems to, M. H. Abrams's description of modernity as "soul-destroying and alienating." If he repudiates self-recognition as intrusive secularism or as self-alienation by another name, what's left in the modernity Jager says he wants that he actually does seem to want? Not much. Certainly not a landscape that enables what Said referred to as effort.

I have been trying to suggest in this chapter that one cannot simply identify Said's secularism with his humanism. Appearances to the contrary, Said's appeals to effort are ways of mediating between humanism and post-structuralism, opening each up to the other. To translate movements and institutions into the shocking neutrality of historical efforts is to come closer to Foucault's postulate of ubiquitous power than any humanist is likely to be comfortable with. It is also to set up a systemic indeterminacy that overlaps with that of Jacques Derrida. A world full of efforts comes dangerously close in its lack of moral criteria or epistemological guidelines to a world full of acts of faith, a world where it is hard to separate political commitment from superstition. In exhorting Western-located intellectuals to transcend the unthinking chauvinism hidden away in disciplinary comfort zones and innocent-seeming habits of interpretation, Said asked us, in effect, to submit ourselves to a practice of modernist estrangement, a worldly version of asceticism. Was this a spiritual practice, or a secular one? Said wanted it to be a secular one, just as he wanted to be able to distinguish superstitions, including those of his fellow scholars, from commitments. What he bequeaths us is his worldly desire, which is both for secularism and for its further secularization.

What sort of effort is required, and where precisely should the effort be focused, in order to change that which must be changed in the world? Said had and has a great deal to say on this all-important subject, which includes such large questions as what kind of empire George Bush was leading (strong or weak) and how much has changed, or how far American imperialism does or does not coincide with global capitalism. But the single largest thing he has to say about it is that this is the question that must be asked, and asked again and again. There are no superhuman beings, angelic or satanic, from which we can take our bearings once and for all. We are not authorized to relax. Secularism is all about effort. Said could have summed up his secular commitment in Derrida's well-chosen words, "Cosmopolites de tous les pays, encore un effort."

# 6 INTELLECTUALS IN PUBLIC, OR ELSEWHERE

If intellectuals are imagined as mysteriously marginal and alluringly homeless, there will be a permanent temptation to look around at home, inspecting the premises with care and discovering, as one must already have known, that, after all, intellectual work is going on and that everyone doing it is susceptible to description in normal, everyday terms. In short, intellectuals are ordinary. For some observers this discovery will come as a relief; for others it will be a disappointment. To my knowledge the most sustained and insightful attempt to locate intellectuals on modest local maps and yet to do so without disappointment is Stefan Collini's *Absent Minds: Intellectuals in Britain.*[1]

The subject of *Absent Minds* is a "rich tradition of debate about the question of intellectuals" in twentieth-century Britain, in particular, debate about "their absence or comparative insignificance" (1). The debate begins with the Dreyfus Affair and its unpredictable British reception (the queen, for example, was a believer in Dreyfus's innocence), it simmers intriguingly through the 1920s and 1930s, and it becomes positively effervescent in the 1950s, perhaps because of a new democratization of the public sphere. Collini is less interested in the possible historical causes than in the rhetorical structure that persists, swirling around figures as different as T. S. Eliot, R. G. Collingwood, George Orwell, A. J. P. Taylor, and A. J. Ayer, each of whom gets a full-length profile.

Other chapters mix shorter profiles—for example, the devastatingly funny discussion of Colin Wilson and the authorities who briefly and embarrassingly made him a star in their firmament—with synthesis of the debate over intellectuals at different scales—for example, how it was shaped by particular periodicals and by the transition to electronic media—and in diverse national settings. Coming closer to the present, Collini admires Edward Said for what he did as an intellectual while disputing what he said about intellectuals: a celebration of rigorous exile from all social belonging which, as we have seen, threatened to leave the category of the intellectual looking almost totally uninhabited. The move turns out to be characteristic: it's as if Collini felt he could win a proper admiration for what intellectuals do only by rejecting most of their self-images, or evasion thereof.

Several libraries' worth of self-reflection are on display here. This is entirely appropriate, for the very magnitude of the debate, as Collini argues, constitutes evidence against the proposition that so often both initiated and concluded it: that intellectuals were indeed absent or comparatively insignificant. Who were the debaters themselves, Collini asks, if not (by a definition to be discussed below) intellectuals, unconsciously indulging in "the paradoxes of denial" (2)? Demolishing the denials and the "intellectuals are absent" premise is the central and most satisfying accomplishment of this deeply satisfying book.

But *Absent Minds* also expresses a secondary desire: to establish the positive significance of intellectuals or at a minimum to refute their "comparative insignificance." The idea that intellectuals in the United Kingdom were and are no more insignificant than the intellectuals of other nations is a matter of setting the historical record straight. To establish that they are of absolute significance, or significant in comparison with other domestic social actors, is a larger, more pressing question, at least to the would-be intellectuals who are likely to made up a sizeable proportion of the book's readers. This is more of a reach. Collini is oblique about this argument. He builds a case largely by doing the historian's work of reanimating a largely forgotten world, honoring the intelligence and commitment that went into minor periodical disputes, ephemeral radio talks, and so on. But properly accounting for the social significance of intellectuals might seem to entail moving to a higher level. Intellectuals would have to be compared with social actors other than intellectuals and with nonintellectual modes of action (supposing these exist). There would have to be reference to standards of significance that are pertinent beyond the domain of statements uttered by and about intellectuals. In making the "anti-absence" argument, on the other hand, Collini can stay within that domain. He is very much at home there, marking his points by means of scrupulous attention to the debaters' words and to the tones and contexts in which they are delivered. His skillful registering of this sort of contextual nuance shapes itself little by little into a kind of ideal, the image of a certain intellectual civility. Civility is not one of Collini's explicit topics, but it is an ethic for intellectuals that must be counted as part of his argument and maybe even as crucial to its appeal. The question of how much or what kind of significance Collini's readers are finally willing to ascribe to intellectuals will perhaps depend on how personally or how passionately this ethic motivates them.

In twentieth-century Britain, Collini suggests, the intellectual makes its presence felt more often than not as an elsewhere, a collectivity in which the writer himself resists membership. Some very amusing pages are devoted to documenting the ingenious ways in which British writers on the topic of intellectuals manage to pretend, for better or worse, that they themselves have nothing to do with that category. Collini pares down this resistance to two essential premises: (1) there are no intellectuals here, though they exist in France or Russia or somewhere else, and (2) once upon a time we used to have intellectuals, but today they have disappeared or are in the process of disappearing. Each premise is then illustrated with examples from a number of decades as well as from various countries other than Britain. The resulting dossier is so very imposing in its bulk as to become a quietly devastating piece of mockery. Refutation is unnecessary; the premise collapses under the weight of its excessively numerous and various adherents. Anything that has been asserted as a description of so many different times and places is very unlikely to be true in a useful or important sense about any of those times or places, least of all the present. Like laments for the loss of organic community or anticipations of the coming of the messiah, the story of the absence or decline of the intellectuals is too transhistorical to serve as the key that fits this particular moment in history, too temporally and geographically promiscuous to seem a convincing account of our dilemmas now and here.

For readers who have tended to nod with instinctive approval at the (always safely rhetorical) question, where are the intellectuals?, and Collini makes it clear that their name is legion, *Absent Minds* can be taken as a plea that they try a little harder to formulate the precise grounds of their disaffection from the present. Some of the contentious reviews the book has received probably indicate a reluctance to do so.[2] It's certainly easier to declare roundly that the present is the worst of times, securing thereby some intellectual credibility (I am one who takes the more rigorous, more uncompromising view) while hinting at the complacent Whiggery of one's opponents, than it is to subject either the present or the familiar litany of antiprogressive reproaches to the fresh scrutiny they deserve. Other readers, already suspicious of the devious comforts and political ambiguities of decline-story ritual, will feel gratitude is owed to Collini for performing the no doubt unpleasant work of collecting so many numbingly repetitive samples. The collection features some bright spots, for example, when Collini discovers British intellectuals unexpectedly awarding credit to other British intellectuals *as* intellectuals: Perry Anderson on John Maynard Keynes and F. R. Leavis, or Francis Mulhern paralleling the oppositionality of *Scrutiny* with that of the Frankfurt School. And there are sparkling sections where Collini devotes himself to the careers of more or less kindred spirits, like the chapters on A. J. Ayer and A. J. P. Taylor. But there are also stretches where the only news is bad: a steady diet of clichés about absence and decline. No historian can envy Collini the time spent tracking a rhetorical structure that appears to go its merry self-propagating way, generating praise of the distant and blame of the here-and-now without any troublesome friction from empirical particulars. It is a tribute to Collini's much-remarked grace as a writer that the experience of reading the book manages to be so very different from what it must have been like to do the research.

At the same time, the excellence of Collini's style could be seen as putting a perverse strain on his argument. The better he sounds, the less inclined one is to say the same of his subjects. More often than not those he describes are culpably self-deluded, at least on the topic of the category to which he would assign them. Why should anyone so scrupulously clear-eyed as Collini be eager to associate himself with a category that allows for and perhaps encourages quite so much vagueness and self-delusion? If it is so tolerant of fools, is this a club he would really want to join? The very massiveness of the evidence by which Collini makes his first argument (against absence/decline) threatens to undermine his second argument (in favor of positive significance) and even to risk tipping it over into its opposite. That is, it risks turning *Absent Minds* into another, more circuitous version of the received wisdom that we have few if any intellectuals, at least of the right sort. And if that received wisdom can be interpreted, even more circuitously, as a backhanded or performative encouragement to the reader to *become* the right sort of intellectual, then the same would have to be said of the whole melancholy discourse Collini has taken so much trouble to unearth. That would be quite a turnabout. But as a book about rhetoric, *Absent Minds* has to acknowledge the rhetorical principle that makes this interpretation conceivable.

The question of how its author imagines himself fitting into the category of the intellectual does not arise directly in this book. But *Absent Minds* would sacrifice much of its emotional and even existential intensity, which is palpable throughout, if the reader did not sense this as a question lurking between the paragraphs. Collini is clearly trying to establish the proper dignity of people like himself, academics who have successfully "crossed over," winning for themselves a more than academic readership on issues well beyond their official expertise. At its heart, the book is about how to evaluate that achievement. It is to Collini's credit that he leaves the results of the evaluation in some doubt. Are you certain it's a point in your favor that, having emerged from your specialization, you have managed to catch and hold the public's notice? Collini would like to believe that it is, but he does not appear entirely certain. After all, as he shows, many have become publicly recognized by spouting nonsense. The particular sort of nonsense about intellectuals that Collini so fervently and properly derides might even be considered a royal road to public approval. His own elevated public status came well before this book was published. Still, can he be sure he is not part of the pathology he is diagnosing?

The critic James English has astutely noticed a resemblance between Collini's voice and that of certain of his subjects, like Kingsley Amis and Philip Larkin, toward whom he is extremely critical.[3] Like Amis and Larkin or, for that matter, in the United States, Louis Menand, Collini is a gifted comic writer. Like all of them, he does not mind occasionally entertaining his readers at the expense of the academy. Summing up his argument, Collini begins the book's epilogue with a powerful and positive invocation of Larkin: "Here no elsewhere underwrites my existence" (499). As we have seen, intellectuals generally do allow their existence to be underwritten by elsewheres. In that sense, among others, Collini shares Larkin's impatience with intellectuals. There is a moment toward the close of his discussion of the 1950s, perhaps the crucial period for his narrative, when he nicely ventriloquizes the Orwellian, no-nonsense, man-in-the-street antagonism toward intellectuals that is his book's own major antagonist: "And for God's sake, man, keep your voice down" (169). It takes nothing away from the force of this sentence to consider that Collini too keeps his voice down. (Well, not at the moment when he utters this wonderful sentence, but most of the time.) When he accuses Raymond Williams of "self-dramatizing" (191), one might say that he too is policing the range of acceptable tones and doing so in the name of the common man and what the common man finds tolerable. But as the "keep your voice down" line indicates, Collini is also struggling (like Orwell at his best) to free himself from some of the visceral aspects of his historical inheritance. This internal, gut-level struggle helps account for the power of the writing, which could not have come from sweet reason alone.

The more important issue here is not personal, however, but conceptual. It has to do with the intellectual's public authority: where it comes from and how one should feel about it. According to Collini, this authority is the intellectual's defining attribute. One gets to be an intellectual only by being recognized as an intellectual; to be an intellectual is to be seen as one in public, by the public. This definition may seem self-evident, but it takes for granted a set of unarticulated political limits that, whether finally accepted or not, need to be made explicit. Both Gramsci's concept of the organic intellectual and Foucault's concept of the specific intellectual have been greeted as necessary additions to the critical debate over intellectuals be-cause they salvage the importance of intellectual activities that exceed those limits, that might not count as public in Collini's sense. Foucault and Gram-sci were wary of granting too much conceptual power to a public under-stood as singular, socially or nationally central, and thus presumptively socially conservative. Collini seems aware of this problem: he declares that he does not want his definition to rely on the illusory criterion of acknowl-edgment by "society as a whole" (55), a phrase he judges "unhelpful" (55). On the other hand, he does not allow the multiplication of publics to express itself in a promiscuous proliferation of kinds of existing intellectuals, varying conceptions of the general interest that authorize each, or cultures that each might express. Like his concept of the public, his concept of culture tends to drift away from an acknowledged empirical plurality, gravitating back in the direction of an idealized Arnoldian singularity.[4] Collini is left with a conception of the intellectual which, though bowing to heterogeneity, often seems functionally homogeneous. The final jurisdiction over what an intellectual is resides in culture, which becomes almost coterminous with a singular public opinion. The intellectual is defined as one who enjoys "public standing" or "cultural authority"—the same thing, and only one thing.

But what is cultural authority? It is not specialized expertise, which is too small. It is not mere celebrity, which is too large. Nor do these extremes point conveniently to a size in between that would be just right. Collini notes the concept's unresolved "puzzles" and "complexities" (56). The notion of "cultural authority," Collini notes, "may in fact be conceptually the trickiest of all" (56). This admission is generous but not quite adequate. Collini seems not to want to fall into cultural relativism, which would allow the intellectual to be anyone at all whom the culture decides is an intellectual, but he also doesn't want to admit how far the intellectual's stature hinges on who precisely is doing the recognizing, whose version of cultural authority is being bestowed and under what circumstances. The more limited the public that bestows it, the more contestable the authority. The enigma of recognition and of the scale of the public that accords that recognition is not dispelled even by Collini's rather elegant treatment of the plurality-of-publics problem. His working definition of public artfully combines the concept's desirable singularity with its awkward but unavoidable multiplicity. Modern society, he says, is fragmented by the division of labor into numerous specializations. In such a society, publicness begins, from the perspective of the intellectual, at the border of any one of those multiple specializations. The intellectual enters the public sphere when she or he makes use of the authority gained in that specialization in order to speak on a subject for which that specialized expertise does not provide a source of legitimate authority.

As Collini presents it, this process of conversion remains something of a mystery. How does it happen? When and why does it fail to happen? Are certain currencies of knowledge more easily converted into public standing than others? Is there a conceptual or rhetorical talent by which the intellectual herself can facilitate this exchange? Or is it once again a matter of what "the" public (but which one?) is prepared to perceive as valid and valuable? Without venturing theoretical answers to these questions, Collini's account manages to explain a good deal of what has been and continues to be said about intellectuals, most strikingly, why the topic should have generated so much vituperation and self-misapprehension. If intellectuals are obliged by definition to oscillate between the poles of (1) genuine expertise in a particular specialization and (2) speaking generally in the public sphere, they are permanently vulnerable to the opposite charges of having sold out to journalism, on the one hand, and of having retreated from the public sphere into the ivory tower, on the other. Out of this tension within the concept itself come disappearance narratives, according to which particular intellectuals or intellectuals as a group have prostituted themselves in the media, or gotten caught up in masturbatory self-involvement, or whatever. Such narratives make sense only if they are extracted from the putative details of individual careers and historical moments and are taken instead as the diachronic workings out of the contradictory demands that the concept itself places on intellectuals. As Collini says, "Movement between these two poles is inherent in the logic of the role itself" (58).

This is an immensely useful point.[5] One can only hope it will induce some hesitation in the persistent tellers of those very trite tales. Given Collini's structural analysis, on the other hand, one cannot in fact be very hopeful that the tales will disappear any time soon. What then should we legitimately hope for? In arguing so effectively against a mode of rhetorical exhortation that easily becomes self-dramatization and self-aggrandizement, Collini sometimes seems a bit strict on the question of hope. And his strictness is relevant to the issue of how to measure the significance of intellectuals, how much desire the category should legitimately excite.

Collini's definition of the intellectual, which involves trading on the limited authority of professional credentials in order to obtain a new, more public sort of authority, derives from the Dreyfus Affair. It is reembodied for postwar France in the figure of Jean-Paul Sartre, who manufactured a politically prophetic role for the intellectual by crossing distinct sorts and sources of authority: in particular, that of philosophy at the École Normale Supérieure and that of the successful novelist and playwright.[6] Again and again Collini catches his subjects in the act of taking the regime-shaking strenuousness of the French model as a standard for the evaluation of intellectuals as such; this is one of his most effective polemics. But his own account might itself be taken as too reverential to the French transcendence-of-specialized-expertise paradigm. At any rate, it seems worth asking whether there perhaps exists a form of intellectual authority that might *not* involve a transfer of qualifications or cultural capital from one domain to another. Can one become an intellectual without trading on a capital amassed elsewhere, but simply by means of work done at one's workplace? Are we sure that some sort of conversion or crossover is essential to being an intellectual? After all, the sort of creative synthesis often associated with interdisciplinary scholarship is also a phenomenon that necessarily occurs *within* disciplines, not to speak of other professions and institutions. It's something for which a good journalist or labor union organizer or representative of Doctors Without Borders might receive a normal salary. If publics are multiple and if address to a singular, comprehensive public is illusory, if there is no "society as a whole," then some specializations may already be public enough, in this diminished sense of public, to boast their own intellectuals.

The Dreyfus Affair paradigm also raises a related question about the presumed centrality of professional credentials in the making of the intellectual. Are we sure it is a rise in the status of specialized knowledge that is the definitive source of the new counterauthority? Collini quotes the right-wing riposte of Ferdinand Brunetière: "I don't see that a professor of Tibetan is qualified to govern his fellow men." Some of the force of this remark seems to come from the irrelevance of academic knowledge as such, but some surely comes from the particular geographical randomness ascribed to knowledge of Tibet. Brunetière seems to be ridiculing the idea that knowledge of a distant and exotic nation might be of pertinence to the issues facing turn-of-the-century Frenchmen. If so, then perhaps xenophobic ridicule and cosmopolitanism deserve a more than incidental place in the birth-of-the-intellectual story. At a moment of crisis when national loyalty was so much at issue—Dreyfus's but also that of the Jews and of all those, recently named as intellectuals, who came to Dreyfus's defense—it seems reasonable to speculate that there may also have been something peculiarly constitutive about what Collini calls "the 'foreignness' of intellectuals"

(126). The Dreyfus Affair might be read, from this perspective, as offering a different sort of founding myth, not so much one in which professional credentials get mobilized as newly authoritative but one in which, with or without the mobilizing of those credentials, the category of the intellectual arises in response to accusations of national betrayal. That would help explain why the category has remained affiliated with the problematic of cosmopolitanism.

This line of thought would lead to the question of whether and how cosmopolitanism—roughly, the ability to take a distance from the interests of one's nation, to weigh one's national loyalty against loyalty to the interests of humanity as a whole—might paradoxically become a source of local authority, something to be valued within one's nation. This question is interesting in part because of its formal resemblance to the contradiction that Collini himself takes as central to the intellectual. While asking how anyone can turn professional credentials into public authority, we could also ask how antinationalism can ever turn into national influence, how it can confer cultural authority within a given nation. In other words, perhaps the tension between specialized knowledge and public standing is itself only one specialized version of a more general paradox. One way to phrase this more general paradox (probably not the best) would be to set opposition to society against reward by society. How does it happen that society is willing and even eager to reward its opposition? Why should there be a social place for social criticism? How can a dissident be socially influential while remaining a dissident?

Tom Nairn sees intellectuals as embedded in the British social order, very much there rather than absent and indeed quite influential, but influential in a conservative cause. Collini comments, "Before our very eyes, the absence-thesis removes its false beard and stands revealed as its opposite, the little-known Peculiar-Strength-of-Intellectuals-in-Britain thesis" (181). The thesis may seem unfamiliar, but its logic is firmly implied by just the paradox Collini has been considering, now raised from the level of publicness to the level of politics. There could be no clearer demonstration of the contradiction on which the concept of the intellectual seems to be founded. Intellectuals are not present if they are defined as dissident. And if they *are* present, then they *cannot* be dissident; they are necessarily conservative. The concept of the intellectual demands two things, dissidence and presence, that are felt (wrongly) to contradict each other. Thus the crowning moment of their coexistence must be projected outward or backward, along with intellectuals themselves, to the elsewheres of the past and of foreign countries. A core of idealization is preserved, but at a high price: by insisting that anything found in an actual historical context cannot genuinely express or embody that ideal.

Cutting off access to these elsewheres is a strong response to this compulsive incoherence, but it is not, perhaps, the strongest. Better would be to dispute the understanding of contradiction that exiles it from history. That's the problem with the conceptualizations of society that beget cultural pessimism and narratives of decline. If society cannot be conceived as providing locations within itself for social criticism, then society is being conceived too narrowly or schematically. As supposed proponents of a dialectical view of history, Nairn and Anderson can be taken to task for using France, the putative society in which historical progress of an imperfect sort has been realized, to stand in for a properly dialectical view of Britain, which is strangely missing from their accounts—a view in which imperfect but actually existing intellectuals could be seen as bearers of and participants in the imperfect forces by which historical progress has in fact been realized, when and where it has. France enables them to chide Britain but also to avoid engaging with Britain's own peculiar mix of progress and ongoing catastrophe, its failure to do nothing but decline and disappoint.

In rephrasing Collini's paradox in the more general terms of dissidence and influence, I have been tugging him in a direction he does not seem to want to go: from publicness to politics. For Collini, politics is one subset of the larger category of publicness: "Being politically active is one form which that public role will frequently, but not necessarily, take" (50). The demand that intellectuals engage in some sort of political intervention or activity, especially a revolutionary one, is a demand that in many times and places may well go unsatisfied. As a requirement for the existence of intellectuals, politics therefore does what Collini most distrusts: it threatens to make their absence seem genuinely plausible. So his resistance to the criterion is logical enough. But is it possible to keep publicness, seen as politically neutral, as the more universal, hence the definitive category?

Collini accuses E. P. Thompson of tendentiousness on this point. Thompson, whose colorful Dickensian retort to Anderson on the subject of Britain's dependence on the French is clearly one of Collini's inspirations, shared unexpected common ground with his *New Left Review* interlocutors, as Collini acutely notes. Thompson too thought that "one of the distinguishing marks of 'a real intelligentsia' is to produce 'a systematic critique' and that this entailed a certain intensity of conflict with its political opponents" (173). In other words, he thought that to be a real intellectual you have to be "Marx or Lenin or Gramsci" (174). Collini comments that this is a "blatant case of building certain preferred characteristics into the very meaning of the terms 'intellectuals' and 'intelligentsia'" (174). This seems true enough. When Collini shifts the center of his definition from the wild-eyed prophet to the socially accepted reformer, however, he seems to be doing exactly the same thing, but on behalf of different characteristics. Is his enlargement of the frame via the criterion of public recognition really neutral, or does it quietly restrict the sort of politics that would count as a subset of it? Collini notes, as a rebuttal to the usual charges against intellectuals, that an apparent falling-off after the Second World War of the prestige and effectiveness of intellectuals might be accounted for by a general loss of prewar deference to the educated classes. If this is right, as it seems to be, then it is a strong argument against the somewhat restrictive criterion of cultural authority by which Collini allows intellectuals to be defined. For it suggests that some large component of that authority or public standing was, precisely, class deference. Class deference would not favor, say, labor organizers, let alone left-wing revolutionaries.

A better definition, then, would have to allow for the existence of intellectuals without such deference, which is to say, without cultural authority, at least in the strongest, most deferential sense. It would allow for the term to cover, among other things, those working in the unpublic or not-yet-public social sites indicated by Foucault and Gramsci. The point of Gramsci and Foucault is that if you understand politics differently it can be seen to be happening without publicness of this sort, and intellectuals can thus be intellectuals without being public. This might help explain large political events that have caught the pundits by surprise, like the fall of the Berlin Wall in 1989 and the toppled North African dictatorships of 2011. It is at least conceivable, working on these different premises, that publicness or publicity could be seen as a means to the higher end of politics and as a means that is merely contingent.

"I have been arguing," Collini writes, "that the relationship with politics is only one form of the larger structure implicit in the relevant sense of 'the intellectual' in English usage, that is to say, the reaching out to a public and an issue that is 'general' in relation to the primary activity or initial source of cultural standing" (216). Collini is aware that by this reclassification he is not merely contesting the power of the revolutionary French model over British thinking, but deliberately dedramatizing intellectuals. For some readers, as he notes, he may thus be undercutting the significance of intellectuals and the desire to become one. On the last page before the epilogue, Collini arrives at a conclusion of exemplary balance: "Once we shed the unrealistic ambition nurtured by the illusion that previous generations of intellectuals reached and directed a public that was coextensive with society as a whole, then we are better placed to see how intellectuals can make use of existing media to reach those publics who, being neither as doped up nor as dumbed down as fashionable commentary suggests, *do* want to see issues of common interest considered in ways less instrumental or less opportunistic, more reflective or more analytical, better informed or better expressed" (495–96). He immediately adds that some will find this "a dispiritingly unambitious job description" (496). For it means giving up on the "self-dramatization" that goes with "that heavily romanticized conception of the intellectual as the acknowledged legislator of the world, marching at the head of mass movements, political or other programme in hand . . . the barricades have never been a very good platform from which to try to conduct rational argument" (496).

Collini may be right to worry that as a job description his account of the intellectual is not as inflammatory or ambitious as it might be. But if so, it's not because he forces his readers to choose an insipid liberalism that shuns movements and marches over a red-blooded Marxism that is properly ready to send us all to the barricades. Collini values rational discussion, but he is hardly a predictable liberal. He refuses to judge British intellectuals by their deviation from a supposed standard of capitalist development and anti-capitalist reaction. He would have to count as a liberal as measured by the more radical French norm of Sartre. But when Jeremy Jennings asks him to acknowledge Raymond Aron's "committed observer" as an alternative to Sartrean *engagement*, Collini will have none of it. His alignments, he says, are not those of the Cold War.[7] Another sense in which the tag "liberal" fails to do him justice appears in his discussion of Ayer. Commenting on a passage in which Ayer declines to advise the public on politics and morals—for the philosopher, "his professional task is done when he has made the issues clear" (395)—Collini writes, "The passage, like Ayer's writing more generally, is not in fact as self-effacing or transparent as it pretends to be. There is, on closer inspection, plenty of 'prescribing' going on here. . . . [Ayer] does a fair amount of pontificating after all" (395–96). It's a wonderful analysis, not least because it serves (and is I think meant to serve) as an acknowledgment that the same is true of Collini himself, whose liberalism never contents itself with the supposed rational virtues of transparency and self-effacement.

It has not been sufficiently noted that if this book is a defense of the existence of intellectuals against those who persist in seeing them as absent, it is also a defense of academics against those who persist in judging them by their failure to become intellectuals. Few public voices are brave enough to take this position. The majority view, amply sanctioned by the market, tends to be satiric. If some have found the book's commitments lukewarm or otherwise hard to read, the explanation may lie not in Collini's politics, which are none the less indignant for being well modulated, but in his seemingly outrageous desire to give proper credit to the ordinary workings of university teaching and research.[8]

That desire should not be taken as a definitive resolution of the book's struggles over the proper significance of intellectuals, whether the significance of the achievement of public status or the significance of intellectual work as such, assuming (as the academic subtheme suggests) that scholarship can be labeled intellectual in the honorific sense without the extra qualification of crossing over. The question of significance is left open, as is that of whether Collini would like to see the discourse of elsewheres simply closed down. An inability to believe in habitable elsewheres is one plausible cause of Larkin's pathological xenophobia. By contrast, the sort of generous citizenly and cosmopolitan engagement that Collini models for his reader, here and in his other writings, seems to indicate that the freedom to imagine things otherwise and to speak out accordingly—a freedom that is as mysterious, under analytic scrutiny, as any exotic elsewhere—is one of his firmest commitments, even if it is far from being the hero of his historical narrative. In this sense *Absent Minds* does not try to put an end to the tradition it describes. It is an upstanding dues-paying member, if a richly ambivalent one.

In the United States a quick way to test out the usefulness of Collini's public or cultural authority model of the intellectual is to examine the editorial pages of the *New York Times*. How much room do they make, or fail to make, for unpopular cosmopolitan viewpoints like those of an Edward Said or a Noam Chomsky?

One would have to be very naive to think of the *Times* Op-Ed page as public in a neutral sense, equally ready to lend its acknowledgment to any cultural expression or distinguished achievement regardless of political slant. It is one of the most exposed spots in the battle over common sense, and what gets to count as public there is obviously subject to relentless ideological strategizing and pressure. Balance is permitted and even encouraged, but balance around central points that have been carefully preselected. It is not a shock to discover that the *New York Times* editorial team has never solicited the opinions of the man the *New York Times* itself has called "the most important intellectual alive," Chomsky. It's true, Chomsky was interviewed by Deborah Solomon in November 2003, but this was in the *Times Magazine*, and the opinions on display in the very brief interview were mainly Solomon's. Apropos of Chomsky's criticism of Israel, for example, Solomon tritely and unhelpfully informs him that he sounds like a "self-hating Jew," thereby taking the subject of Israel and the Palestinians off the table. The only other *Times* appearance I could find in the past decade was when, speaking at the United Nations in 2006, Hugo Chavez mistakenly referred to Chomsky as being dead. (Chavez regretted the missed chance to meet him.) By reminding its readers that Chomsky was in fact alive, the *Times* could both catch Chavez in a careless error and indulge in a bit of guilt by association.

It seems plausible that the *Times*'s no-Chomsky policy, like that of the mainstream media in general, has to do both with Chomsky's uncompromising position on Israel and with his scathing critiques of the *Times* and of the mainstream media in general, especially for their misreporting and nonreporting of stories involving interventions by the United States around the world.[9] What is most remarkable is that Chomsky earned his reputation as an intellectual entirely without the mainstream media's platforms or endorsements. If he counts as an intellectual, and it's hard to say by what criteria he could be kept from so counting, then it's only by putting a certain strain on Collini's model of the public.

That model finds some confirmation, however, in the unlikely person of Slavoj Žižek. From the perspective of ordinary public opinion, Žižek could easily be made to look like a monster. A strong critic of liberalism in all its forms, he defends violence (for example, in the book entitled *Violence*) while castigating liberalism for the violence it both performs and denies.[10] As it happens, he is by no means lacking in civility, but he is often described as being a clown or a buffoon, and he describes his thinking as Lacanian and Leninist, schools of thought to which the major media have not usually felt compelled to give respectful attention. He is also a self-declared atheist. In short, he would seem an improbable choice for so central and highly scrutinized a spot as the *New York Times* Op-Ed page. Yet he has in fact appeared on the *Times* Op-Ed page—four times, by my count. Moreover, he has not said anything different there than he has said elsewhere. (At least one Op-Ed piece was recycled almost word for word in *Violence*—see below.) So what can we learn from these spicy journalistic sightings? Perhaps only that celebrity is enough, especially if accompanied by amusing paradoxes and the intriguing translation of high philosophy into pop culture. But perhaps it is something more: about the possible stretching of the editorially possible and of Collini's public-based definition of the intellectual.

Each of the four Op-Eds Žižek has published in the *Times* has dealt in some fashion with the touchy subjects of secularism and cosmopolitanism. Disengagement from God and disengagement from country are arguably the issues on which would-be or self-nominated intellectuals are most likely to feel their differences from American public opinion and from journalism, which is directly responsive to it and which by Collini's theory gets to do the actual nominating of intellectuals. They are certainly the topics on which academics are most likely to incur attacks on academic freedom and most vulnerable to calls for public scrutiny and regulation.[11] But Žižek seems undeterred. In an Op-Ed of 11 October 2007 called "How China Got Religion" he manages to infuse both secularism and cosmopolitanism into a very unfashionable statement on behalf of the official Chinese position on Tibet:

"The problem with Tibetan Buddhism resides in an obvious fact that many Western enthusiasts conveniently forget: the traditional political structure of Tibet is theocracy, with the Dalai Lama at the center. He unites religious and secular power—so when we're talking about the reincarnation of the Dalai Lama, we're talking about choosing a head of state. It's strange to hear self-described democracy advocates who denounce Chinese persecution of followers of the Dalai Lama—a non-democratically elected leader if there ever was one."

This is exactly the sort of point Chomsky might have made: a critique both of religion and of the complacent, hypocritical American critique of another country.[12] Why can Žižek can get away with this while Chomsky cannot, at least in the *Times*? But what interests me more is the question of how far the mainstream's editorial limits can in fact be stretched. After offering a proper and necessary criticism of Chinese "military coercion"—one that Chomsky himself could not be guaranteed to make, lest it distract the reader from the inconsistency of the official American attitude—Žižek suggests that when the Chinese government passed a law concerning the reincarnation of Tibetan Buddhas, effectively "prohibit[ing] Buddhist monks from returning from the dead without government permission," the gesture of an atheistic state regulating something that in its eyes doesn't exist is no less ridiculous than Western policy vis-à-vis religion. In the West we "dismiss fundamentalist believers" like the Taliban as "'barbarians' with a 'medieval mindset'" because "they dare to take their beliefs seriously," as evidenced by the blowing up of the Buddhist statues at Bamiyan. Western outrage at the blowing up of those statues stemmed not from belief in the divinity of the Buddha, but from respect for the statues as cultural heritage. *Culture* is our word for the things we respect and keep doing even though we don't actually believe in them. In this, Žižek says, we resemble the People's Republic of China after all. We too aim to manage ideas without taking them seriously.

The strong implication is that we *should* take them seriously, which might mean dismissing them outright. At its most radical, this would entail giving up liberal tolerance of religion in the name of something like Kierkegaardian Leninism: being prepared to kill the innocent, as Abraham was prepared to sacrifice Isaac, on the grounds that faith, or revolution, trumps and suspends the domain of the ethical. In a less violent, less revolutionary version, it might entail exchanging liberal secularism for an active disputation of theological premises and practices. Žižek spells this out in another *Times* Op-Ed, this one from March 2006. There he again contrasts belief with respectful liberal tolerance. "Respect for others' beliefs as the highest value can only mean one of two things: either we treat the other in a patronizing way and avoid hurting him in order not to ruin his illusions, or we adopt the relativist stance of multiple 'regimes of truth,' disqualifying as violent imposition any clear insistence on truth. What, however, about submitting Islam—together with all other religions—to a respectful, but for that reason no less ruthless, critical analysis? This, and only this, is the way to show a true respect for Muslims: to treat them as serious adults responsible for their beliefs."[13]

Žižek's viewpoint here is simultaneously American and anti-American, national and transnational. No doubt he owes some of his editorial success in part to the coincidence between critiques of liberalism (and of Islam) from the left, like his own, and an American public opinion informed in large part by critiques of Islam, diversity, and multiculturalism from the right. The *Times* could well have accepted him as a cultural conservative, though an eccentric one. Yet his position is hardly a reassuring one for American public opinion, which rejects militant atheism as violently as it rejects Islamic terrorism and the authoritarianism of the People's Republic of China. Like it or not, Žižek is giving voice to a version of cosmopolitanism. Recall the Brunetière line cited by Collini: "I don't see that a professor of Tibetan is qualified to govern his fellow men." In grabbing Tibet away from its part in the comfortable American sense of moral superiority over China for its human rights violations, Žižek makes it clear that knowledge of Tibet is now anything but irrelevant to governance in distant lands like France and the United States. For better or worse, acts of government cross borders. One's "fellow men" include Tibetans, Han Chinese, and many others who will be affected by decisions taken in foreign capitals without, as yet, having their opinions solicited. The scale of democracy remains under dispute and under construction. Intellectuals participate in both processes. It is extraordinarily difficult work. That is one reason it is possible to say that they are ordinary—citizens of real localities and nations, like the rest of us—without sinking into melancholy and disappointment.

The problem is not too dramatic or heroic a portrait of the intellectual;

rather, it is too narrow and dispiriting a sense of the landscape in which intellectuals operate. No nation can afford utterly to ignore foreign realities or even foreign ideas. There is no national landscape that is not simultaneously transnational. Though Chomsky has not had Žižek's luck with the *New York Times* Op-Ed page, he too counts as an intellectual in Collini's sense because the media of the rest of the world have paid him more than enough attention to make up for the unreceptiveness of organs like the *Times*, and there is no nation, not even the United States, that does not need and want to hear at least some of what is said beyond its borders. Cosmopolitanism can become a source of national recognition and local authority —its version of the paradox of empowered dissent—because even the most parochial understanding of "the public" has to leave room for something other than the flattering of national prejudices. Elsewhere is already here.

The word *public* has been most frequently used about collectivities up to but not exceeding the scale of the nation. This fits the word's association with zones of actual conversation and self-consciously shared destiny, which have historically been limited. On the other hand, the meaning of the term also refers to a zone of causal connectedness: to those actions relevant to or significant for the welfare of a given group, whether or not the group is in conversation with itself or with the begetters of the actions. This zone is much vaster. In the era of the world market, not to speak of official and unofficial violence across borders, it has become increasingly international. Thus the restrictively national scale of public (in the sense of conversation and control) is seen to be stretching, or to need stretching. One way of describing the challenge of so-called global democracy is the challenge of enlarging the scale of international attention, conversation, and opinion so it will match the scale of international causal connectedness—in other words, to re-set the boundaries of the relevant moral community so that those likely to be affected by a course of action, wherever they live, are included among those invited to debate it. This is probably the best mortals can do at present against the threat of perpetual war. It cannot claim to define the identity or responsibilities of intellectuals, but the challenge does guarantee to anyone who takes it up a nonnegligible shot at significance.

# 7  WAR WITHOUT BELIEF
Louis Menand's *The Metaphysical Club*

The concern that animates my argument in this chapter and indeed in the book as a whole might be described, adapting John Dewey's title, as the global public and its problems. What are we to make of Dewey's heroic attempt to extend the concept of the public into society at the new industrial scale at a moment when, thanks to so-called globalization, the scale at which the concept of the public is required to function has expanded still more dramatically, obliging us to speak and listen transnationally? In order to reflect on this general question, I will focus on Louis Menand's prize-winning, best-selling history of pragmatism, *The Metaphysical Club: A Story of Ideas in America* (2001).[1] It is clear enough that Menand's account of Dewey and pragmatism carries forward the call for patriotism associated with Richard Rorty. It is perhaps less clear that it also takes for its center the topical issue of American military intervention.

Thinking about Dewey and his legacy in the summer of 2006, while watching television news of the Israeli invasion of Lebanon, an incursion supported by the United States, as well as of the increasingly bloody, chaotic consequences of the U.S. occupation of Iraq, accompanied by background threats that the United States might bomb Iran or invade it or both, I found it difficult not to think back to the notorious disagreement between Dewey and

Randolph Bourne over America's entry into the First World War. Like many others, I have always thought that Bourne and Jane Addams were right to resist entry by the United States in the war and that Dewey was wrong to support it. But how much ought these personal positions matter now? Should we allow ourselves to draw conclusions about Dewey's ideas and about pragmatism in general on the basis of that episode? According to Rorty, an author's personal politics ought to be irrelevant to one's evaluation of his or her ideas. Literary criticism, the discipline I work in, mainly agrees with Rorty on this; if it didn't we might well be out of business. Yet Menand, who is also a literary critic, gives a great deal of importance to the person behind the ideas. Indeed, one might say that this is how he makes the pragmatists into a narrative: by supplying a personal dimension, integrating the ideas into the lives of those who had them. What it means to tell a story about pragmatism, what it means to present pragmatism in the form of a story as opposed to presenting it in some other, nonnarrative form, is therefore not an incidental or unimportant theme, whether in the context of pragmatism or in the context of United States entry into wars.

On the first page of his book *Achieving Our Country* (1998), in a chapter called "American National Pride: Whitman and Dewey," Rorty says that those who want the United States to improve must "remind their country of what it can take pride in as well as what it should be ashamed of. They must tell inspiring stories about episodes and figures in the nation's past—episodes and figures to which the country should remain true" (3–4).[2] This is the project on which Menand had already been engaged for some time. Three years later, when *The Metaphysical Club* appeared, it told a story—the word appears in the subtitle, "A Story of Ideas in America"—that is also in a complicated sense a patriotic story, a story in which patriotism is initially questioned but in which the pragmatism that questions it comes itself to represent what is most inspiring in the American past. As in Rorty's own book, pragmatism becomes one of the few uncontroversial things that Americans are entitled to feel legitimate pride about. The theme of national pride cannot be irrelevant to questions of pragmatism's relation to entering into war, whether then or now. But what precisely is that relation? I'll come back to the hint of possible contradiction between the telling of inspiring stories about the past and pragmatism's self-defining concern with action in the present.

The fact that Menand's book is a story and not a work of philosophy is also consistent with its pragmatist subject matter. Rorty has famously suggested, for example in his Amnesty Lecture on human rights, that storytelling is what philosophers ought properly to be doing and to declare that they are doing.[3] This is not just because people enjoy stories more than they enjoy philosophy and will listen to them more attentively. It's also because storytelling is more honest than philosophy: it doesn't pretend to be universal truth. So in this sense too one might say that Menand is acting out or embodying Rorty's view of pragmatism. Yet, as I said in the critique of Rorty on human rights that I published in *Feeling Global*, it all depends on what stories you tell.[4] Pulling rank as a literary critic, which is to say as a sort of disciplinary authority on stories, I felt then, as I feel now, that philosophers are mistaken if they think stories don't make claims of their own, claims that, precisely because they go down easily and don't seem to demand as much assent, are in some ways more influential. Thus they can be even more dangerous than philosophical universals. One has to pay attention to the particular stories told.

I want to pay attention here to the view of pragmatism embodied in Menand's story, a view that turns on military intervention and on why military intervention even in a good cause is a bad idea. *The Metaphysical Club* opens with an argument about the entry of the United States into the Civil War. The illustration facing the title page is a drawing by William James of his brother Wilky, who is seen in bed in 1863 recovering from his war wounds. And the first part of the book is devoted to the military service in the Civil War of Oliver Wendell Holmes Jr. Holmes is the most creative of the narrative choices, since by comparison with Menand's three other main characters— James, C. S. Peirce, and Dewey—he is by far the least closely associated with pragmatism. Yet he is the one who in a sense gets to tell us what pragmatism really is. And what pragmatism really is is an attitude toward going to war. The first sentence of the first chapter reads as follows: "Oliver Wendell Holmes, Jr. was an officer in the Union Army" (3). As Menand tells the story, Holmes became an officer because the antislavery movement in the North generated support for the otherwise unpopular cause of the Civil War. In retrospect, this is presented as a terrible mistake. Menand writes, "He had gone off to fight because of his moral beliefs, which he did with singular fervor. The war did more than make him lose those beliefs. It made him lose his belief in beliefs" (4). Versions of this slogan are repeated again and again: "The lesson Holmes took from the war can be put in a sentence. It is that certitude leads to violence" (61). In the book's epilogue, Menand underlines his moral once more: "Pragmatism was designed to make it harder for people to be driven to violence by their beliefs" (440).[5]

This seems absolutely unambiguous. But the story that begins with Holmes ends with Dewey, who dominates the book's final section. If one were to judge by these two main characters, one dominating the beginning and the other the end, it might seem that the story begins with why it was wrong for the North to enter the American Civil War and ends with why the United States was right to enter the First World War.[6] How the story could end with this prowar position, after pragmatism had been defined as resistance to being "driven to violence by [one's] beliefs," is a bit of a conundrum.

Menand makes no direct reference to this conundrum. He does note the apparent structural contradiction within his view of pragmatism between these two positions on military intervention, one anti and one pro. Perhaps such notation does not fall within the responsibilities of the storyteller. Menand himself does not seem enthusiastic at all about Dewey's position in 1917. His treatment of the falling out between Dewey and Bourne over America's entry into the First World War does not take Dewey's side. He does not prettify Dewey's support for the position taken by the administration of Woodrow Wilson, and, once that support had been challenged by Bourne, he is quite forthright about Dewey's active and somewhat unprincipled efforts to stop Bourne from getting published. Menand suggests that both of these gestures were unrepresentative of Dewey: "His momentary advocacy of violent means during the First World War is a peculiar episode in his career" (406), Menand writes, and he uses the word *peculiar* about Dewey's unforgiving reaction to Bourne as well. Yet he stops short of saying —perhaps stopping short is another of the prerogatives of telling a story, as he does, rather than entering into the contest of ideas more directly—that in 1917, when a choice had to be made about staying out of the war or not, Bourne, not Dewey, was the true pragmatist. So one can't see whether or not the book is true to the "certitude leads to violence" version of pragmatism.

One impulse toward narrative resolution of this seeming contradiction can be detected when Holmes comes back many years later, toward the end of the book. Now Chief Justice of the Supreme Court, he is asked to decide on the convictions under the Espionage and Sedition Act of 1918, in *Abrams v. United States*, of Eugene V. Debs and other antiwar figures who had been found guilty of encouraging people to resist conscription into the army. Debs had been sentenced to ten years in prison. The war was already over, but Holmes affirmed the convictions and had Debs sent back to prison (424). Menand suggests that this judgment is entirely coherent with Holmes's pragmatism. Holmes removed from the law any transcendent appeal or sanction that would interfere with the way things are already working, insisting that "what the law ought to be is what it pretty much already is" (344): "In the case of Debs, Holmes said, it did not matter if the suggestion that the war was wrong was just an incidental remark in a plea for socialism. If 'the opposition was so expressed that its natural and intended effect would be to obstruct recruiting,' he argued, ' . . . if, in all the circumstances, that would be its probable effect, it would not be protected by reason of its being part of a general program of and expression of a general and conscientious belief' " (424). The lesson about belief that Holmes learned in the Civil War, which seemed to be a lesson about the horror of war, becomes something very close to its opposite: a way of justifying society's decision both to make war and to defend itself against any voices that would try to stop it from making war. Menand does not make this point. He does not say that the situation of the conscript whose right not to die Debs seems to be defending closely parallels the hypothetical situation Holmes himself would have faced had he come to his loss of belief in beliefs before rather than after his military service in the Civil War. Yet this is crucial to the story he tells.

Menand does not openly take Holmes's side. But he ends this paragraph in a deftly characteristic way: when Debs went back to prison after Holmes's judgment in order to serve out the rest of his sentence, Menand writes that "he brought with him his most prized possession: the candlestick holder John Brown had used at Harpers Ferry" (424). Menand has made much of the violence of John Brown's attack on slavery. The caption under Brown's portrait, which faces the book's first chapter, reminds readers that in 1856 Brown abducted five proslavery settlers "and split their skulls open with cutlasses." The violence of this editorializing caption—"split their skulls open"—marks a line that by his own violence Brown appears to have stepped over. Thus when Debs is revealed to be an admirer of Brown, the violence suddenly seems to be on the side of the antiwar protester, not on the side of the government that is prosecuting him and that has been involved in the deaths of millions. This tiny touch gives the aesthetic impression that Holmes was consistent, that is, consistently antiviolence, even though Menand cannot actually say in good faith that he *was* consistent. It's an artful narrative twist. Yet the moral we are forced to draw about what Menand has presented as the essence of pragmatism is a somewhat frightening one. It suggests at the very least that the loss of belief in beliefs after all offers very little protection against making war, even making a very bad war.[7]

The reference in the Holmes/Debs sequence to the abolitionist John Brown also suggests another, more central area in which Menand is using the resources of narrative to resolve, or to escape having to resolve, the contradictions in his vision of pragmatism and war. I'm referring to the area of race. When Holmes comes back from the Civil War having lost his belief in beliefs, since beliefs lead to wars, the hidden content of the word *belief* is slavery. Having made antislavery the key to the war, Menand is suggesting but not quite saying, and not even allowing Holmes to say, that the cause of putting an end to slavery was not worth it. Perhaps this statement cannot be made explicitly, as an arguable ethical and political position. Yet the point is in fact suggested, and protected, at the level of story. The closest Menand comes to an open acknowledgment of what his story is doing is when he suggests that the price of reform in the United States between 1898 and 1917, that is, the period of pragmatism, was the "removal of the issue of race from the table" (374). Were it not for this sentence, one might almost say that this removal of race from the table is something his own story acts out. Having used the situation of slaves in the South to explain the beliefs that led to the war, Menand neglects to ask what would seem to be the obvious question about the war's consequences: whether the fate of blacks in the United States would have been significantly better or worse had there been no emancipation. He refuses to go back to the former slaves, after the war, in order to see from their point of view whether the war was indeed worth fighting. In the model town meeting staged by this text, their voices need not be heard.

Perhaps this is simply good storytelling. Menand respects the centrality of the character he has chosen; he never steps outside the story of Holmes and Holmes's ideas in order to seek verification of whether the cause by some independent criterion was worth fighting for or not. Pragmatism, like a certain version of storytelling, says that there *is* no outside. Menand tells us, or his version of pragmatism tells us: Don't think about the slaves. You don't have to think about them, you just have to listen to the story I'm telling you. For a story is responsible only to itself. It has no foundation in historical fact; its only verification comes from its effects. The effect of persuading people to wear their beliefs lightly and ironically, to suspend their belief in beliefs, might collapse if it turned out that large numbers of African Americans did indeed feel themselves to be significantly better off as a result of emancipation.

Other than simply forgetting about the consequences of the war for African Americans, the only case Menand can make is that they were not in fact better off as a result of emancipation. This seems an unpromising argument, and it is only mentioned once and very obliquely. The mention comes apropos of the same James brother who, now recovered from his wounds, visits Florida and sees "that the emancipation for which he had fought had only brought a new kind of misery to black people in the South" (146). There is a kind of truth here. But if followed up, this truth would undermine a good deal of the relatively proud, relatively patriotic story Menand has been telling. It would offer support for just that deep pessimism about the prospects for social justice in America that Rorty and his followers like Todd Gitlin castigate in what they call the academic left. As a storyteller, Menand prefers to forget it.

It's tempting to think that the forgetting that is essential to good storytelling (cutting out what doesn't directly concern your chosen characters, your central plot) fits only too well the forgetting of primal violence and structural inequality—that is, the forgetting of what is most primal and most structural about violence and inequality, what is least open to immediate improvement—that Rorty and Menand alike present as essential to pragmatism. What makes *The Metaphysical Club* so wonderfully good as a story is the astonishing, if also evasive, consistency between its narrative form and its philosophical content. But to say this is to do something of an injustice both to Menand and to story as such. On some level at least, the book does seem to recognize that having begun with slavery, it has an obligation to bring the subject of race back—not just an ethical obligation but a formal obligation, an obligation to itself as story.

This recognition takes the form of the appearance, toward the end of the book, of two African American intellectuals who were both students of

James: Alain Locke and W. E. B. Du Bois (377). Dewey's case for the First World War, like Wilson's, emphasized the self-determination of peoples. The cultural pluralism that was so distinctive of the United States, Dewey argued, should become a tenet of our foreign policy and should be exported around the world. As James Livingston puts it, "The promise of American life could not be realized, then, except as an international or trans-national proposition." Dewey believed this in part because the U.S. was itself home to many peoples and cultures: it was international or cosmopolitan by definition, by internal composition, and therefore had a vested interest in "promoting the efficacy of human intercourse irrespective of class, racial, geographical and national limits." He wanted, therefore, to "make the accident of our internal composition into an idea, an idea upon which we may conduct our foreign as well as our domestic policy." Along with Horace Kallen, a Jew, and Bourne, a Judaeophile, the champions of cultural pluralism whom Menand discusses are Locke and Du Bois. In discussing them, one might say that Menand tries to solve pragmatism's Civil War problem or its race problem, which is also its First World War problem. Pragmatism allows an expression of the pride of African Americans in their distinct cultural and ethnic identity, to difference as a virtue (392). In effect, Menand suggests, pragmatism has offered African Americans a kind of peaceful emancipation. Yet Menand hints at this response to the Civil War problem without acknowledging that it could not have been articulated for most African Americans unless and until slavery had been abolished—the work of the Civil War that it appears, according to the same pragmatism, should not have been fought. Moreover, at the end of the book Menand obliquely repeats the case against fighting it, putting this case in the mouth of the central African American figure himself, Locke. Locke argues in favor of the necessity of assimilation. As Menand summarizes, "It is a mistake to cling to ethnic identity," even though it is "also a mistake to abandon it. The trick is to use it to overcome it" (398). But for Locke racial pride is a virtue only because it speeds up assimilation, which is to say, pragmatic coping with the conditions of national life as set by the majority. If race seemed to represent a necessary belief in beliefs, here Menand brings forward his most fully developed African American character in order to say, in effect, that, on the contrary, racial identity must be worn lightly, just as any other belief should be worn lightly. One should not, after all, *believe* in race.

Menand seems to be suggesting, then, that Holmes was right both about the Civil War, which should not have been fought, and about the First World War, against which there was no legal appeal. It's the context that decides. Coping with the context, however bad that context may be, is the responsibility of the individual, whether the conscript coping with being sent to the battlefield to die (the context of war) or an African American coping with assimilation to the identity of the majority (the context of domestic racism). As important as race is in itself, it's also a figure for the larger question of whether the belief in beliefs should or should not be abandoned. In the same passage in which he concedes the Progressive Era's need to take race off the table, Menand also admits the following: "Pragmatism explains everything about ideas except why a person would be willing to die for one" (375). Race usually stands in for one answer to this question: why to some people under some circumstances ideas might seem worth dying for, and some wars might therefore seem worth fighting. This is not an answer Menand is ready to give. But, as I've suggested already, he is ready, at some risk of inconsistency, to admit that the loss of belief in beliefs can lead to a prowar position. If the subcommunity of race is not a foundation, the larger community around it is: the community which is larger than belief and serves as the foundation for all, whatever their beliefs or lack of beliefs. Dewey backed America's entry into the First World War without a belief in beliefs, on arguably pragmatic grounds, and even Holmes is presented as backing violence without certitude. If there is nothing beyond belief, so to speak, then losing your belief in beliefs doesn't really matter very much. Belonging to the community ensures that you will go to war whether you believe in it or not.

This is how certain of pragmatism's early critics could see war as, perversely, the very essence of pragmatism, the inevitable result of its worship of worldly success, which is to say, worldly force. So Bertrand Russell writes in 1909 that "ironclads and Maxim guns must be the ultimate arbiters of metaphysical truth" (374). Neither worldliness nor secularism will save us. Today (2011), the fact that we Americans no longer have a born-again president supported by a strong fundamentalist constituency should certainly not lead us to forget the high value of secularism, which Rorty was reminding us of long before George W. Bush was elected. It gives us reason to remember, as written up recently in *The Nation*, that the Founding

Fathers spent less time invoking Jesus Christ than Bush did. But in the larger view, America's penchant for military adventures does not require Bush's Christian messianism. Bush could very easily have lost the presidential elections of 2000 and 2004—some would say he did. It's now obvious that, under a different president, we can go on doing something not very different from what Bush engaged us to do in Afghanistan and Iraq. The long-term logic of such a patriotic engagement in the Muslim world, as Walter Benn Michaels correctly points out, was provided by Samuel Huntington in *The Clash of Civilizations*, and it is nothing if not a pragmatic, relativist, and postmodern logic.[8] No one's beliefs are right or wrong, Huntington insists; our civilization is no better than the Muslim civilization. But there *is* a clash out there, and when the fighting starts, even if you're the one who started it, realism dictates that you fight for your side. That's where the power of community pushes even those without beliefs. Community is the foundation beneath belief.

Menand's book, which was written before the attacks of 11 September 2001, had and has an obvious and acute value as an anticipatory critique of the Bush administration's case for war based on God-given certitude. This line of thinking does not discourage the West's tendency to flatter itself on its liberal irony, to believe itself to have a superior civilization because it wears its own beliefs lightly while the rest of the world continues to take its beliefs with dangerous seriousness.[9] But I'm trying to make a more important point. The suspension of belief in beliefs offers a great deal less protection against going to war than the book's first pages suggest.

According to Alan Ryan, the First World War was "a test case designed by fate to place [Dewey's] instrumentalism in the worst possible light" (157). Is the case of war an unfair test? Is pragmatism a doctrine intended only for peacetime, as Bourne said (338)? War is at the limit of a philosophy that believes confidently in adaptation and problem solving. Indeed, as Menand tells the story, it was Dewey's belief in problem solving that pushed his dispute with Bourne over the edge. In Menand's favor, in his narrative the Dewey/Bourne exchange ends with Dewey failing to understand why Bourne would not have liked the book he's reviewed, a book by F. M. Alexander, a theorist of bodily posture. Alexander argued that posture is a matter of willpower, open to self-control, literally a matter of (self-)construction. As Menand pointedly notes, such an argument would not be welcome to someone who, like Bourne, was "severely disabled" (401) as a result of a forceps delivery that mauled his face along with a later case of tuberculosis of the spine. But Menand does not make the further connection between Dewey's failure to see this and their different positions on America's entry into the First World War. For Bourne, pragmatism "has no place for the inexorable" (342). War, like his disability, is an example of the inexorable. War carries human beings beyond what is open to their control, beyond the limits of self-improvement. "Willing war," Bourne wrote, "means willing all the evils that are organically bound up in it." Like his posture, war, for Bourne, marks a zone of organic inevitability. His analogy for progressive intellectuals who thought they could control the war by joining it was and is memorable: a child on the back of a mad elephant.[10]

Menand remarks that after the First World War Dewey became a pacifist. But he stops short of suggesting that pacifism is the truth of pragmatism. (Which is just as well, in my opinion.) Menand might have told the story differently, as Ross Posnock does, for example, when he writes, "After 1917 Dewey modified his brand of pragmatism in a Bournian direction" (286).[11] Here I return to the issue I mentioned at the outset: the tension between pragmatism's concern for present action and the telling of inspiring stories about the past. In order to be inspiring, in order to be a sort of foundation, the actions of inspiring characters in the past—here, Dewey himself—cannot display all the adaptability that Dewey and Rorty value so highly in the present. The past is, in a positive or inspiring sense, set in stone, inexorable. It seems worth speculating that perhaps it is precisely the pastness of Holmes's military experience that serves Menand's purposes. Consider pastness as an undisclosed ingredient of Holmes's loss of his belief in beliefs. Is Menand's story about pragmatism perhaps less a banal appropriation of Holmes's bravery in action, as it might appear, than an appropriation of Holmes's *having* fought? In other words, is it making use of military violence *in the past*, violence that is inexorable in the specific sense that it is no longer accessible to the decision that fighting is not worthwhile, safely on the other side of any hypothetically transgressive or illegal resolution to defy the will of the majority and not fight at all?

This speculation would help explain Rorty's turn to the humanities and to literary criticism in particular, which specializes in a pastness that is by definition inaccessible to truly pragmatic instrumentalism.[12] One way to put this would be to say that this story of ideas in America has chosen story over ideas, that Menand's is really a story of the irrelevance of ideas in America. Ideas of right and wrong, for example, are only intermittently decisive here. Holmes was always eager to remind the world of his military service. He never said that the Civil War should not have been fought, that it was a bad idea. His story, as Menand tells it, suggests that the highest heroism is precisely to fight for a cause in which you do not believe. For it is only when you don't believe, when ideas do not matter, that it becomes absolutely clear that what you are really fighting for is not an idea at all, but rather solidarity with your community, solidarity as such, completely divorced from objectivity—solidarity without the foundational support of any idea that would be held to transcend the community. This is what Menand quietly finds embodied, even more dramatically than in Holmes, in Holmes's doomed friend and fellow Union officer Henry Livermore Abbott, a nonbeliever in the war who nevertheless fights bravely and is killed. Abbott represents pragmatism in the guise of courage not only without belief, but courage in the past tense, courage protected from interference from any ideas that might discourage its heroic sacrifice.

One can speculate, going back to the relation of pragmatism to war, that, far from being antiwar, pragmatism's loss of belief in beliefs leads to a sort of hunger for war. For what more convincing demonstration can there possibly be that nonbelief can be consistent with the will of the majority, consistent with commitment unto death to the violence that the majority wills? When Menand writes in the epilogue that "pragmatism was designed to make it harder for people to be driven to violence by their beliefs" (440), we must perhaps conclude that he is speaking with almost legal scrupulousness. He is not saying that pragmatism makes it harder for people to be driven to violence or war. He is saying very precisely that pragmatism makes it harder for people to be driven to violence or war *by their beliefs*. The possibility of being driven to violence or war despite their beliefs or, despite their nonbelief, of being driven to violence merely by the will of the majority, by the quiet but awesome power of belonging to a community, is not part of this explicit moral. But it is very much part of the extraordinary story that, perhaps against his will, Menand actually tells.[13]

This is the central point of the chapter. But if I were to end here, I would seem to suggest something I have explicitly denied above: that it is possible to have a pure cosmopolitanism, one that is in no way contaminated by the sorts of dangerous belonging that Menand's story illustrates. Like Menand and Rorty, I think Americans need more rather than less solidarity with other Americans, for example, so as to defend and extend the institutions of the welfare state. At the same time, they need more solidarity with non-Americans, the sort of solidarity that might lead to a better immigration policy and a more constrained, more reflective use of the U.S. military. One cannot speak against solidarity or belonging as such. Nor can one simply speak in its favor. The question is, how to face the shifting demands of the two scales of belonging, the dilemma of simultaneous and perhaps conflicting loyalties?

I can see no easy answer to this dilemma, but one small step in the right direction is to recognize that a dilemma exists. Those of us on the academic left often speak as if we assumed that this is a relation of necessity between Rorty-style democracy at home and American neo-imperialism abroad—that you can't have one without the other. For example, "In this book I explore how international struggles for domination abroad profoundly shape representations of American national identity at home. . . . The idea of the nation as home, I argue, is inextricable from the political, economic, and cultural movements of empire" (1).[14] The banal term *inextricable* marks the site of an assumption, an interesting working assumption but not an established truth or even an argument. Are we sure that domestic democracy cannot be extricated from imperialism, extricated and therefore given its own independent value? Again: "Imperialism has been simultaneously formative and disavowed in the foundational discourse of American studies" (5).[15] The discovery that something was disavowed is not the same as a demonstration that it was formative, and legitimate enthusiasm at the opening up of a rich area for research—research on the question of the degree to which it was or wasn't formative—should not be taken as equivalent to the demonstration that it was indeed formative, in other words, constitutive or definitive. The assumption that imperialism did indeed define the whole field carries with it the assumption that imperialism has been definitive of American identity itself, including every seemingly desirable movement in the direction of domestic democracy, against racism and sexism and so on. This is what my former colleague Nicholas de Genova memorably assumed when he said at a teach-in in 2003, several days after the U.S. invasion of Iraq, that anti-imperialist patriotism was a contradiction in terms and that what he wanted, personally, was "a million Mogadishus."

If this is where "inextricable" leads, then there's much to be said in favor of an earlier, more tolerant sense of the relation between, say, Walt Whitman as poet of democracy and Walt Whitman as backer of the Mexican War: the judgment that such positions can be thought of as "incidental vices," vices that can and must be "extricated," within certain limits and for certain purposes, from the virtues that keep us reading Whitman. Rorty is, of course, on the side of the extricators. "The sort of pride Whitman and Dewey urged Americans to feel," he writes, "is compatible with remembering that we expanded our boundaries by massacring the tribes which blocked our way, that we broke the word we pledged in the treaty of Guadalupe Hidalgo, and that we caused the death of a million Vietnamese out of sheer macho arrogance" (32). His position is that "nothing a nation has done should make it impossible for a constitutional democracy to regain self-respect. To say that certain acts *do* make this impossible is to abandon the secular, antiauthoritarian vocabulary of shared social hope in favor of the vocabulary which Whitman and Dewey abhorred: a vocabulary built around the notion of sin" (32). Rorty is hinting broadly that the academic condemnation of imperialism has been unconsciously complicit with this vocabulary of sin, which makes it possible to maintain the attitude of "a horrified spectator of your own past" (33).[16]

If we academics don't want to succumb to the temptation of spectatorship, we will need to be more secular in this sense than we have been, more skeptical of this updated version of sin. For all our talk of ambiguity and aporia, secularism doesn't seem to come easy. Whatever we think about American expansionism and about Whitman's complicity in that expansionism (whether deep or only incidental), we have no choice but to extricate. We need what Whitman did for democracy at home, and, for that matter, what Menand and Rorty have done as well. We need to struggle both for democracy *in* America (call it, provisionally, the welfare state) and for democracy *between* America and the rest of the world (call it international justice), even when they are not the same struggle, even if we find, as we may, that in trying to do both, very well, we contradict ourselves.

The public sphere is a form of conversation or storytelling in which, as Dewey wanted, the input of all speakers would matter. It is this model that allows Rorty to make Dewey the key figure representing a redeemable America, the America he is thinking of when he talks about taking America "back from the Pentagon and the corporations."[17] The public is also the ideal that Rorty sees the academic left as falling away from. When he tells—before the fact—the sequel to Menand's story about pragmatism, the center is his story of the academy's self-isolation from the American mainstream. Academics isolate themselves by overstressing, like Bourne, the inexorable and the irreparable. The academic left, Rorty says, "thinks that the system, and not just the laws, must be changed. Reformism is not good enough. Because the very vocabulary of liberal politics is infected with dubious presuppositions which need to be exposed, the first task of the Left must be, just as Confucius said, the rectification of names. The concern to do what the Sixties called 'naming the system' takes precedence over reforming the laws" (*Achieving*, 78). This is close to the story that Casey Blake tells in his book *Beloved Community* (1990).[18] The left may be right about America, as Blake agrees that Bourne was right about the First World War. But being right while the majority is wrong brings with it the temptation of losing one's proper social role: "The war had driven Bourne to despair about the immediate possibilities for public action, but this approach seemed to close off forever the role of civic conscience that he had outlined" in his critique of the war (168). Here Bourne becomes the ancestor of Rorty's academic left, withdrawn into self-righteousness, no longer willing to bet on hope for America, no longer willing to tell stories encouraging national pride in order to encourage national improvement: "In Bourne's case, the choice of the prophetic vocation came at the expense of his faith in the public realm" (170).[19]

I have conceded that there is some truth in this story, that my fellow members of the academic left are often overinvested in a self-congratulatory vision that gives us all the credit for the genuine progressiveness we self-protectively refuse to see outside ourselves, in American society or elsewhere. But there is at least one thing I want to say here in favor of the academic left, and in this context I think it is crucial. The academic left has characteristically tried to make itself part of a larger public; it has tried to speak as if it were accountable to a public beyond any particular nation. I have written this chapter as someone who wants his country to stop making wars, not because I'm always and everywhere against war as such but because, with very few exceptions, almost all the wars waged by the United

States have been moral disasters. The moral of what I've argued seems to me the following: democracy at the level of the nation is not enough to stop wars. The only sort of democracy that would have a chance of stopping war is a truly global democracy. That means a democracy in which the decision-making process is not restricted to any given polity, for example, the group of citizens; it means democracy in which, as Dewey said, everyone who is affected by given decisions will have a voice in making those decisions. That may seem utopian, but it is a logical extension of Dewey's project that circumstances have rendered necessary and to which we must therefore learn to adapt.

# COMPARATIVE NATIONAL BLAMING
## W. G. Sebald on the Bombing of Germany

In an article entitled "Israel, Palestine, and the Campus Civil Wars," published in December 2004 in the online journal *Open Democracy*, the British historian Stephen Howe wrote, "There is a good rule of thumb for social arguments, now applicable to almost any subject and circumstance. It goes simply: whoever first mentions the Nazis loses the argument."[1] Consider this one-liner in conjunction with another, not as clever but again emerging from debate about the Middle East. It describes a common response on the Israeli street to political reproaches from foreigners about Israel's treatment of the Palestinians: "Nobody's better than we are, so they should all shut up."[2]

The two slogans differ in how much shutting up they encourage and how much immunity from hostile commentary this silence seems intended to secure. At a certain level of abstraction, however, they can perhaps be said to have the same purpose: to throw a critical light on the rhetorical practice that I will call, for want of a more precise term, comparative national blaming. (A utilitarian alternative might be the calculus of national accountability for infelicity, but I can't see that catching on.) Both sentences seem to object in particular to the use of national comparison in order to seize the high moral ground, invocation of Fascism as absolute evil, for example, in the late Christopher Hitchens's repeated post-9/11 references to Islamo-Fascists, being merely a special instance of such seizure. But is this an exercise that can be conducted only from a moral elevation? It might seem that criticism of one nation's conduct could be legitimately illuminated by reference to another nation's conduct without anyone being obliged to produce a certificate of spotless rectitude. All likeness is inexact, but is this a sufficient reason for prohibiting references to the Union Carbide disaster at Bhopal as the Hiroshima of industrial accidents? Or discouraging parallels between today's Guantánamo prison camps and the Soviet-era Gulag? On what grounds exactly should Toni Morrison be prevented from dedicating *Beloved* to the sixty million, thereby linking the victims of the middle passage to the Jewish victims of the Holocaust? Yet the second and more popular of my initial slogans, expressing a defensive national pride that is surely not confined to Israelis, refuses even a moderate version of national comparison. If one is permitted neither (1) to take sides on a questionable action or situation by identifying it with an earlier, unquestioned figure of wrongdoing (the Nazis) nor (2) to refer to national differences which also involve relative historical inequalities, whether of scale, of degree of guilt, or whatever, then national comparison itself seems ruled out, except to the extent that it always remains implicit in "nobody's better than we are." If forgiveness is what follows and undoes a prior act of blaming, then this discursive state of affairs might be tentatively described as generalized presumptive forgiveness.

In the United States, the assumption on the street would probably be that we're better than anyone else. Within the limits set jointly by this assumption and by our overwhelming ignorance of the rest of the world, national comparison thrives. Perhaps the only place where it does not thrive is the humanities, where the anticomparison position has made a surprising amount of room for itself. While Howe's no-Nazi rule of thumb, which seems representative of the reigning academic common sense, seems intended merely to curb attributions of essential and irredeemable evil, it makes its point by implying that the Holocaust, a product of such evil, is unique in that respect. Accordingly, the sufferings of its victims must remain beyond or above all comparison. But this logic has proved wildly popular and therefore impossible to quarantine. In effect, the uniqueness of the Holocaust has been universalized. After all, whose national suffering is not, in its own way, unique? Whose national particulars cannot claim to be inherently incomparable? If it does not shut down completely all efforts to compare, the incomparability position certainly burdens them with considerable anxiety.

Benedict Anderson takes the title of his book *The Spectre of Comparisons* from José Rizal's masterpiece *Noli Me Tangere*, where it refers to the Filipino hero's inability to "matter-of-factly experience" the municipal gardens of Manila without simultaneously comparing them with the (original, primary) gardens he has seen in Europe (2).[3] This double vision is incurable (2), Anderson says, but with such regret as to suggest that if so, then countries like the Philippines will never enjoy, as they have every right to, a genuine cultural autonomy. The search for a cure, a means of exorcizing the specter of comparisons, thus continues to motivate. As I noted above, it is commonly taken for granted across the humanities disciplines that because any comparison demands a common standard and because any supposedly common standard will in fact favor the interests of some over the interests of others (a frequent example is the discourse of human rights), comparison is imperialistic by its very nature.[4] Although the academic rhetoric of praise and blame is far too deeply ingrained not to find other ways of expressing itself, one might say that where international comparison is concerned the academy has cordoned off a zone of universal blamelessness, dramatically distinct from the strident national name-calling assumed to be going on outside. Within this zone, the one critical act likely to be blamed is national blaming itself.[5]

I begin with these two quotations, which call attention to the apparent but precarious division between academic and nonacademic common sense on the comparing of nations, first of all because they frame the large questions that underlie this chapter (without, unfortunately, finding satisfactory answers within it). How is comparative national blaming actually done? What might it look like if done better or done right? Can we, should we give up on it? These questions are urgent in themselves, but they also provide an essential background to the wider issues of forgiveness, mercy, and clemency. Commonsense notions of justice and fairness, which flow into the law, pressure it, and sometimes expose its shortcomings, have their own shortcomings, for which the law in turn tries to compensate. Nowhere are both sets of shortcomings more obvious than in judgments of events beyond the borders of the nation. In the international realm, a realm to which the adjective *Hobbesian* seems almost as firmly attached now as fifty years ago, the law itself has only a fragile hold. The mass media, not notorious for their responsible attention to domestic matters, seem still more unreliable on foreign affairs. Yet this realm provides us with case after case, past and present, in which the vocabulary of accusing, forgiving, and forgetting, however inappropriate, will nonetheless be asked to do what it can do, that is, to mediate between international politics and an individual scale and sense of what is and isn't right. When pundits advise us not to play the blame game, a phrase insinuating our well-established agreement that the game itself is blameworthy, should we take their advice? Can countries forgive? Can they be forgiven? Surrounded as we are by statements about what Elazar Barkan calls "the guilt of nations," we have no choice but to find out more about the general cultural resources instructing us on these matters.[6] And if comparison reveals a significant difference here between opinion on the street and the credentialed wisdom of the experts, we need to know that as well.

I also find these opening quotations compelling points of reflection because they respond to a situation in the Middle East that is like—if you will permit me an insidious but, to me, unavoidable moment of national comparison—*like* that of the United States after 11 September 2001, a situation in which a claim to victimhood is put forward by a population seen widely from without as victimizers rather than victims. This rhetorical likeness is also one source of uneasy fascination in W. G. Sebald's book *On the Natural History of Destruction* (2003)—in the original German, "The Air War and Literature"—which I will discuss at some length.[7]

The topic of the two lectures that compose this book was, again, a silence that was also a refusal to blame: silence about the sufferings of German civilians in cities devastated by Allied bombers in the Second World War, a catastrophic experience that Sebald argues took half a century even to begin working its way into the national consciousness or the national literature. The most evident explanation for this silence, the explanation Sebald mentions once early on and then returns to at the end of his text, is, again, a practice of national comparison: a comparison with the sufferings Germany caused. It is this comparison, however implicit, that plausibly leaves the Germans, despite more than half a million dead, unable to believe in their absolute victimhood, hence unable to narrate or perhaps even to remember. On the last page, Sebald notes "the fact that the real pioneering achievements in bomb warfare—Guernica, Warsaw, Belgrade, Rotterdam— were the work of the Germans" (104). "The majority of Germans today know, or so at least it is to be hoped, that we actually provoked the annihilation of the cities in which we once lived" (103). If there was never an "open debate" in Germany about the strategic or moral justification for the Allied bombing, he says, it was "no doubt mainly because a nation which had murdered and worked to death millions of people in its camps could hardly call on the victorious powers to explain the military and political logic that dictated the destruction of the German cities. It is also possible . . . that quite a number of those affected by the air raids, despite their grim but impotent fury in the face of such obvious madness, regarded the great firestorms as just punishment, even as an act of retribution on the part of a higher power with which there could be no dispute" (14).[8] What better motive for silence than the conviction, as Hitchens puts it in his review of the book, that "well, what goes around comes around" (186)?[9]

This hypothesis is intriguing, to begin with because it's so obviously not what a majority of Americans decided after 9/11. If not, then why not? What would it take for Americans now to respond the way Germans did after 1945? Am I breaking Howe's rule in conceiving this question? But the hypothesis also invites further, more serious scrutiny because Sebald himself does not appear to believe it. If he did believe it, why would he have written thousands and thousands of words accusing the Germans of their failure to remember? Why did he go on to treat the silence as something like a crime, and an unsolved one? According to Volker Hage in his book on literary reactions to the air war, *Zeugen der Zerstörung* (Witnesses to the Destruction) (2003), German critics have often insisted, against Sebald, that the German silence was self-conscious and entirely appropriate: "If one measured the suffering of the perpetrating nation against the horror that Germany and its henchmen had brought to the conquered peoples of the East and above all those sacrificed to the design of racial elimination," then, as one of them put it, "perhaps the silence concealed a shame that is more precious than any literature" (118–19).[10]

In what he modestly describes as unsystematic notes, Sebald offers several very different interpretations of the German silence. Sometimes he suggests, restricting all blame to the bombers, that these "true stories . . . exceeded anyone's capacity to grasp them" (23). The word *capacity* is stressed: "The death by fire within a few hours of an entire city, with all its buildings and its trees, its inhabitants, its domestic pets, its fixtures and fittings of every kind, must inevitably have led to overload, to paralysis of the capacity to think and feel in those who succeeded in escaping" (25). The magnitude of the experience seems, like Kant's mathematical sublime, to defy all comparison, making a demand for representation that cannot be refused, on the one hand, while at the same time and by the same token, that very magnitude makes adequate representation impossible. The absolute horror of the firestorms, the inhuman scale and speed of the death and destruction, simply exceeded the capacities of the human senses and the categories of the human mind. As in media discussions of so-called compassion fatigue, the size and shape of the human container are considered to set more or less absolute limits to how much suffering can be taken in and digested before people turn off or tune out.

According to Andreas Huyssen, this account of the German response to the bombing is less than totally accurate: "There always was a lot of *talk* about the bombings in postwar Germany."[11] Another problem with Sebald's hypothesis might be called its technologism. Like Walter Benjamin's parable in "The Storyteller" of how the technology of long-distance killing in the First World War undermined the experience of the soldiers, hence also their ability to tell stories, it suggests that technology, whether expanding our destructive powers or expanding the scope of our senses, necessarily collides with the capacities of the individual rational mind, conceived as fixed and finite. The ability to kill from further and further away, so that the combatants finally need not see each other at all, is a real truth about the history of modern warfare. Yet the conclusions drawn from it seem to rely on implicit contrast with a universal face-to-face norm or model of comprehensible, communicable violence. And this model lends itself to all sorts of ethical and political confusions, among them (1) a naturalizing of local and national belonging at the expense of long-distance affiliations and commitments, as if the latter were less natural and less real, and (2) the delusion that physical proximity acts as a kind of natural brake or impediment to violence. The canonical wisdom on bombing is articulated in Eric Hobsbawm's history of the world from 1914 to 1991, *The Age of Extremes*. Hobsbawm describes "the new impersonality of warfare, which turned killing and maiming into the remote consequences of pushing a button or moving a lever. Technology made its victims invisible, as people eviscerated by bayonets, or seen through the sights of firearms could not be. . . . Far below the aerial bombers were not people about to be burned and eviscerated, but targets. Mild young men, who would certainly not have wished to plunge a bayonet in the belly of any pregnant village girl, could far more easily drop high explosives on London or Berlin, or nuclear bombs on Nagasaki. . . . The greatest cruelties of our century have been the impersonal cruelties of remote decision, of system and routine" (50).[12] By flattering the mildness of the mild young men, this indictment of technologically mediated impersonality cries out for the sarcasm it receives from the media critic Thomas Keenan, encountering a version of it in a recent online discussion of the war in Iraq: "Yeah, I think we all share a longing for the good old days when killing was up close and personal, when you really had to see your enemy ('whites of their eyes,' and all that) before the slaughter could begin, when war was real and effective, not this inefficient but easy virtual game stuff. Like, um, in April and May and June of 1994, when those interahamwe guys . . . in Rwanda set the current world record for temporally-concentrated killing, 800,000 to 1,000,000 people dead in 100 days."[13] Or, to take another sort of example, when the ancient Israelites killed all of the neighboring Midianites except the nubile virgins, one cannot say the genocide was hindered by the primitiveness of their weaponry. It's possible to negotiate between these two positions, for example, by insisting, as in Mahmood Mamdani's book on Rwanda and Joanna Bourne's book on "face-to-face killing in 20th century warfare," on how much ideological work has become necessary in order to turn everyday mildness into face-to-face murder.[14] Still, the automatic ethical effects supposedly caused by the military technology of remoteness seem as questionable in relation to bombing as in relation to video games.

The remoteness-makes-cruelty-easier argument, which seems obscurely linked to the being-bombed-makes-narrative-difficult proposition, often comes accompanied by just that ironic corollary to which Keenan alludes: the suggestion that bombing doesn't actually work. This may well have been the case in the Second World War, as Sebald claims, correctly, according to most authorities.[15] It was certainly the case in Vietnam and again, from the perspective of "winning the peace," in Iraq. But there is something strange in the repeated yoking of remoteness both to psychological ease and to strategic ineffectuality. There are blatant historical cases like the Gulf War and the ousting of Saddam Hussein and the many other colonial wars documented by Sven Lindqvist in his *History of Bombing* in which, for better or worse, bombing did work, at least in the sense of achieving its aims. We seem to be in the presence here of a counterfactual but deeply embedded cultural narrative.

Sebald suggests at first that the bombing, strategically irrelevant, was pursued nonetheless as an attempt to break the morale (17) of the Germans, while it was also seen as "essential for bolstering British morale" (18). Then he goes further. The bombing was not merely a piece of bad planning, based on nothing more solid than phantasmatic projections of future morale. It was not merely a strategic mistake, something the Allies hoped would shorten the war but didn't. It was irrational in its very essence. Sebald quotes with approval Elaine Scarry's conclusion from *The Body in Pain*: "The victims of war are not sacrifices made as the means to an end of any kind, but in the most precise sense are both the means and the end in themselves" (19–20). In effect, this is an alternative explanation of the failure of German memory.[16] If the bombing was fundamentally irrational, if it did not even respond to the strategic self-interest of the Allies as the Allies perceived it, if in that sense it was incomprehensible, then its incomprehensibility would also make it harder for the victims to fix the bombing in narrative or in memory. And it would become that much easier to nudge the bombing and the Holocaust closer to equivalence.

This oblique commitment to incomprehensibility would also explain why Sebald lays the responsibility of remembering on literature rather than on some other form of discourse, while simultaneously making it impossible for literature to fulfill this responsibility. He asks literature not merely to preserve "traces of pain," as eyewitness accounts might do just as well, but to make the pain comprehensible (10), to tell us "what it all actually meant" (4). Telling us what it all actually meant entails something much more strenuous. Indeed, for Sebald it is self-contradictory and ultimately unattainable. He speaks of literature as an attempt "to make sense of the senseless" (49)—a characteristically no-win formulation that somehow leaves him free to accuse anyway, even though sense itself, could it be achieved, might then be understood as proof of literature's failure to do justice to the event or to *be* literature. Logically enough, he accuses every literary text that did treat the bombing of doing so badly, and badly precisely to the extent that it is, indeed, literary: because it uses plot, style, self-conscious artifice, and so on rather than simply recording the observed facts.

The cultural narrative that subtly turns the inefficiency of bombing into the irrationality of bombing is a strangely comforting one, I would suggest, for it allows the system to replace the individual as the source or site of a fundamental irrationality, and thus—what seems to be the intent of Scarry's overeager embrace of the irrationality of war as well—it manages to save the rationality of the individual. In preserving the freedom to remember or not, it also preserves a responsibility to remember, and with the responsibility it allows leverage for Sebald's indignation that they did *not* remember. Psychoanalysis, which rejects such assumptions about the fundamental rationality of the individual, is not one of Sebald's preferred modes of explanation. Though he occasionally refers to repression, quoting, for example, Hans Magnus Enzensberger's theory that the "mysterious energy" behind the German economic recovery came in part from repression of their "total degradation" (12–13) in the bombings, he more often seems to prefer a humanistic vocabulary which suggests a greater degree of individual freedom to remember or not. In that freedom, as I said, lies a mandate for Sebald's indignation. Sebald comes closer than Enzensberger to saying, indignantly, that his postwar compatriots wanted to forget merely in order to concentrate on making money.

Here I open a brief parenthesis concerning national comparison in general. One of its functions is to affront. Explaining the bipartisan French vote in 2004 for Jacques Chirac in order to stop the far-right nationalist Jean-Marie Le Pen, Perry Anderson writes, "The second round duly gave him a majority of 82 per cent, worthy of a Mexican president in the heyday of the PRI. On the Left Bank, his vote reached virtually Albanian proportions" (14).[17] Albania and Mexico are terms of abuse, yes, but there is no obvious inaccuracy here to which a Mexican or Albanian chauvinist might legitimately object. (For contrast, consider Michael Moore's visual references to "the coalition of the willing" in *Fahrenheit 9/11*.) Objection might perhaps be made to the assumption that France really is, or ought to be, different in its expectations of democratic diversity from Mexico and Albania. Is Anderson expressing a sort of Great Power arrogance? If so, he is also, unexpectedly, holding open a zone of free will. Playing on the presumed incongruity between French and Albanian versions of democracy, he appeals to the possibility of doing a better job than the French, at least, seem to be doing. If you are proud enough to think that your democracy works better than Albania's, he tells the French, then prove it. You *can* prove it. In the same mode he tells the English that if the French could make a bourgeois revolution, then they can too; comparison reveals that it can be done, for somewhere it *has* been done. Anderson, whose structural, antihumanist, somewhat deterministic version of Marxism makes him constitutionally skeptical of all appeals to the will, finds in the language of national comparison an oblique, somewhat backhanded means of expressing exhortation, which is to say, implying the existence of freedom, hence accountability—his equivalent of Sebald's indignation at his fellow Germans.

The link between Sebald's equivocations as to the cause of the German silence and his defense of the rational individual appears in an early passage where he speaks of the so-called "literature of the ruins" as "probably influenced by preconscious self-censorship—a means of obscuring a world that could no longer be presented in comprehensible terms" (10). If the world could no longer be presented in comprehensible terms, then one would think it was already obscure enough. What was there to be gained by seeking to obscure it further? It's as if Sebald wants to blame the survivors (they were surely trying to gain *something*) without being quite sure on what grounds the blame is deserved. The next two lines compound this ambiguity: "There was a tacit agreement, equally binding on everyone, that the true state of material and moral ruin in which the country found itself was not to be described. The darkest aspects of the final act of destruction, as experienced by the great majority of the German population, remained under a kind of taboo like a shameful family secret, a secret that perhaps could not even be privately acknowledged" (10). This "not to be described" (in German, "nicht beschrieben werden" [18]) does not suggest something by its very nature indescribable, as one might think, so much as a self-imposed imperative not to describe—an imperative that, like any other imperative, one could choose either to obey or not to obey and might be blamed for not obeying.

Yet this same passage also gives an indication that the forces involved might *have* to be obeyed, might be too unquestionably overpowering for even the staunchest will to withstand.[18] The German term translated above as "ruin" is *Vernichtung*, more literally "destruction" or "annihilation" but also "extermination," the very word (translated "elimination" in the Hage passage above) that has stuck to the Nazi extermination camps. This is a strong verbal hint of equivalence between what was done by the Nazis in the extermination camps and what was done by the Allies in the German cities. It attributes the silence of the German survivors in the cities to a trauma of memory no less cataclysmic than that suffered by the survivors of the camps.

Here Sebald is breaking Howe's "whoever first mentions the Nazis" rule. Or perhaps I should say that he is breaking down that rule, playing the game of comparative national blame so as to undermine the absolute, incomparable authority of the Nazi example. As I suggested earlier, it remains unclear whether this authority is something that Howe himself, while eager to reject a rhetorical figure of instantly legitimized hatred, is also eager to preserve.

How should we feel about this comparison? We would certainly be within our rights if we protested, worrying, for example, about how comparison threatens to devalue the privileged term and thereby takes an apparent step toward the normalization of the Holocaust. But perhaps a better response would be to take seriously the comparison of Allied bombing to German camps and, like Lindqvist, follow it out. "In both cases," Lindqvist writes,

> it was a question of a well-organized mass murder of innocent people, sanctioned at the highest level but contrary to international law. . . . But the difference between the German and the British war crimes is . . . also very clear. In the first place, the order of magnitude in the two cases is completely different. . . . The allied bombing offensive against Germany claimed about half a million civilian lives. That is less than the margin of error surrounding the Germans' crime. In the second place, the victims of the Germans were almost completely defenseless. . . . Up to the conclusion of the war, Germany's cities defended themselves energetically; the graves of 56,000 British airmen testify to that fact. . . . And in the third place, the British had no plans for a conquest that would require the killing of Germans in order to make room for British settlement. . . . The air attacks against Germany stopped as soon as the German armed forces had surrendered. The German war crimes, on the other hand, were committed for the most part after the surrender of their opponents. (97)[19]

Reading this instructive page, one wishes that Sebald had focused less on the experience itself, horrific as it was, and more on national comparison. For comparison, risky as it is, does not necessarily end in the equivalence of all suffering.

But wait: maybe the equivalence of all suffering is precisely where we want to end? The warm welcome Sebald's lectures have received outside Germany undoubtedly owes a great deal to what might be called the human rights consensus. By "human rights consensus" I mean, in this context at least, a general willingness to extract civilian suffering from its historical (national, causal) contexts, from all narratives of provocation, collective responsibility, just retaliation, or "what goes around comes around." If we have come to feel —I concede it's a genuine "if"—that remembering what the Nazis did in the Holocaust and to cities like Guernica should not stop us from remembering the sufferings inflicted by the Allies on German civilians, the obvious reason would be that we have ceased to identify German civilians sufficiently with the Nazis, or even as Germans. We have come to think that they can and must be detached from their national belonging, at least for this purpose, that they must be protected from it and treated instead as abstract individuals. If human rights has become a new secular religion, as is sometimes proposed, this might be described as an essential precept of the new creed.[20] Each human rights violation, we now believe, is absolutely unique and must be looked at alone, without regard for mitigating circumstances, guilty histories, yesterday's actions by today's victims, comparisons of any sort. The discourse of human rights radically amends the Israeli street wisdom with which I began: nobody's country is any better than anybody else's country, and therefore no one should shut up. Everyone has a right to speak about their own as well as everyone else's country, no matter what their own country may have done. Belonging to a given country is morally irrelevant. The nervous backward glance at one's own national history and the guilt or shame it carries should be no impediment to speech or, indeed, to action. This is a version of cosmopolitanism, but not a self-evident one.

Sebald's success in resuscitating the memory of how Germany's cities were destroyed owes something to the passage of time, which, in contrast to what is usually said about time in Sebald, here seems to indicate not melancholy decay but, more happily, the lifting of a burden, the removal of a blockage.[21] But time does not work this miracle alone. Sebald also gets direct support from human rights cosmopolitanism as I've just described it. His defense of the abstract rational individual is consistent with a nonnational, radically individualist, and relatively guilt-free worldview, a worldview he would perhaps have been more exposed to in England than in Germany. Speaking for myself, I can't imagine ever stepping entirely outside this worldview, and especially not on the subject of saturation bombing. And yet I think it's also necessary to consider its possible limits, limits that are relevant both to an understanding of Sebald and to an understanding of the world since 9/11, and that may lead us back after all to the practice of national comparison that human rights cosmopolitanism would seem to be trying to supersede.

To articulate the human rights position is to be aware immediately that it is not quite Sebald's position, or not all of it. In various ways, in this text and others, Sebald tries quite hard to seek out a connection between the bombing and his infant life, to show that "this catastrophe . . . left its mark on my mind" (viii). Like references to the great American novel, his complaint that no one has written the great German epic of this period can only be read as the demand for a certain affirmation of nationhood. Notorious self-exile and fervent cosmopolitan that he was, Sebald also seemed to be trying to negotiate some new mode of belonging to Germany.

This does not seem to me an effort with which anyone, even a would-be cosmopolitan, should want to interfere. There is no excuse for the Allied commanders who, knowing they were bombing civilians and facing evidence that they were doing so to no rational end, nevertheless imposed national belonging on Germany's civilians from above. Yet national belonging, whether imposed or negotiated, can never be far from the mind of anyone trying to prevent or redress or even win recognition for atrocities like these. Here we cosmopolitans may have something to learn from the wisdom of the street, which (like the psychoanalysis of national trauma) takes for granted on manifestly insufficient evidence that nations can be treated as if they were persons and hence capable of such actions as forgiving, showing mercy, and apologizing. Consider some of the progressive political causes that cannot possibly succeed without an increase in the sentiment of national belonging. Efforts to win agreement about reparations and restitution (for slavery in the United States, say, or for our treatment of Native Americans) often founder on the issue of national belonging, especially across time. They run up against a refusal to acknowledge, on the part of descendants of the perpetrators, that they do belong in a sufficiently powerful sense so as to justify present sacrifices in compensation for acts they themselves did not commit. And they run up against a refusal to acknowledge that the descendants of the victims deserve to receive reparations for harms done not to them directly but only to their ancestors. The cohesiveness and continuity of national belonging are stretched even more drastically in the case of recent immigrants who are asked to accept (in the form of taxation, for example) part of the guilt for crimes against slaves or native inhabitants even though neither they nor their ancestors were present when the crimes were committed.[22] Radical individualism in the human rights style, which asserts that nothing done by the collectivity ought to have any weight for you unless you yourself choose it as your own, will discourage people from acknowledging the benefits they inherit, without having lifted a finger, on the basis of someone else's primordial crimes. Yet white Americans continue to benefit from a racialized structure of property ownership that goes all the way back to slavery. Immigrants who come to former settler colonies like the United States, Canada, and Australia benefit directly from the land that others took away from the indigenous people. The crimes and benefits constitute an unconscious belonging that only political effort can perhaps render conscious and eventually channel into compensatory policy.

All these devious tracks of causality are relevant to my own life, but I should perhaps confess that the causal line leading to this essay is also more direct and more personal. During the Second World War my father was the pilot of a B-17, or Flying Fortress, the largest bomber the Army Air Corps possessed. His squadron flew out of the area of southeastern England where Sebald would later visit and describe the lonely remains of the bases. When he took his plane over Germany in 1944 and 1945, he wanted above all to get back all in one piece, and I don't think he could afford to be overscrupulous about where his bombs fell. In trying to hit his assigned targets, which he told me were industrial targets, he certainly wasn't trying to give the postwar U.S. economy the huge relative advantage that he would discover when he got home in 1946, an advantage that would ease the way to precipitous upward mobility for him and to a much easier childhood for me than he or my mother had had. But in this sense, among others, my childhood, like

Sebald's, is part of the bombing. One might say the two childhoods are two tiny points on the enormous circle of the same event.

I say this with a mixture of pride and shame. In its emotional logic, at least, acknowledgment of benefits received as the result of an earlier generation's acts of violence and injustice would seem to resemble the more traditional acknowledgment of indebtedness to the heroic deeds and virtuous sacrifices of founding fathers. (In my own father's case, at least, it's probably too late for me to disentangle the two.) In their insistence that one is indebted to those who came before, both will inevitably seem to restate a position—the premise of a debt too large ever to be repaid—that is essentially theological. To see oneself as an accomplice after the fact to theft and other crimes is the functional equivalent, that is, of seeing oneself as born into a state of sin and requiring divine grace. Ideally one would like a less theological foundation for the need to temper the law with forgiveness, for the risky regress of looking *before* as well as *at* any individual's actions and thus diluting or dispersing personal responsibility for them, for the imperative to hold the law open, allowing at least intermittent entry to varieties of extralegal supplement.

My argument here has been that this debt explains why national belonging cannot be simply disavowed and also why we cannot wholeheartedly embrace the blithe cosmopolitan individualism of the human rights consensus, which would encourage us to condemn the Allied bombardment of Germany simply, without giving any thought to the German actions that preceded it. (How much and what kind of difference that thought should make are questions too complex for me to take on here.) Such debts are not necessarily shared with fellow nationals alone; like our strongest loyalties, they do not magically disappear the moment we step across the nation's borders. So if this argument leads away from cosmopolitanism in one sense —in its hesitation toward the individualist impulse of human rights discourse—it leads back to cosmopolitanism in another, enriched sense. In its insistence that stepping outside one's nation in order to criticize it or apologize for it or both, thereby acknowledging a transnational or cosmopolitan standard, it seems to require a prior psychological identification with the nation, a sense of national belonging. It seems entirely plausible, to take the case most pertinent to this essay, that Sebald refused to accept the possibility that his fellow Germans blamed themselves for the Allied bombing, and that he refused at the same time the practice of comparative national blaming, in part because of a failure or deficiency in his own sense of national belonging. Pursuing the parallel, it would seem to follow that if we want to make Americans more cosmopolitan, we may have to start by first trying to make them better Americans, and this even though the process is in fact less a logical sequence than an endless and endlessly demanding dilemma.

As I said at the outset, this chapter has been largely inspired by the fraught, controversial parallel between Americans since 9/11 and other possible claimants to the title of victimhood who accepted—more (like the Germans since 1945) or less (like the Israelis since 1948 or 1967)—the responsibility for having victimized others. A great deal more might be said about each of these parallels. Huyssen has written very powerfully against the abusive mobilization of German memories of the Allied bombardment, even in the excellent cause of opposing recent American bombing campaigns.[23] As for the United States, the rage for retribution that led the American public to accept its government's invasion and occupation of Iraq, even in the glaring lack of any evidence of Iraqi involvement in the 9/11 attacks, would seem to indicate that American mechanisms of national blame are functioning only too well. But this is not to say that what Americans need is a more fervent commitment to forgiveness.

"Forgiveness is a power held by the victimized," Martha Minow writes, "not a right to be claimed."[24] To decide in advance that peace must be privileged over justice, reconciliation over truth, is to exercise a form of moral absolutism every bit as oppressive as the familiar claim to victimized innocence. To live in the world as a responsible political agent is to forego the dubious certainty that one can foreknow such things about each and every situation that will present itself. There is no permanent title to the high moral ground. Thus Minow suggests, in my view correctly, that "perhaps forgiveness should be reserved, as a concept and a practice, to instances where there are good reasons to forgive" (17). Theological and, for that matter, deconstructive arguments for forgiveness, which share an insistence on forgiveness in the absence of good reasons to forgive, usefully insist on the inadequacy of those reasons which are offered and accepted, whether for forgiveness or for blame.[25] But surely there would be no rejoicing in either camp if reasons were taken as good at the level of the individual but not at the level of the nation, so that individuals could be blamed but nations could not—if nations were taken to enjoy a sort of corporate-like limited liability that, grounded in the supposed incommensurability of scale between moral individual and impersonal state, prevented questions of responsibility from ever being asked. The word we use in order to insist on the connection between those scales is *politics*. Politically speaking, the state of the world does not permit us the luxury of a universal, preemptive absolution where national blame is concerned.

I have suggested here that in order to blame our own nation, as modern Americans have no ethical choice but to learn to do, modern Americans must forego the pleasures of pure detachment, pleasures that human rights individualism has made dangerously accessible and that overlap with the presumed ethical superiority of forgiveness. In order to be forgiven, and perhaps eventually also in order to forgive others, we must first acknowledge that we belong.[26] Detachment needs belonging. In the concluding chapter of *The Spectre of Comparisons*, Anderson proposes an effectively low-key mode for such an acknowledgment: not national pride, but national shame. One can see the difference between nationalism and religion, he says, "if one tries to transform 'My Country, Right or Wrong' into 'My Religion, Right or Wrong.' The latter is an inconceivable oxymoron. How could Islam for Muslims, Christianity for Christians, Hinduism for Hindus possibly be Wrong?" (360). But one's country can be wrong. And this conviction coexists with, indeed, is made possible by, the complementary conviction that one's country can and should be made right. The country can be blamed because, like the individual, it is a site of some quantity of free will. Anderson declares his desire to propagate the slogan "Long Live Shame!" (362). Cosmopolitanism could be represented by worse slogans.

# NOTES

## INTRODUCTION

1. *Three Kings* (1999), directed by David O. Russell.
2. Consider the Academy Award–winning movie *The Hurt Locker*, which portrays the other side as demonically cruel and almost faceless. Is this really just the enemy as seen by troops in action?
3. At whatever scale and by whatever definition, cosmopolitanism is always suspicious of the all-too-human tendency to favor people and groups that are close to you simply because they are close to you and not for some other reason. Parental pride, which might easily be forgiven in some other context, looks a bit odd, therefore, in this one. Nevertheless, I ask the reader to take my son's reaction to *Three Kings* (of which I was and am proud) as the principle of the book that follows.
4. Israel's three-week-long devastation of Gaza in 2008–9 was a test of our cosmopolitanism that we Americans by and large failed. The prevailing American discourse obediently followed the American government in its identification with a reliable American ally. Assuming the blameworthiness of Israel's target, Hamas, it assimilated the invasion of Gaza to the American-sponsored metaphor of a war on terror—a metaphor that made a brief reappearance even in President Barack Obama's inaugural—and it therefore assimilated some fourteen hundred civilian casualties, roughly one-third of them children, to the category of collateral damage, inevitable and therefore, however horrible, ultimately acceptable. Or else it has blamed the outrage of the civilian deaths on the Palestinians themselves.
5. Gaëlle Krikorian, "A New Era of Access to Rights?," in Michel Feher with Gaëlle Krikorian and Yates McKee, *Nongovernmental Politics* (New York: Zone Books, 2007), 247–59.
6. Alex Williams, "Love It? You Might Check the Label," *New York Times*, September 6, 2007, C1, C6.

7. The chapter on pragmatism below repeats a point that others have made before me but that can stand another iteration: a community that takes an ironic stance toward its identity or identities is not thereby protected against the temptation to mete out violence against others, especially when it can perceive those others as being less ironic about *their* beliefs.

8. There are ambiguities here. The larger unit to which loyalty was to be transferred obviously changed over time, swelling and sometimes shrinking with the set of strangers known or imagined or intersected with on a regular basis. Other questions include how much detachment is possible and how much of a transfer is required. Leaders like Giuseppe Mazzini and Sun Yat-sen, who saw themselves as simultaneously nationalists and cosmopolitans, were a reminder that some nations would claim to embody the universal and that under certain circumstances national and planetary loyalties might coexist. But usually the term imagined a collision between them, actual or potential, head-on or oblique. The honor that accrued to the term depended on the certainty that nations would not be pleased if their citizens threatened to withdraw from obligations to their government in the name of higher obligations elsewhere.

9. Bruce Robbins, "Comparative Cosmopolitanism," *Social Text* 31/32 (spring 1992), 169–86, reprinted in Pheng Cheah and Bruce Robbins, eds., *Cosmopolitics: Thinking and Feeling Beyond the Nation* (Minneapolis: University of Minnesota Press, 1998); *Feeling Global: Internationalism in Distress* (New York: New York University Press, 1999); translated into Chinese as *The Cultural Left in Globalization* (Beijing, 2000).

10. John C. Hawley, ed., *India in Africa, Africa in India: Indian Ocean Cosmopolitanism* (Bloomington: Indiana University Press, 2008). Other recent works in the social sciences include Gavin Kendall, Ian Woodward, and Zlatko Skrbis, *The Sociology of Cosmopolitanism: Globalization, Identity, Culture and Government* (London: Palgrave Macmillan, 2009), and Pnina Wernber, ed., *Anthropology and the New Cosmopolitanism: Rooted, Feminist and Vernacular Perspectives* (Oxford: Berg, 2008).

11. One could suggest, following the argument of Richard Rorty, that cosmopolitanism was always plural in the sense that the reattachment was never to justice as such or to humanity as a whole but always a growth of larger loyalties which were themselves as particular as the smaller loyalties they impinged upon or even superseded. I am drawn to this pragmatist reformulation. The key for me is whether the phrase *larger loyalties* adequately encourages the perception of impingement or superseding—that is, some degree of eventual collision between scales of loyalty. The abstraction "humanity" has the virtue of pushing harder on this necessary eventuality.

12. This was a question that Paul Rabinow had posed explicitly in 1986 in a book Clifford coedited, when he spoke of a "critical cosmopolitanism." He described

critical cosmopolitanism as "an oppositional position, one suspicious of sovereign powers, universal truths." Yet universalism has not been banished from it, for it is also described as being "suspicious [both] of its own imperial tendencies" and of "the tendency to essentialize difference" (258). It seems intended to lie in between local identities and universal ones. In other words, the universal is not simply alien to it.

13. Werbner, "Introduction," *Anthropology and the New Cosmopolitanism*, 17.

14. A random sample of Google hits from a few weeks in 2010 included claims to cosmopolitanism on behalf of cities (Shanghai, Vancouver, Addis Ababa), nations (Pakistan), regions (the Caribbean, the Hudson Valley), and smaller groups and localities (a bakery in Pune, a railway station in northern Nigeria, Liverpool fans at Leeds United, LGBT supporters in Latin America).

15. David A. Hollinger, *Postethnic America: Beyond Multiculturalism*, rev. edn. (New York: Basic Books, 2000); Ross Posnock, *Color and Culture: Black Writers and the Making of the Modern Intellectual* (Cambridge: Harvard University Press, 1998). See also Paul Gilroy, *Against Race: Imagining Political Culture beyond the Color Line* (Cambridge: Harvard University Press, 2000).

16. David A. Hollinger, "Not Pluralists, Not Universalists, the New Cosmopolitans Find Their Own Way," *Constellations*, June 2001, 236–48.

17. In a critique of Hollinger, the Canadian Will Kymlicka argues, for example, that, however appropriate to the United States, Hollinger's "open, fluid, and voluntary conception of American multiculturalism" has a "pernicious influence in other countries" (73), countries to whose minority nationalisms, more deeply rooted in history, it does not apply. Thus Hollinger's position "is more accurately called 'pan-American' than 'cosmopolitan'" (78). Will Kymlicka, "American Multiculturalism in the International Arena," *Dissent* (fall 1998), 73–79.

18. Arjun Appadurai, "Patriotism and Its Futures," *Public Culture* 5:3 (spring 1993).

19. Benedict Anderson, "Ice Empire and Ice Hockey: Two Fin de Siècle Dreams," *New Left Review* 214 (November–December 1995), 146–50. Anderson's examples suggest that prosperous North America has been exporting violence, born out of its peculiar ethnic dynamics, to less prosperous areas of the world but has been doing so in ways that are not aligned with U.S. foreign policy; the U.S. government has supported Zionism but not Hindutva or the IRA.

20. Craig Calhoun, "The Class Consciousness of Frequent Travelers: Towards a Critique of Actually Existing Cosmopolitanism," *South Atlantic Quarterly* 101:4 (2002), 869–97. On the need to engage with the communitarian critique of cosmopolitanism, see Janna Thompson, "Community Identity and World Citizenship," *Re-Imagining Political Community: Studies in Cosmopolitan Democracy*, ed. Daniele Archibugi, David Held, and Martin Köhler, 179–97 (Cambridge: Polity, 1998).

21. See my "Commodity Histories," *PMLA* 120:2 (March 2005), 454–63.

22. Thomas L. Haskell, "Capitalism and the Origins of the Humanitarian Sensibility, Parts One and Two," *American Historical Review* 90:2 (April 1985), 339–61, and 90:3 (June 1985), 547–66.

23. I will be arguing that, as far as the theory of power is concerned, Chomsky needs Wallerstein (the world system), and Wallerstein in turn needs both Giovanni Arrighi (for his attention to significant action by states) and Michel Foucault (for his critique of a centered, pyramidal model of power). The more we see power as distributed in a nonpyramidal way, the more groups and countries cosmopolitanism will apply to.

24. This is a point that Orwell himself suggested in a different vocabulary. I recognize the possibility that I can be accused, as Orwell was, of evading the guilt of class privilege by assuming that fellow nationals of whatever class, poor as well as rich, benefit illicitly from the metropolis's ability to drain resources away from the periphery. Things would be much simpler politically if only one had the luxury of talking about class privilege at home without also talking about privilege at the global scale.

25. As I have argued elsewhere, Martha Nussbaum surrounds cosmopolitanism with contiguous, supplementary nouns, a process that closely resembles the adjectival modification that Hollinger sees in his new cosmopolitans. The latter try to reconcile cosmopolitanism, seen as an abstract standard of planetary justice, with a need for belonging and acting at levels smaller than the species as a whole. Adding adjectives to cosmopolitanism, they try to bring abstraction and actuality together. This is precisely what Nussbaum is doing when she adds emotion, time, imagination, and institutions to her version of cosmopolitanism. Though she does not announce the modification with a catchy logo-like adjective, she too has been modifying cosmopolitanism. See my "Cosmopolitanism, America, and the Welfare State," "Theories of American Culture/Theories of American Studies," ed. Winfried Fluck and Thomas Claviez, REAL—*Yearbook of Research in English and American Literature* 19:5 (2003), 201–24; *Genre* 38:3/4 (fall/winter 2005), 231–56.

26. My theoretical differences with Gitlin depend on different readings of the political moment. Though Gitlin willingly concedes the embarrassing record of interventions by the United States around the world, for all practical purposes that record disappears when a choice must be made, as he assumes it must, between us and them and when them, Gitlin assures us, means terrorists. Definitive victory is necessary over "al Qaeda *and its allies*" (152, emphasis added). The seemingly casual addition of the open-ended phrase "and its allies" commits us in effect to a stigmatizing of political Islam as such, which is to say, to Bush-style unending war against both absolute and inexplicable malevolence and those who don't join us in making war on that evil. There is no hint that we might be reasonably accused of such malevolence ourselves. There is no hint that Islamic parties, whatever their sins (they are arguably no more imperfect in their historical record than the

United States), have played a respectable role in various countries (like Lebanon and Turkey) and often carry the hopes of democracy against corrupt regimes (like the Mubarak regime in Egypt, during which the United States protected the government torturers). "The question remains: what should the United States do about thousands of actual and potential present-day killers who set no limits to what and whom they would destroy?" (137). Here again there is a telltale phrase: "set no limits." If there are no limits to the evil of our enemies, then there are no limits in our pursuit of them. Thus this question that remains becomes the only question, decisively throwing the reader back into with-us-or-against-us. If Gitlin's hope in calling for a draft is to stop American military adventures, I can only say that this piece of otherwise principled democratic policy is conjuncturally misguided. What historical reasons do we have for thinking that a draft would be any more successful in stopping present or future military aggressions by the United States than it was in Vietnam? Gitlin espouses "the principle that wars must be popular with their soldiers" (142). Well, maybe, if it were more obviously difficult to make bad wars popular with those who fight them, or popular enough. The seizure of Texas from Mexico? The extermination of the Indians? The invasion of Panama and the Dominican Republic? Popular enough. Note that the Civil War cause of eliminating slavery, arguably a better though also a bloodier war, was notoriously not popular with many of those asked to sacrifice for it.

27. See my *Upward Mobility and the Common Good* (Princeton: Princeton University Press, 2007; pb. 2010) and "Cosmopolitanism, America, and the Welfare State."

28. Gitlin's patriotism includes support for the U.S. invasion of Afghanistan. Aside from the familiar position that the implacable evil of Muslim terrorists justifies any and all responses, at whatever scale, the argument would presumably be that under international law, the United States had the right to invade because the Taliban regime had harbored the al-Qaeda planners of the 9/11 attacks. I would take this mature, pragmatic argument more seriously if the same people added that after the Bay of Pigs attack in 1961 Cuba had an even better right in international law to bomb and invade the United States and topple the Kennedy regime, which played a much more active role in supporting the Bay of Pigs than the Taliban did when they did not expel the organizers of 9/11. (This is one reason why, while I take the force of the criticisms of Chomsky by my friend Michael Bérubé in *The Left at War*, I don't see Chomsky as Bérubé does.) This would be a good time for the defenders of the Afghanistan war to admit that under international law the Palestinians have the right of every occupied people to resist their occupiers by violent means. If supporters of the United States and Israel do not say these things, they forfeit the right to be considered as anything other than apologists for a given nation, which is to say, nationalists.

29. Feher, Krikorian, and McKee, *Nongovernmental Politics*. I speak about this book at greater length in "Du cynisme et des droits" (Cynicism and Rights), *Revue*

*Internationale des livres et des idées* (Paris), 7 (September–October 2008), 33–38; published in English as "Progressive Politics in Transnational Space," *Radical Philosophy* 153 (January–February 2009), 37–44.

30. In some cases the new movements have tried to make a virtue of their fragmentariness, a natural temptation, given how far away the ultimate goal continues to seem. Yet whether they want to or not these groups and movements do add up to something that is not merely random or eclectic. I do not feel I am doing them a disservice in assimilating their diversity to the larger problematic of cosmopolitanism, a cosmopolitanism that in our time cannot debate anything less than the good of a multivoiced, polycentric humanity.

31. See also Stephen P. Marks, "Access to Essential Medicines as a Component of the Right to Health," *Realizing the Right to Health: Swiss Human Rights Book*, ed. Andrew Clapham, Mary Robinson, and Claire Mahon, 80–99 (Zurich: Rueffer & Rub, 2009).

32. Though the regime of intellectual property is doggedly supported by the United States, the United States is not the sole or central villain of this story, as Gitlin suggests it will always be for the cosmopolitan left. No less mainstream an American than William Jefferson Clinton continues to play a very active role in the struggle for access to generic drugs through the Clinton Foundation. Nor does Clinton's role mean that this effort is merely humanitarian, though the person with AIDS is a classic propaganda exhibit for humanitarianism. These are among the inescapable complexities of real politics in our (global) time and place.

33. See, for example, Tom Hazeldine, "The North Atlantic Counsel: Complicity of the International Crisis Group," *New Left Review* 63 (May–June 2010), 17–33.

34. Thanks to Bonnie Honig for the phrase and for much else.

35. Through no fault of my own, hundreds of freshmen have been forced to work their way through this essay, which was in no sense intended for them, in the Columbia University Writing Program, where it has been taught as a sample of academic writing. I am grateful, mainly, to Hannah Gurman, who initiated this ongoing ordeal, and to the various students who have emailed me with interesting and difficult questions about what I meant.

1. COSMOPOLITANISM, NEW AND NEWER

1. Reprinted as "Cosmopolitan Patriots" in Martha C. Nussbaum and respondents, *For Love of Country: Debating the Limits of Patriotism*, 21–29, ed. Josh Cohen (Boston: Beacon Press, 1996); Kwame Anthony Appiah, *The Ethics of Identity* (Princeton: Princeton University Press, 2005); Kwame Anthony Appiah, *Cosmopolitanism: Ethics in a World of Strangers* (New York: Norton, 2006).

2. "I want to propose cosmopolitanism as an educational ideal and cultural mine for our work," Domna Stanton declared in her presidential address to the Modern Language Association in 2005. Stanton makes a strong case that this isn't an

empty piety by pointing out that "two-fifths of all Americans live in states that have officially adopted English-only statutes" (630). Domna Stanton, "Presidential Address 2005: On Rooted Cosmopolitanism," PMLA 121:3 (2006), 627–40.

3. Jacqueline Loss, *Cosmopolitanisms and Latin America: Against the Destiny of Place* (New York: Palgrave Macmillan, 2005). Loss kindly credits me with "contributions to cosmopolitan studies" (11). I appreciate the gesture but must disavow the intention of contributing to any such institution.

4. Gita Rajan and Shailja Sharma, eds., *New Cosmopolitanisms: South Asians in the US* (Stanford: Stanford University Press, 2006).

5. Here the move is clearly away from the "emphasis . . . on the traumatic history of dislocation or expulsion" (7) characteristic of the category of diaspora. *New Cosmopolitanisms* does not deal with the enthusiastic support of diasporic Hindus for the destruction of the Ayodhya mosque. The episode gets no entry in the index. Benedict Anderson's insistence that much of what is praised as cosmopolitanism would be more accurately and more skeptically described as "long-distance nationalism" is mentioned only in a note (30).

6. In the name of the purity of the aesthetic, some, I imagine, will be outraged. Others will perhaps be intrigued to watch the concept of cosmopolitanism take over the undeclared evaluative functions of aesthetic terms like *irony*, *ambiguity*, and *indeterminacy*, rewriting them as an enterprise of geopolitical loyalty-in-multiplicity and thus quietly offering aesthetics some ethico-social backup. The strongest, most provocative case I know for the equating of cosmopolitanism with aestheticism is made in Rebecca L. Walkowitz, *Cosmopolitan Style: Modernism beyond the Nation* (New York: Columbia University Press, 2006).

7. James Seaton, *Weekly Standard*, 9 October 2006.

8. Jessica Berman, *Modernist Fiction, Cosmopolitanism, and the Politics of Community* (Cambridge: Cambridge University Press, 2001). Another aesthetic example is Malin Pereira, *Rita Dove's Cosmopolitanism* (Urbana: University of Illinois Press, 2003).

9. Mitchell Cohen, "Rooted Cosmopolitanism," *Dissent* 39:4 (1992), 483–87.

10. Berman has a chapter (on Proust) in which Zionism figures, but for her there seem to be no Palestinians lurking in the concept's future.

11. In *In My Father's House: Africa in the Philosophy of Culture* (New York: Oxford University Press, 1992), Appiah makes a similar but interestingly distinct point: "My father is my model for the possibility of a Pan-Africanism without racism" (ix).

12. Joseph Appiah, *Joe Appiah: The Autobiography of an African Patriot*, foreword by Henry Louis Gates Jr. (New York: Praeger, 1990).

13. Upon inspection, what Appiah describes as his father's patriotism turns out to be a domestic politics. Admirable as it is, Joseph Appiah's willingness to fight his country's rulers (and in his case to sacrifice for the good of the country as a whole) could be described in entirely nonnational terms, terms lacking patrio-

tism's special emphasis on one country as apart from and sometimes against others. One might say he was willing to fight for the common good where he happened to live, and to do so both for and with that portion of humanity he knew best and could affect most easily. The use of the term *patriotism* here may be good politics, and not just in a demagogic sense, but it doesn't even begin to acknowledge the hard questions.

14. When a writer uses family anecdotes, the material of the writer's familial relations are fair game. Readers are within their rights if they make sense of what they are given in ways the writer may not have intended. And the writer's intention in using her or his family history is at much in play as the family history itself.

15. In this piece he tells the story of how, as a child, he asked his father in a crowd of people "whether one of the people there was really my aunt." It turns out that though he has always called her auntie, she was in fact "the descendant of a family slave" (15). The father is angry because his son has embarrassed her, and the lesson learned is not to "inquire after people's ancestry in public" (15). Yet Appiah fends off the larger embarrassment—that his African family owned African slaves in the first place—in part by separating his father from it ("I don't think he regarded her ancestry as an embarrassment himself" [15]) and in part by blaming the victims, as it were: it is the descendants of the slaves, he suggests, who insist on seeing themselves as genealogical inferiors. Kwame Anthony Appiah, "A Slow Emancipation," *New York Times Magazine*, 18 March 2007, 15–17.

16. One difference between Nussbaum's "sympathy" and Appiah's metaphor of "conversation" is that Appiah's forces the reader into a more active and two-sided engagement.

17. The phrase Appiah chose for his subtitle, "a world of strangers," belongs to the free-market apologetics of books like Paul Seabright's *The Company of Strangers*, which sees strangers as properly bound together by the market and argues for the privatization of water. Paul Seabright, *The Company of Strangers: A Natural History of Economic Life* (Princeton: Princeton University Press, 2004). Jeremy Waldron spells out a similar commerce-centered version of cosmopolitanism in his response to Seyla Benhabib, where "custom" (the custom of merchants) precedes law and produces norms rather than the other way round. A useful contrast can be found in Bonnie Honig's contribution to the same volume. For Honig, the time in which norms gradually become actualities is better thought of as a time in which there is the freedom (and the necessity) for maneuvering. Indeed, norms would be better thought of as maneuvers. Seyla Benhabib, *Another Cosmopolitanism*, with commentaries by Jeremy Waldron, Bonnie Honig, and Will Kymlicka, ed. Robert Post (Oxford: Oxford University Press, 2006).

18. Jeremy Waldron, "Minority Cultures and the Cosmopolitan Alternative," *The Rights of Minority Cultures*, ed. Will Kymlicka, 93–119 (New York: Oxford University Press, 1995).

19. In refusing to dissociate cosmopolitanism from elitism, Appiah is in good company. See, for example, Domna Stanton's presidential address for 2005 to the MLA, which disagrees explicitly with James Clifford's brief for cosmopolitanism "from the bottom up" (637).

20. Hollinger is well aware of the need to balance or negotiate commitments to justice on a global scale against solidarity with the most disadvantaged of one's fellow citizens, solidarity that has found no better form for the moment than the welfare state. Cosmopolitanism in his new, plural, modified sense involves "respecting the instincts to give special treatment to those with whom one is intimately connected and by whom one is socially sustained, and respecting, further, the honest difficulties that even virtuous people have in achieving solidarity with persons they perceive as very different from themselves. It is out of respect for these instincts and honest difficulties that the New Cosmopolitanism looks toward nation-states, as well as toward transnational organizations, as potential instruments for the support of the basic welfare and human rights of as wide a circle of humanity as can be reached." It is as sharers in these "honest difficulties," willing to face rather than ignore "the contradiction between the needs of the ethnos and the needs of the species," that Hollinger can suavely enlist most of Nussbaum's supposedly anti-cosmopolitan critics in the new cosmopolitans' camp.

21. Alan Ryan, "Cosmopolitans," *New York Review of Books* 53:11 (22 June 2006).

22. "Going Green," unsigned editorial, *The Nation*, 7 May 2007, 3–4.

23. For more on this issue, see my *Upward Mobility and the Common Good: For a Literary History of the Welfare State* (Princeton: Princeton University Press, 2007).

## 2. NOAM CHOMSKY'S GOLDEN RULE

1. For a nuanced but not unrepresentative version of this argument, see Natalie Melas, *All the Difference in the World: Postcoloniality and the Ends of Comparison* (Stanford: Stanford University Press, 2007). The premise of Melas's book is that it is paradoxically possible to have "a ground of comparison, but no given basis of equivalence" (xii)—in other words, a mode of comparison that fully respects "incommensurability" (xii).

2. Noam Chomsky, *Hegemony or Survival: America's Quest for Global Dominance* (New York: Metropolitan Books, 2003).

3. Franco Moretti, "Conjectures on World Literature," *New Left Review* 1 (n.s.) (January–February 2000), 55–67.

4. Noam Chomsky, "Commentary: Moral Truisms, Empirical Evidence, and Foreign Policy," *Review of International Studies* 29 (2003), 605–20.

5. "'Exterminate All the Brutes': Gaza 2009," Noam Chomsky, chomsky.info, 19 January 2009, http://www.chomsky.info/articles/20090119.htm.

6. Noam Chomsky, *9-11* (New York: Seven Stories, 2001), 40.

7. This is cited from Arthur Schlesinger.

8. Why take for granted that, like Steven Spielberg's E.T., an extraterrestrial would be nice, that he or she or it would like us? If one pays attention to Chomsky's rhetorical figure—never an easy thing to do with Chomsky's rhetoric, which seems designed to look innocent, transparent, not like rhetoric at all—this is exactly what Chomsky does take for granted. His extraterrestrial seems surprised by human self-destructiveness. Why so surprised? In its intergalactic travels, did the visitor from space encounter only life forms that were naturally peace loving and ecologically friendly? One wonders whether this visitor has really done any traveling at all. Perhaps, at heart, the extraterrestrial is really rather provincial, an indignant but basically friendly American human, equipped with the standard set of humane values, and unusual only in its willingness to apply those values to the mystifications and hypocrisies of America's official discourse.

9. See below for further discussion of Chomsky's anarchism, which stops him from seeing the value in state action of any sort.

10. As an astute graduate student at Wayne State University noticed during an earlier oral version of this chapter, Chomsky's rational-comparative view of justice does not demand any response from the subjectivity or opinions of others. This avoids the threat to justice that would arise from recognition of a chaotic swirl of potentially incommensurable subjectivities, but it also closes down any sense of the public sphere as a site where these subjectivities might nonetheless reach some degree of agreement. The distinctive authority of Chomsky's voice comes in part from the premise that he does not have to stop and listen to anyone. On the Americanness of Chomsky's critique, see also Joe Lockard, "Chomsky on 9-11," *Judaism* 51:2 (spring 2002), 249–52.

11. This looser definition presents a more than merely hypothetical danger that soon very little will be excluded from it, that we will approach the fatal indistinction of the formula "*everything* is cosmopolitanism." If some rough distinctions can't be drawn both around and within it, then, politically speaking, the term will have been murdered by its success.

12. Note the contradiction between this and Chomsky's other rhetorical effect, which is to suggest that we are all aliens. If one reads Chomsky for tone, there is something a little strange about the "visitor from another planet" rhetoric. Chomsky is indignant, but he is also bemused, as if he can't quite believe that people continue doing and saying things that are so obviously counter to justice and common sense. And he does not seem to worry that we might disagree with him. It's as if he imagined himself telling all this to the Martians back home, who could be counted on to chuckle along with him. And it's also as if we were guaranteed to react in the same way as those Martians. Hence the strangeness: on the one hand, there are no Martians, or none we know of. On the other, the Martians are us.

13. Michael Bérubé, *The Left at War* (New York: New York University Press, 2009).

14. This is just what the current crop of dictators never tires of saying. It's a betrayal of those struggling against them.

15. Walter Benn Michaels, *The Trouble with Diversity: How We Learned to Love Identity and Ignore Inequality* (New York: Metropolitan Books, 2006).

16. Quoted in Robert F. Barsky, *Noam Chomsky: A Life of Dissent* (Cambridge: MIT Press, 1997), 178. See also page 188, where the ethical emphasis falls on "atrocities for which [one] shares responsibility and knows how to bring to an end, if [one] chooses]."

17. Differences of power are also the key to the eloquent critique of comparison in comparative literature in Rey Chow's *The Age of the World Target*. Comparison cannot be the basic ethical act if, as Chow argues, all comparison presupposes norms of comparison which implicitly favor one side over the other. Comparison is grounded, "as the etymology of the word suggests, in the notion of parity—in the possibility of peer-like equality and mutuality among those being compared" (72–73). Yet the notion that such equal common ground exists in some natural or unproblematic way has been troubled. Chow's citation of Foucault's citation of Comte de Lautréamont—"the fortuitous encounter on an operating table of a sewing machine and an umbrella" (76)—makes the act of comparison seem at once random and violating, epistemologically untrustworthy and sneakily aggressive. At the same time, Chow is unwilling to discontinue comparing, and, as I have argued elsewhere, the alternative, self-consciously tentative versions of comparison she offers are probably close to the best practice standard that already exists. Among these alternatives is, in effect, comparison as the study of the uneven distribution of power that keeps comparison from ever assuming the ideal parity on which it depends and in that sense keeps it from being what it claims to be. Rey Chow, *The Age of the World Target: Self-Referentiality in War, Theory, and Comparative Work* (Durham: Duke University Press, 2006). See also Bruce Robbins, "Afterword," "Remapping Genre," PMLA 122:5 (October 2007), 1644–51.

18. This point could be made cynically: look, one might say, even the rhetorical figure of the extraterrestrial assumes a degree of power that needs to be spelled out. Like Spielberg's E.T., who could make bicycles fly and perform other neat tricks, Chomsky's extraterrestrial would also have to possess superhuman powers merely in order to have arrived on Earth in the first place. Those powers may go unmentioned, but they must be part of what the figure actually means to us. One might argue that in this respect, too, the alien is secretly American.

19. Talal Asad, *On Suicide Bombing* (New York: Columbia University Press, 2007).

20. Compared to Foucault, Chomsky does indeed come off as a stalwart defender of norms. He rejects Foucault's idea that "the notions of justice or of 'realization of the human essence' are only the inventions of our civilization and result from our

class system. The concept of justice is thus reduced to a pretext advanced by a class that has or wants to have access to power" (138). Chomsky, on the contrary, speaks up for "fundamental human rights" (139). If one looks deeper, however, his position is more complicated.

21. For reflections on consistency as a criterion in Chomsky and his "mistake . . . that hypocrisy is the principal evil of our time" (534), see Jeffrey C. Isaac, "Hannah Arendt on Human Rights and the Limits of Exposure, or Why Noam Chomsky Is Wrong about Kosovo," *Social Research* 69:2 (summer 2002), 505–37.

22. The rule, Chomsky writes, is "that only the most powerful are granted the authority to establish norms of appropriate behavior—for themselves." The exception, a sarcastic one, is when this authority is "delegated to reliable clients. Thus, Israel's crimes are permitted to establish norms: for example, its regular resort to 'targeted killings'" (24).

23. It is this same assumption that seems to underlie his rhetorical opportunism about humanitarian intervention to stop genocide.

24. An interesting alternative to Chomsky on India and Vietnam would be the practice of comparison in Perry Anderson, who refuses to cite authorities whose political credentials are less than impeccable. Since there are few, if any, such authorities, Anderson could logically find himself being extremely critical of the movement against the Iraq War in 2002–3 on the grounds that the antiwar movement looked to the United Nations or to Europe, each of them compromised in the extreme, as useful counterweights to U.S. militarism. Politically speaking, this takes Anderson out of the game, or at any rate forces him into a posture of analytic spectatorship. It's perhaps worth asking which, Anderson or Chomsky, is the more extraterrestrial.

25. A cosmopolitan theory of power would have to insist that power is not located in one place. This was Foucault's point about not having cut off the king's head in the domain of political theory, and though Foucault is widely thought of as an anti-statist (I've said this myself), looking back to the debate between Foucault and Chomsky makes it clear that of the two, it's Chomsky who is more of an antistatist and more mistaken, therefore, in his theory of power. No state has all the power. But the all-important corollary to this is that cosmopolitanism also has power.

26. But there is also large, transnational power in the norms by which Israel's slaughter of civilians is condemned around the world—in those voices, like Asad's and like Chomsky's, that gather around those norms and speak them.

27. Judith Butler, *Frames of War* (London: Verso, 2009).

28. Chomsky created a great deal of trouble for himself by making a similar move with regard to the French literature professor Robert Faurisson, who was fired from his position on the grounds that he had denied the existence of the gas chambers. Chomsky signed a petition in his defense and wrote the following: "I

have nothing to say here about the work of Robert Faurisson or his critics, of which I know very little, or about the topics they address, concerning which I have no special knowledge" (Barsky, *Noam Chomsky*, 180).

29. *Is Critique Secular? Blasphemy, Injury, and Free Speech* by Talal Asad, Wendy Brown, Judith Butler, and Saba Mahmood (Berkeley: Townshend Center for the Humanities and University of California Press, 2009). Asad's term *sensibility* is worth comparing with Amanda Anderson's *ethos*. Arguing that "the appeal to ethos in Foucault's late work—and more importantly in the reception of that work by the Anglo-American academy—actually functions to cloud the ways that character and ethos might redress the underdeveloped normative and practical dimensions of much current theory" (136), Anderson tries to reconnect ethos "to the progressive projects of liberalism and socialism" (137–38). Hegelian *Sittlich-keit* (171) is by no means her highest ideal, but it helps her see some value in a cosmopolitanism that manages to express a normative impulse while it also "artfully avoids any overly explicit avowal of norms" (172). My rough sketch of a very subtle argument can at least indicate the existence of common ground between Anderson and the notion of a Hegelian (rather than Kantian) cosmopolitanism as articulated above. Amanda Anderson, *The Way We Argue Now: A Study in the Culture of Theory* (Princeton: Princeton University Press, 2006).

30. Here one might say it is Chomsky himself who takes the unmarked place of the United States.

## 3. BLAMING THE SYSTEM

1. Luc Boltanski, *Distant Suffering: Morality, Media and Politics*, trans. Graham Burchell (Cambridge: Cambridge University Press, 1999).

2. For Boltanski, one criterion of politics is generalizability. Politics cannot be about the merely particular. He follows Hannah Arendt in arguing that compassion is for particular individuals (6) and hence is not generalizable. But pity, he says, can be generalized. Later he will seem to say that pity, too, is necessarily particular.

3. Boltanski's major institutional inspiration, Médecins sans frontières, came into existence because of a perceived need for a humanitarianism that would be less neutral, in other words more ready to blame, than the Red Cross.

4. In *Blaming the System*, forthcoming from the University of Chicago, Clifford Siskin suggests that the system as an object and a genre came into being *in order* to be blamed, that is, to draw off impulses to criticize that would have been better directed at particular individuals and actions.

5. Boltanski treats rhetoric not as weighted down with local cultural baggage, but as a set of transcultural, transhistorical tropes, closer in this sense to universalizing accounts of the aesthetic. In his discussion of the aesthetic, he does not follow Kant's emphatic contrast between the two.

6. Immanuel Wallerstein, *The Modern World-System: Capitalist Agriculture and the Origins of the European World-Economy in the Sixteenth Century* (New York: Harcourt Brace Jovanovich, 1974).

7. Paul Gilroy, *The Black Atlantic: Modernity and Double Consciousness* (Cambridge: Harvard University Press, 1993).

8. Jan Pieterse writes, for example, "In the indexes to Wallerstein's books . . . one looks in vain for any reference to 'system' and from the outset it is clear that we are dealing with an untheorized use of 'system'" (30). "No reasons are given as to why the existence of a division of labor over an area should be considered to give rise to a social system. Why a *system*? And why a *social* system? It would be more obvious to speak of an economic system" (31). Jan P. Nederveen Pieterse, *Empire and Emancipation: Power and Liberation on a World Scale* (London: Pluto Press, 1990). Pieterse goes on: "The unit of analysis (classes, strata, nations) remains unclear, and is switched ambiguously from one to another" (40).

9. Immanuel Wallerstein, "The Rise and Future Demise of the World Capitalist System: Concepts for Comparative Analysis," in *The Essential Wallerstein* (New York: New Press, 2000), 71–105.

10. When Wallerstein describes the world capitalist system as "a unit with a single division of labor and multiple cultural systems" (75), one notes that cultures are themselves recognized as systems, hence presumably endowed with their own coherence. (This becomes an issue for other commentators, who claim either that Wallerstein denies such coherence to subworld units, whether cultural or social, or that he is inconsistent on this point.) Yet even if this coherence exists, it is irrelevant to that larger coherence in which the multiple cultures reside, the singleness that overrides cultural multiplicity and determines the proper unit of analysis: a single, shared division of labor.

11. Raymond Williams, *Culture and Society, 1780–1950* (London: Chatto and Windus, 1958).

12. Matthew Arnold, quoted in *The Eagleton Reader*, ed. Stephen Regan (Oxford: Blackwell, 1998), 174.

13. This is a bit unfair, as readers are sometimes too quick to draw from Foucault's diagnosis of system the conclusion that Foucault was hostile to system or hostile to it as such.

14. Edward W. Said, "Criticism between Culture and System," *The World, the Text, and the Critic* (Cambridge: Harvard University Press, 1983), 178–225. The essay was originally published in 1978.

15. *Edward Said: Criticism and Society* (Verso, 2002). I will not insist here on the prosystemic side of Said's work, which is obvious enough. In dialogue with Tariq Ali in 1994 Said described the genesis of his book *Orientalism* as a discovery that "distortions and misrepresentations [of the Arabs in Western discourse] were systematic, part of a much larger system of thought that was endemic to the West's whole enterprise of dealing with the Arab world" (62). I will suggest only

that Said's sense of what sort of enemy we are up against—a category from which, as he had learned from his French interlocutors, we can never exclude ourselves—does not permit any simple distinction between system and antisystem, humanism and antihumanism.

16. Wallerstein, "The Rise and Future Demise of the World Capitalist System."

17. Arjun Appadurai, ed., *The Social Life of Things: Commodities in Cultural Perspective* (Cambridge: Cambridge University Press, 1986). In his introduction to the book Appadurai explains that many of the commodities dealt with "have a strong luxury dimension and thus appear to constitute a sample that is bound to favor a cultural approach in a way that humbler, more mass-produced commodities might not" (40). He proceeds to deny the line, so that the cultural approach is made to work for all. There is perhaps some doubling here, as culture is itself often imagined as a luxury.

18. Steve J. Stern notes how much support the Caribbean experience of slavery lends to "Wallerstein's theoretical stance on units of analysis and capitalist combinations of free and coercive labor" (35). Yet after long examination he concludes that local factors were more decisive than systemic ones in explaining, say, recourse to coerced labor in the Caribbean and Brazil (46). Steve J. Stern, "Feudalism, Capitalism, and the World-System in the Perspective of Latin America and Africa," *Confronting Historical Paradigms: Peasants, Labor, and the Capitalist World System in Africa and Latin America*, ed. Frederick Cooper et al., 23–83 (Madison: University of Wisconsin Press, 1993).

19. In *The Decline of American Power* (New York: New Press, 2003), Wallerstein refers to many causal factors and attributes varying degrees of power to them. His account of 1968, for example, carries a suggestion that culture matters quite a bit after all. The decline of American power can be dated from events whose significance was mainly symbolic: "The direct political consequences of the world revolutions of 1968 were minimal, but the geopolitical and intellectual repercussions were enormous and irrevocable" (19). The same could be said of 11 September 2001, which "posed a major challenge to U.S. power" (22). Admittedly this book is a popularization, hence looser and more narrative than the work that produced Wallerstein's account of the world-system. Still, there remains some question about how far the original work is itself narrative in its essence, an account of a single, unrepeatable sequence of events rather than a theory, properly speaking, which would have to extend to other times and places.

20. Marshall Sahlins, "Cosmologies of Capitalism: The Trans-Pacific Sector of 'the World System,'" *Proceedings of the British Academy* 74 (1988), 1–51.

21. Talal Asad, *Genealogies of Religion: Discipline and Reasons of Power in Christianity and Islam* (Baltimore: Johns Hopkins University Press, 1993).

22. Paul Jay, "Beyond Discipline? Globalization and the Future of English," PMLA, 116:1 (2001), 32–47.

23. Appadurai, *The Social Life of Things*.

24. This assumption is concealed by the fact that the word *system* continues to appear with regularity in Appadurai's work, as in *Fear of Small Numbers: An Essay on the Geography of Anger* (Durham: Duke University Press, 2006), 26, 129–30, and passim.

25. Appadurai, "Disjuncture and Difference in the Global Cultural Economy," *The Phantom Public Sphere*, ed. Bruce Robbins (Minneapolis: University of Minnesota Press, 1993). Its last two paragraphs are explicitly about the question of whether some flows are "always prior to and formative of other flows" (292) or, as he says, "radically context-dependent" (292).

26. Eric Wolf's version of what Wallerstein does is similarly a choice, as if it were nothing but a choice: "to understand how the core subjugated the periphery, and not to study the reactions of the micro-populations habitually investigated by anthropologists" (23). Eric R. Wolf, *Europe and the People without History* (Berkeley: University of California Press, 1982).

27. James Ferguson, "Decomposing Modernity: History and Hierarchy after Development," *Postcolonial Studies and Beyond*, ed. Ania Loomba, Suvir Kaul, Matti Bunzl, Antoinette Burton, and Jed Esty, 166–81 (Durham: Duke University Press, 2005).

28. Ferguson reveals the power of the culture concept, even in an anthropologist as clear-eyed as himself, when he talks of "relatively fixed global statuses." It might have seemed that the category he was looking for was not status but class, which puts the emphasis where he wants it: on forms of structural inequality that are unyielding and systematic. Status, on the other hand, which is somewhat more subjective, allows for a more disordered, less hierarchical diversity; it makes the global hierarchy seem *merely* cultural, exactly the position Ferguson is trying to get away from.

29. Pieterse, *Empire and Emancipation*.

30. Perry Anderson, "Confronting Defeat," *London Review of Books* 20 (17 October 2002), 10–17.

31. For a recent reiteration of the same vision—the decline of the United States and the rise of East Asia, without any questioning that this might constitute a significant shift in the system itself—see Immanuel Wallerstein, "The Curve of US Power," *New Left Review* 40 2d ser. (July–August 2006), 77–94.

32. "The Rise and Future Demise of the World Capitalist System." On decolonization, compare, for example, Stephen Howe, for whom decolonization was "one of the most profound transformations that the world political system ever experienced" (104). Stephen Howe, *Empire: A Very Short Introduction* (Oxford: Oxford University Press, 2002).

33. If they became part of the system, which seems the implication when he says, "The antisystemic movements were in power" (40), then why continue to call them antisystemic?

34. Wallerstein, *The Decline of American Power*.

35. The recent relegation of Pluto to subplanetary status does not seem to me to interfere with this conclusion.

36. It would be interesting to speculate at length about the role of force in Wallerstein's work. If he rescues coercion from its neglected place in Marx, where it is upstaged by free wage labor, does he also bring it back as a cause (in the form of strong nation policy) of the core–periphery system? And if so, does coercion make a sort of deconstructive return to unsettle the coherence of a world-system defined by the supposed long-term capacity to function at a deeper level, relatively untroubled by the surface tumult of wars and rebellions? There was a system, it seems, before there were states, but didn't you need strong states in order to create the modern world-system?

37. Immanuel Wallerstein, *Historical Capitalism* (London: Verso, 1983).

38. Wallerstein is scornful of "the 'progressive' politics of the past several hundred years" (104) as resulting merely in a "diminution of the unequal distribution of world surplus-value among the small group who have shared it" (104).

39. Robert S. DuPlessis, "The Partial Transition to World-Systems Analysis in Early Modern European History," *Radical History Review* 39 (1987), 11–27.

40. Note how Wallerstein's lack of epistemological anxiety here rejoins Appadurai's insistence on the trouble that uncertainty brings into the modern (non)system. (Appadurai, *Fear of Small Numbers*, 88ff.) And Wallerstein's certainty about the causal power and knowability of the system converges with a common version of antisystem in the humanities, which makes unknowability similarly programmatic and irremediable. "Auschwitz, Gulags, and ethnic purification all occurred within the framework of a historical social system, the capitalist world-economy," Wallerstein writes. "We have to ask what it is about this system that produced such phenomena and allowed them to flourish in the twentieth century, in ways and to a degree that hadn't occurred before" (41). He insists that "the explanation must be found in the functioning of the system" (42). One can raise an eyebrow at the outlandish confidence of the claim that the system can explain Auschwitz without committing oneself in advance to the impossibility of explanation. Surely it would be better to remain agnostic on the point of when, where, and how much of the unknown must remain unknown.

41. Is there a zero-sum relation between foregrounding the victim and foregrounding the agent/rescuer, in particular the morally risky agency of the interventionist state? Blaming goes on in both cases but with mutually exclusive objects. The ultimate foregrounding of the victim is genocide, which makes the call for action peremptory and absolute. This allows the agent called on to do the acting to remain invisible, instinctively legitimate, as protected from blame as possible.

## 4. THE SWEATSHOP SUBLIME

1. David Lodge, *Nice Work* (Harmondsworth: Penguin, 1988).
2. I owe the Baudelaire reference (from "L'Invitation au Voyage") to Philip Fisher, *Hard Facts: Setting and Form in the American Novel* (Oxford: Oxford University Press, 1987), 133.
3. Roz Chast, cartoon, *The New Yorker*, 29 November 1999, 88.
4. Immanuel Kant, *Critique of Judgment*, trans. J. H. Bernard (London: Collier Macmillan, 1951), 88, 91.
5. See Gary Shapiro, "From the Sublime to the Political: Some Historical Notes," *New Literary History* 16:2 (winter 1985), 213–35. Apropos of this "sinking back," Shapiro finds in both the Burkean and the Kantian sublime "a dual structure of communication and the possibility of withdrawal which constitute society" (219). See also Jonathan Arac, "The Media of Sublimity: Johnson and Lamb on *King Lear*," *Studies in Romanticism* 26 (summer 1987), 209–20. Arac argues that this valued moment when our usual categories break down and we find ourselves suddenly defenseless in the face of the new is also about the paradoxical comforts of nonrealization.
6. "Wal-Mart's Shirts of Misery," a report by the National Labor Committee (New York, July 1999).
7. George Eliot, *Middlemarch* (New York: Norton, 1977 [1871–72]), 544. Dorothea's direct dependence on these people is not really clarified by this passage, which does not capture them in the moment of productive labor, nor does it state, as the Lodge passage does, that were it not for that labor she would not enjoy good clothing or shelter. On the sublime in *Middlemarch*, see Neil Hertz, *The End of the Line: Essays on Psychoanalysis and the Sublime* (New York: Columbia University Press, 1985), chap. 5.
8. *Middlemarch*, chap. 19, p. 135.
9. Steven Marcus, "Literature and Social Theory: Starting In with George Eliot," *Representations: Essays on Literature and Society* (New York: Columbia University Press, 1990), 204. As a female member of the landed gentry, Dorothea is neither expected nor permitted to work for a living; she lives purely in the domain of consumption. This passage can thus also be construed as her revolt against her exclusion from the domain of production.
10. Raymond Williams, *Culture and Society, 1780–1950* (London: Chatto and Windus, 1958), 108–9.
11. "Are My Hands Clean?," *Sweet Honey and the Rock*; lyrics and music by Bernice Johnson Reagon, Songtalk Publishing Co., 1985:
    I wear garments touched by hands from all over the world
    35% cotton, 65% polyester, the journey begins in
    Central America

In the cotton fields of El Salvador
In a province soaked in blood, pesticide-sprayed
workers toil in a broiling sun
Pulling cotton for two dollars a day
[ . . . ]
Far from the Port-au-Prince palace
Third World women toil doing piece work to Sears
specifications
For three dollars a day my sisters make my blouse
It leaves the Third World for the last time
Coming back into the sea to be sealed in plastic for me
This third world sister
And I go to the Sears department store where I buy my blouse
On sale for 20% discount
Are my hands clean?

12. Francis Mulhern, *Culture/Metaculture* (London: Routledge, 2000).

13. Quoted ibid., 66.

14. Durkheim, who looked more favorably on the division of labor than the "Culture and Society" tradition, nevertheless joined with it in defining the role of the intellectual in relation to the division of labor. As Frank Parkin writes, "Durkheim placed a lot of faith in people's willingness to bear burdens provided they could see themselves as part of some meaningful and just design. His entire theory of the division of labour as the basis of solidarity depended upon the general readiness to make such a connection. If individuals saw their daily toil in isolation, rather than as one important element in a purposeful whole, social solidarity would be sabotaged by the division of labour" (64–65). Frank Parkin, *Durkheim* (New York: Oxford University Press, 1992). We are rescued from fragmentation only by consciousness of the whole, and it is intellectuals who specialize in providing this consciousness.

   The division of labor, while responsible for the disguising of systematic economic inequality, is also responsible for the beginnings of a positive attitude toward social difference: "Different kinds of different human beings appeared to be able to live harmoniously with each other. Indeed, it became possible to *define* a society as the harmonious interplay of very different kinds of human beings living very different kinds of lives without the social whole dissolving into chaos. It takes something like a leap of the imagination to grasp the difference between the old view and the new. The new view meant that differences between men were socially integrative. The old view that a society was better the more its members were the same was simply overturned." J. S. McClelland, *A History of Western Political Thought* (London: Routledge, 1996), 433.

15. Dana Frank, *Buy American: The Untold Story of Economic Nationalism* (Boston:

Beacon Press, 1999). Note the toaster, an American equivalent to Lodge's electric tea kettle.

16. As Kim Moody notes, "The campaign against PNTR status for China [was] really about the fear of rising, ever-cheaper imports, not human rights." And he goes on, "There is also more than a little hypocrisy in singling out China's labor rights record with its implication that labor rights in the United States—or Mexico, or South Korea—are some sort of model. . . . Finally, there is the fact that focusing exclusively on China brings out the jingo and the cold warrior still under the skin of many labor leaders. This was exemplified by Teamster President Jimmy Hoffa, who invited Pat Buchanan to speak at a Teamster rally on April 12." Kim Moody, "Protectionism or Solidarity?," *Against the Current* 87, 15:3 (July–August 2000), 34–38; see also Kim Moody, "Global Capital and Economic Nationalism," *Against the Current*, 88, 15:4 (September–October 2000), 26–30.

17. Randy Shaw, *Reclaiming America: Nike, Clean Air, and the New National Activism* (Berkeley: University of California Press, 1999).

18. Naomi Klein, *No Logo: Taking Aim at the Brand Bullies* (New York: Picador USA, 1999).

19. Barbara Ehrenreich, "Maid to Order," *Harper's*, April 2000, 69. See also Ehrenreich, *Nickel and Dimed: On (Not) Getting By in America* (New York: Metropolitan Books, 2001). Ehrenreich's insistence on the working, cleaning body can be balanced by Ann Cvetkovich's analysis of sweatshop rhetoric in *Capital*. Cvetkovich sees Marx using the sensationalism of the suffering body even as his analysis demonstrates that the suffering body is not the key to capital's working. Ann Cvetkovich, *Mixed Feelings: Feminism, Mass Culture, and Victorian Sensationalism* (New Brunswick: Rutgers University Press, 1992), 165–97.

20. Ehrenreich is writing about corporate housecleaning agencies that systematically overwork and underpay their employees. It is to be assumed that a private individual who chooses to pay good wages for housecleaning, however uncomfortable the exchange might be, would at least avoid the sweatshop charge.

21. This will mean after-hours work; it can't be the content of our teaching and writing.

22. Gayatri Chakravorty Spivak, *A Critique of Postcolonial Reason: Toward a History of the Vanishing Present* (Cambridge: Harvard University Press, 1999).

23. Fredric Jameson, *Postmodernism, or, The Cultural Logic of Late Capitalism* (Durham: Duke University Press, 1991), 314–15. The passage continues, "Indeed, it 'violates' the intimate space of your privacy and your extended body. For a society that wants to forget about class, therefore, reification in this consumer-packaging sense is very functional indeed."

24. Spivak seems to think the sort of subject represented by contemporary feminists, and the sort of subject contemporary feminists seek to produce, resembles Jane Eyre in the sense that she has a missionary zeal to act, even when action involves

the objectification of the Third World woman. For better or worse, I don't think this is accurate. The teaching of culture can certainly politicize, but the sort of consciousness it produces is more likely to be unhappy. If we collectively can be said to teach commitment, we also teach hesitation.

## 5. EDWARD SAID AND EFFORT

1. Among the works by Said discussed here are *Orientalism* (New York: Vintage, 1978); *The World, the Text, and the Critic* (Cambridge: Harvard University Press, 1983); *Culture and Imperialism* (New York: Knopf, 1992); *Representations of the Intellectual* (New York: Pantheon, 1994); "Palestine: Memory, Invention, and Space," *The Landscape of Palestine: Equivocal Poetry*, ed. Ibrahim Abu-Lughod, Roger Heacock, and Khaled Nashef (Birzeit: Birzeit University, 1999), 3–30; *Reflections on Exile and Other Essays* (Cambridge: Harvard University Press, 2000); and *From Oslo to Iraq and the Road Map: Essays* (New York: Pantheon, 2004).

2. Stefan Collini, *Absent Minds: Intellectuals in Britain* (Oxford: Oxford University Press, 2006).

3. Bruce Robbins, "The East Is a Career: Edward Said and the Logics of Professionalism," *Edward Said: A Critical Reader*, ed. Michael Sprinker (Oxford: Blackwell, 1992), 48–73.

4. See Caren Kaplan, *Questions of Travel: Postmodern Discourses of Displacement* (Durham: Duke University Press, 1996).

5. Gil Anidjar, "Secularism," *Critical Inquiry* 33 (2006), 52–77. See also Bruce Robbins, "Secularism, Elitism, Progress, and Other Transgressions: On Edward Said's Voyage In," *Social Text* 40 (1994), 48–73, and Aamir Mufti, "Critical Secularism: A Reintroduction for Perilous Times," *boundary 2* 31 (2004), 1–9.

6. Rob Nixon, "London Calling: V. S. Naipaul and the License of Exile," *South Atlantic Quarterly* 87:1 (1988), 1–38.

7. Anidjar adds that Christianity is sometimes "inchoate, unintentional" (60) and does not always act "knowingly" (61). So it may be functionally ubiquitous and omnipotent, but it is not quite omniscient.

8. Aijaz Ahmad, *In Theory: Classes, Nations, Literatures* (London: Verso, 1992).

9. Akeel Bilgrami, "Occidentalism, the Very Idea: An Essay on the Enlightenment and Enchantment," *Critical Inquiry* 32:3 (2006), 381–412. Ian Buruma and Avishai Margalit, *Occidentalism: The West in the Eyes of Its Enemies* (New York: Penguin, 2004).

10. What Said seems to resent so much in Orwell, for example, is less his not unwilling exploitation in the Cold War than the faked or wannabe homelessness that launched his early career: the fact that, whether among the Burmese, the miners of the North, or the tramps of the South, he always knew he could return. In an article called "Tourism among the Dogs" (Said 2000), Said describes the exile's genuine loss of identity as something Orwell never approached: "Losing your identity as

defined for you by where you come from and where most of the time you know (as Orwell certainly knew from membership in the lower-upper-middle-class) you can return" (95). Orwell wrote, Said says, "from the perspective of someone who very definitely felt, and really was, at home *somewhere*" (95). Orwell's "political excursions," he says, were "tours in the garden, not . . . travels abroad," not "harrowing exposures to real politics" (96).

11. Akeel Bilgrami, "Preface," Edward W. Said, *Humanism and Democratic Criticism* (New York: Columbia University Press, 2004).

12. Tariq Ali, *Conversations with Edward Said* (London: Seagull, 2006).

13. Abdirahman Hussein, *Edward Said: Criticism and Society* (London: Verso, 2002).

14. In one of my own first published essays, I posed the question as follows: "How can a set of theoretical terms that assume the permanent, irremediable homelessness of our condition coexist side by side with the practical terms of political discourse (common humanity and dehumanization, repression and liberation, experiential reality and its denial) that inevitably seem to present struggle as an effort to retrieve the (natural or given) homes from which people have been forcibly removed?" (Bruce Robbins, "Homelessness and Worldliness," *Diacritics* 13:3 [1983], 69–77). François Cusset, in *French Theory: Foucault, Derrida, Deleuze & Cie et les mutations de la vie intellectuelle aux Etats-Unis* (Paris: La Découverte, 2003), arguing that Said's "dialogue . . . avec la théorie française est resté cruciale" (221), traces Said's identification of the cause of liberation with the figure of the intellectual in exile back to Gilles Deleuze and Félix Guattari. The key passage is, "Liberation as an intellectual mission, born in the resistance and opposition to the confinements and ravages of imperialism, has now shifted from the settled, established, and domesticated dynamics of culture to its unhoused, decentered, and exilic energies, energies whose incarnation today is the migrant, and whose consciousness is that of the intellectual and artist in exile, the political figure between domains, between forms, between homes, and between languages" (Said 1993, 332). In Cusset's translation, however, the intellectual and the "political figure" are clearly the same person. In Said's original, that reading is not impossible, but the more likely possibility is that the "political figure" is a separate person, distinct from the intellectual and the artist but resembling them in being a migrant. This would suggest that Cusset, like many others, is misreading Said as celebrating the solitary, lonely figure of the intellectual as a political force at the expense of other sorts of political character and group.

15. Giles Gunn, "On Edward W. Said," *Raritan* 23:4 (2004), 71–78.

16. Said, *The World, the Text, and the Critic*.

17. Nubar Hovsepian, "Connections with Palestine," *Edward Said: A Critical Reader*, ed. Michael Sprinker (Oxford: Blackwell, 1992), 5–18.

18. Eve Kosofsky Sedgwick, *Touching Feeling: Affect, Pedagogy, Performativity* (Durham: Duke University Press, 2003), 139–40.

19. Colin Jager, "Introduction," "Romanticism, Secularism, and Cosmopolitanism," in *Romantic Circles* (online journal), August 2008. The following paragraphs are adapted from my afterword to the same collection.
20. Said, *Representations of the Intellectual*.

## 6. INTELLECTUALS IN PUBLIC

1. Stefan Collini, *Absent Minds: Intellectuals in Britain* (Oxford: Oxford University Press, 2006).
2. Representative examples are Ben Macintyre in the *Times* (14 April 2006), who proudly reasserts the premise of anti-intellectualism that Collini is questioning, and Kenan Malik in the *Sunday Telegraph* (14 May 2006), who takes Collini to be threatening the idea that culture is special and important. In these reviews Britain's practical good sense (reaffirmed by Macintyre) does precisely the same work as its commitment to Arnoldian high culture (reaffirmed by Malik): each is supposed to offer a British alternative and antidote to Continental ideology and thus a standard against which the present can be condemned for its slide into ideology.
3. James English, "Hazards of the Higher Debunkery," *Journal of the History of Ideas* 68:3 (July 2007).
4. The adjective *Arnoldian* is mine, not Collini's. In arguing that intellectuals are ordinary, Collini sides with Raymond Williams against Arnold. In arguing that culture is important because it is capable of changing the world, he is on common ground with both Williams and Arnold. The issue of where each stands vis-à-vis culture's multiplicity—not to be confused with culture's ordinariness—is too complex to enter into here.
5. At the same time, this point has to be somewhat qualified if, as Dolan Cummings suggests in *Culture Wars* (18 April 2006), one looks behind the conceptual contradiction and the repetitive rhetorical structure it generates, inquiring into the historical reasons why people at a given time and place care about intellectuals at all.
6. See Anna Boschetti, *The Intellectual Enterprise: Sartre and Les Temps Modernes*, trans. Richard C. McCleary (Evanston: Northwestern University Press, 1988).
7. See Jeremy Jennings, "The View from Calais," in the *Journal of the History of Ideas* symposium and Collini's response.
8. Reluctance to see credit given to the university helps explain another characteristic note struck in reviews, as when David Womersley (in *Social Affairs)* notes a Cambridge ring in Collini's prose (though this could as well be an Oxford/Cambridge affair, I suppose) or when Terry Eagleton (in the *New Statesman*, 3 April 2006) complains that there is "something of the view-from-King's-Parade about this book."
9. There is a great deal more evidence of the same kind, though it is merely circumstantial and hardly conclusive. As I write (14 March 2011), Frank Rich has just claimed in his valedictory column for the *New York Times* (12 March) that he was

never censored in any way. Rich did in fact make space to register Palestinian suffering on at least two occasions. What followed was a series of vicious personal attacks on him by the pro-Israel lobby (again as a "self-hating Jew") along with threats to boycott the *Times*. The result was years of near-complete silence on Israel–Palestinian issues. The website *U.S. Media and Israel*, which tells this story, has a very similar one about the Op-Ed columnist Thomas Friedman. See Rich, "Confessions of a Recovering Op-Ed Columnist," *New York Times*, 12 March 2011, and usmediaandisrael.com/?p=353 and usmediaandisrael.com/?p=134. I found two Op-Ed pieces by Edward Said, one of them devoted to a critique of his fellow Palestinians.

10. Slavoj Žižek, *Violence: Six Sideways Reflections* (New York: Picador, 2008).

11. Here more might be said about Mark Taylor's *New York Times* Op-Ed from April 2008 entitled "End the University As We Know It," which asks that higher education be "rigorously regulated and completely restructured" and takes religion as one of those exemplary problems, replacing existing departments, around which this restructuring should take place. Does the university need restructuring *because* it does not give religion the centrality that it holds in the mind of the American majority?

12. Here is Chomsky on Tibet: "China's actions in Tibet, whatever one may think of them, are no proof of aggressive expansionism, unless one wants to say the same of Indian suppression of tribal rebellions, for example. Tibet has been recognized internationally as a region of China. This status has been accepted by India as well as Communist and Nationalist China, and to my knowledge, has never been officially questioned by the United States. Although it is of no relevance to the issue, it is a bit too simple to say that 'China did indeed take over a country that did not want to be taken over.' This is by no means the general view of Western scholarship. For example, [George] Ginsburg[']s and [Michael] Mathos[']s comment that 'the March 1959 uprising did not, by and large, involve any considerable number of lower-class Tibetans, but involved essentially the propertied groups and the traditionally rebellious and foraging Khamba tribes opposed to any outside public authority (including sometimes that of the Dalai Lama)' (*Pacific Affairs*, September 1959). But whatever the complexities of the situation may be, it does not substantiate the charge of boundless Chinese expansionism." http://www.chomsky.info/debates/19670420.htm.

13. This Op-Ed appears more or less as is in *Violence*, 135–39.

## 7. WAR WITHOUT BELIEF

1. Louis Menand, *The Metaphysical Club: A Story of Ideas in America* (New York: Farrar, Straus and Giroux, 2001).

2. Richard Rorty, *Achieving Our Country: Leftist Thought in Twentieth-Century America* (Cambridge: Harvard University Press, 1998).

3. Richard Rorty, "Human Rights, Rationality, and Sentimentality," *On Human Rights: The Oxford Amnesty Lectures 1993*, ed. Stephen Shute and Susan Hurley, 111–34 (New York: Basic Books, 1993).

4. Bruce Robbins, "Sad Stories in the International Public Sphere: Richard Rorty on Culture and Human Rights," *Public Culture* 9:2 (winter 1997), 209–32; reprinted in *Feeling Global: Internationalism in Distress* (New York: New York University Press, 1999).

5. The last paragraph of the first part of the book describes a scene in which Holmes, near the end of his life, tries to read a poem about the Civil War and breaks down in tears. The tears, Menand comments, are not for the war but for what the war destroyed, the fact that all the learning and brilliance of the prewar world were "powerless to prevent" (69) the war.

6. James Livingston writes, "The field of American action had broadened to the world, whether Americans understood that or not. In 1916, Dewey noted: 'Facts have changed. In actuality we are part of the same world as that in which Europe exists and into which Asia is coming. Industry and commerce have interwoven our destinies. To maintain our older state of mind is to cultivate a dangerous illusion.' The promise of American life could not be realized, then, except as an international or trans-national proposition. Dewey believed this in part because the U.S. was itself home to many peoples and cultures: it was international or cosmopolitan by definition, by internal composition, and therefore had a vested interest in 'promoting the efficacy of human intercourse irrespective of class, racial, geographical and national limits.' He wanted, therefore, to 'make the accident of our internal composition into an idea, an idea upon which we may conduct our foreign as well as our domestic policy.'" James Livingston, "War and the Intellectuals: Bourne, Dewey, and the Fate of Pragmatism," *Journal of the Gilded Age and Progressive Era* 2 (2003), 431–50

7. Although Menand describes in detail Debs's role in the Pullman Strike of 1894, a strike that Dewey observed very closely, and although this is how Dewey came to call himself a socialist in Menand's account, that account does not pause, when it gets to the neighborhood of the First World War, to observe that Dewey had, in fact, voted for Debs in 1912—a fact that might have made Dewey's sudden support for America's entry into the war more like a submissive bowing to the pressure of the surrounding community.

8. Walter Benn Michaels, *The Shape of the Signifier: 1967 to the End of History* (Princeton: Princeton University Press, 2004), 41ff.

9. When Menand claims in the final pages that pragmatism is now coming back because of the end of the Cold War, one wishes he had been more prophetic, that we were not now involved in what so many commentators have described as a new Cold War, the self-proclaimed war on terror that perpetuates the sensibility of the Cold War by substituting a new version of the supposed Communist

menace. One wishes it had not become necessary, amidst all this zealotry and polarity, to renew the question of realism, with its acceptance both of national interest and of the limits of national interest, as an important ally of the internationalist left.

10. Bourne writes, "The realist thinks he can at least control events by linking himself to the forces that are moving. Perhaps he can. But if it is a question of controlling war, it is difficult to see how the child on the back of a mad elephant is to be any more effective in stopping the beast than is the child who tries to stop him from the ground" (316). Randolph Bourne, *The Radical Will: Selected Writings 1911–1918*, ed. Olaf Hansen (Berkeley: University of California Press, 1977).

11. Ross Posnock in *The Trial of Curiosity* appreciates Bourne's term the *inexorable* as well as *irony*: you can, Posnock suggests, have both, and perhaps they imply each other. Ross Posnock, *The Trial of Curiosity: Henry James, William James, and the Challenge of Modernity* (New York: Oxford University Press, 1991).

12. John Kerry's failure to make his combat service into a decisive political asset in the presidential election of 2004, coupled with the Bush campaign's success in preventing Bush's questionable record, or lack of one, from telling against him, suggests that the American public may be more pragmatic in this temporal sense than Rorty thinks, less eager to identify with their country's past, either in the mode of pride or in the mode of shame, and more concerned with the here and now. It's possible that it comes natural in America to forget about, say, the heritage of slavery, as Menand allows his story to do.

13. In *The Shape of the Signifier* Michaels speaks of "the complete continuity between the pragmatism of *Contingency, Irony, and Solidarity* and the patriotism of *Achieving Our Country*. Pragmatism has always been committed," he goes on, "to treating your beliefs as if they *were* your country, perfecting 'my country, right or wrong' (a slogan that acknowledges considerations of right and wrong but subordinates them to a higher loyalty) with 'my beliefs, neither right nor wrong' (which eliminates the need for any higher loyalty and which makes fighting for your beliefs—rather than arguing for them—the appropriate course of action" (78, emphasis added). Aside from its dangerous confusion between epistemological right and wrong and ethical right and wrong, this seems to me exactly right.

14. Amy Kaplan, *The Anarchy of Empire in the Making of U.S. Culture* (Cambridge: Harvard University Press, 2002).

15. Amy Kaplan, " 'Left Alone with America': The Absence of Empire in the Study of American Culture," *Cultures of United States Imperialism*, ed. Amy Kaplan and Donald E. Pease, 3–21 (Durham: Duke University Press, 1993).

16. I think there is something in this. Unfortunately, Rorty links spectatorship of this sort to cosmopolitanism, especially toward the end of the book, where the idea that "our country has little to be proud of" is attributed to "the point of view of a detached cosmopolitan spectator" (105). But why should the political roles of

agent and even lover, engaged in working toward "an ideally decent and civilized society" (106), be restricted to the borders of the United States? Especially when, from agricultural subsidies on, there are so many ways that struggling for decency for one's fellow Americans can become collateral damage for non-Americans.

17. Richard Rorty, "The United States as Republic and Empire," talk delivered at American Studies conference in Nepal, 19–20 September 2001. Whitman has also figured significantly in the larger conversation provoked by Rorty's "Unpatriotic Academy" Op-Ed in the *New York Times*, a conversation setting Rorty and patriotism against Martha Nussbaum and cosmopolitanism—though Nussbaum's chapter on Whitman in *Upheavals of Thought* is almost entirely celebratory. Nussbaum is not horrified by the prospect of the bard of democracy horrifying foreign despots (645). Martha Nussbaum, *Upheavals of Thought: The Intelligence of Emotions* (Cambridge: Cambridge University Press, 2001).

18. Casey Nelson Blake, *Beloved Community: The Cultural Criticism of Randolph Bourne, Van Wyck Brooks, Waldo Frank, and Lewis Mumford* (Chapel Hill: University of North Carolina Press, 1990).

19. For Casey Blake, Bourne explains Dewey's acquiescence in the war in terms of Dewey's attachment to reason and deafness to the aesthetic (158).

## 8. COMPARATIVE NATIONAL BLAMING

1. Stephen Howe, "Israel, Palestine, and the Campus Civil Wars," *Open Democracy* (14 December 2004). The passage continues, "By that measure, *all* sides in polemics over the middle east have long since lost: comparing each other to Nazis has become the routine, shop-soiled and ever-devaluing currency of dispute."

2. Quoted in John Leonard, "Motherland" (review of Amos Oz's *A Tale of Love and Darkness*), *New York Times Book Review*, 12 December 2004, 16–17 (16).

3. Benedict Anderson, *The Spectre of Comparisons: Nationalism, Southeast Asia, and the World* (London: Verso, 1998).

4. See, for example, Charles Bernheimer, ed., *Comparative Literature in the Age of Multiculturalism* (Baltimore: Johns Hopkins University Press, 1995). In his introduction, entitled "The Anxieties of Comparison," Bernheimer writes, "The more literatures you try to compare, the more like a colonizing imperialist you may seem. If you stress what these literatures have in common—thematically, morally, politically—you may be accused of imposing a universalist model that suppresses particular differences so as to foster the old humanist dream of man's worldwide similarity to man. If, on the other hand, you stress differences, then the basis of comparison becomes problematic" (9).

5. The famous debate between the British Marxist historians E. P. Thompson and Perry Anderson might be seen as, among other things, a reflection on the practice of comparative national blaming. In his essay "The Peculiarities of the English" (1965), reprinted in *The Poverty of Theory and Other Essays* (London: Merlin, 1978),

Thompson accuses Anderson and Tom Nairn of making illegitimate use of "an undisclosed model of Other Countries" (37), or what he refers to as "inverted Pod-snappery" (36). Podsnap, in Charles Dickens's *Our Mutual Friend*, is the patriot who proclaims, "No Other Country is so Favoured as This Country." Thompson imagines Anderson and Nairn as answering the question of how other countries do as follows: "They do—we are sorry to be obliged to say it—in Every Respect Better. Their Bourgeois Revolutions have been Mature. Their Class Struggles have been Sanguinary and Unequivocal. Their Intelligentsia has been Autonomous and Integrated Vertically. . . . Their Proletariat has been Hegemonic" (37). In his defense, Anderson might have insisted on the difference between using a national model and not disclosing that model. In *English Questions* (London: Verso, 1992), which reprints the original essays of the early 1960s to which Thompson was objecting, Anderson accepts "the justice of [Thompson's] criticism" (4) and discloses the model: "The standard is provided by France" (5). Anderson acknowledges that he was excessively influenced by Antonio Gramsci, whose comparison of advanced France with belated Italy inspired Anderson's own comparison of a mature France with a premature England. Whatever the failings of the French model, there surely exists a better case in favor of national comparison in general than Anderson, a master of the art, seems willing, for the moment, to make.

6. Elazar Barkan, *The Guilt of Nations: Restitution and Negotiating Historical Injustices* (New York: W. W. Norton, 2000).

7. W. G. Sebald, *On the Natural History of Destruction*, trans. Anthea Bell (New York: Randon House, 2003); the German edition is *Luftkrieg und Literatur* (Munich: Carl Hanser, 1999).

8. Even in the immediate aftermath Germans may well have agreed with Winston Churchill, Sebald writes, that there was "a higher poetic justice at work" (19).

9. Christopher Hitchens, *Atlantic Monthly* 291:1 (January–February 2003), 182–89. This formula is more mysterious and intriguing than the banal "they started it."

10. Volker Hage, *Zeugen der Zerstörung: Die Literaten und der Luftkrieg Essays und Gespräche* (Frankfurt: S. Fischer Verlag, 2003). "Das 'Schweigen der Betroffene' . . . sei zu begrüssen, wenn man das Leid des Tätervolks messe an den Entsetzen, 'das Deutschland mit seinen Schergen über die unterworfenen Völker im Osten und, das vor allem, über die Opfer des rassistischen Vernichtungs-Wille' gebracht habe. . . ." "Das Schwiegen verbarg vielleicht eine Scham, die kostbarer ist als alle Literatur." (My translation.) On the troubled German reception of Sebald's book, see Mark Anderson, "The Edge of Darkness," *October* 106 (fall 2003), 102–21. For another judicious contextualization of this debate, see Noah Isenberg, "Dresden Mon Amour: Realism or Revisionism? Germans Revisit the War," *Bookforum* (summer 2005), 4–8.

11. Andreas Huyssen, *Present Pasts: Urban Palimpsests and the Politics of Memory* (Stanford: Stanford University Press, 2003), 147.

12. E. J. Hobsbawm, *The Age of Extremes: A History of the World, 1914–1991* (New York: Pantheon, 1994). Thus the supposed ease and geometrical clarity of bombing, seen from the bomber's aerial point of view, could be counterposed to the difficulty of remembering bombing, from the point of view of the victims on the ground.

13. Available from the author, Department of English, Bard College.

14. Mahmood Mamdani, *When Victims Become Killers: Colonialism, Nativism, and the Genocide in Rwanda* (Princeton: Princeton University Press, 2001); Joanna Bourne, *An Intimate History of Killing: Face to Face Killing in 20th Century Warfare* (New York: Basic Books, 1999).

15. Hitchens writes, "Few historians or strategists now argue that the bombing made much difference if any to the outcome of the war" (189). See also Robert Pape, *Bombing to Win* (Ithaca: Cornell University Press, 1996); Daniel Byman and Andrew Waxman, *The Dynamics of Coercion: American Foreign Policy and the Limits of Military Might* (Cambridge: Cambridge University Press, 2002); and Andrew Stigler, "A Clear Victory for Air Power: NATO's Empty Threat to Invade Kosovo," *International Security* 27:3 (winter 2002–3). Thanks to Jack Snyder for these references.

16. This romantic tendency in Sebald, visible also in other works, seems sometimes to be complaining more about the modernization that followed the bombs than about the bombs themselves, as when he speaks, for example, of "a second liquidation . . . of the nation's own past history" (7).

17. Perry Anderson, "Union Sucrée," *London Review of Books*, 23 September 2004.

18. And if they were, then the individual would be redeemed from the shame of having chosen not to remember.

19. Sven Lindqvist, *A History of Bombing*, trans. Linda Haverty Rugg (New York: New Press, 2000).

20. I discuss related complexities of human rights blaming in "Temporizing: Time and Politics in the Humanities and Human Rights," *boundary 2* 32:1 (spring 2005), 191–208.

21. Time seems Sebald's enemy, elsewhere in his writing, in that it makes atrocities into classics, whitens the bones, dilutes the moral absoluteness of suffering.

22. In *Nation and Identity* (London: Routledge, 1999), Ross Poole writes interestingly, for example, about the issue of whether recent Australian immigrants from Europe and Asia can and should be induced to share responsibility for white crimes against aboriginals, even though they obviously weren't there to participate in the crimes.

23. Andreas Huyssen, "Air War Legacies: From Dresden to Baghdad," *New German Critique* 90 (fall 2003), 163–76.

24. Martha Minow, *Between Vengeance and Forgiveness: Facing History after Genocide and Mass Violence*, foreword by Judge Richard J. Goldstone (Boston: Beacon Press, 1998), 17.

25. See, for example, Jacques Derrida, *On Cosmopolitanism and Forgiveness*, trans. Mark Dooley and Michael Hughes (London: Routledge, 2001).

26. No one belongs only to the nation, and the diversity of debts to other collectivities loosens the individual's responsibility to each. Acknowledging debts to the nation, even unliquidatable debts, need not entail treating the nation, in the manner of Alcoholics Anonymous, as a single, higher power.

# BIBLIOGRAPHY

Ahmad, Aijaz. *In Theory: Classes, Nations, Literatures.* London: Verso, 1992.

Ali, Tariq. *Conversations with Edward Said.* London: Seagull, 2006.

Anderson, Amanda. *The Way We Argue Now: A Study in the Culture of Theory.* Princeton: Princeton University Press, 2006.

Anderson, Benedict. "Ice Empire and Ice Hockey: Two Fin de Siècle Dreams." *New Left Review* 214 (November–December 1995), 146–50.

——. *The Spectre of Comparisons: Nationalism, Southeast Asia, and the World.* London: Verso, 1998.

Anderson, Mark. "The Edge of Darkness." *October* 106 (fall 2003), 102–21.

Anderson, Perry. *English Questions.* London: Verso, 1992.

——. "Union Sucrée." *London Review of Books,* 23 September 2004.

Anidjar, Gil. "Secularism." *Critical Inquiry* 33 (2006), 52–77.

Appadurai, Arjun, ed. *The Social Life of Things: Commodities in Cultural Perspective.* Cambridge: Cambridge University Press, 1986.

——. "Disjuncture and Difference in the Global Cultural Economy." *The Phantom Public Sphere,* ed. Bruce Robbins, 269–95. Minneapolis: University of Minnesota Press, 1993.

——. "Patriotism and Its Futures." *Public Culture* 5:3 (spring 1993), 411–29.

——. *Modernity at Large: Cultural Dimensions of Globalization.* Minneapolis: University of Minnesota Press, 1996.

——. *Fear of Small Numbers: An Essay on the Geography of Anger.* Durham: Duke University Press, 2006.

Appiah, Joseph. *Joe Appiah: The Autobiography of an African Patriot.* Foreword by Henry Louis Gates Jr. New York: Praeger, 1990.

Appiah, Kwame Anthony. *In My Father's House: Africa in the Philosophy of Culture.* New York: Oxford University Press, 1992.

——. "Cosmopolitan Patriots." Martha C. Nussbaum and respondents, *For Love of Country: Debating the Limits of Patriotism*, ed. Josh Cohen, 21–29. Boston: Beacon, 1996.

——. *The Ethics of Identity*. Princeton: Princeton University Press, 2005.

——. *Cosmopolitanism: Ethics in a World of Strangers*. New York: W. W. Norton, 2006.

——. "A Slow Emancipation." *New York Times Magazine*, 18 March 2007, 15–17.

Arac, Jonathan. "The Media of Sublimity: Johnson and Lamb on *King Lear*." *Studies in Romanticism* 26 (summer 1987), 209–20.

Arnold, Matthew. *Culture and Anarchy*. New Haven: Yale University Press, 1994 [1869].

Asad, Talal. *Genealogies of Religion: Discipline and Reasons of Power in Christianity and Islam*. Baltimore: Johns Hopkins University Press, 1993.

——. *On Suicide Bombing*. New York: Columbia University Press, 2007.

Asad, Talal, Wendy Brown, Judith Butler, and Saba Mahmood. *Is Critique Secular? Blasphemy, Injury, and Free Speech*. Berkeley: Townshend Center for the Humanities and University of California Press, 2009.

Barkan, Elazar. *The Guilt of Nations: Restitution and Negotiating Historical Injustices*. New York: W. W. Norton, 2000.

Barsky, Robert F. *Noam Chomsky: A Life of Dissent*. Cambridge: MIT Press, 1997.

Benhabib, Seyla. *Another Cosmopolitanism*. With commentaries by Jeremy Waldron, Bonnie Honig, and Will Kymlicka. Edited by Robert Post. Oxford: Oxford University Press, 2006.

Berman, Jessica. *Modernist Fiction, Cosmopolitanism, and the Politics of Community*. Cambridge: Cambridge University Press, 2001.

Bernheimer, Charles, ed. *Comparative Literature in the Age of Multiculturalism*. Baltimore: Johns Hopkins University Press, 1995.

Bérubé, Michael. *The Left at War*. New York: New York University Press, 2009.

Bilgrami, Akeel. "Preface." Edward W. Said, *Humanism and Democratic Criticism*. New York: Columbia University Press, 2004.

——. "Occidentalism, the Very Idea: An Essay on the Enlightenment and Enchantment." *Critical Inquiry* 32:3 (2006), 381–412.

Blake, Casey Nelson. *Beloved Community: The Cultural Criticism of Randolph Bourne, Van Wyck Brooks, Waldo Frank, and Lewis Mumford*. Chapel Hill: University of North Carolina Press, 1990.

Boltanski, Luc. *Distant Suffering: Morality, Media and Politics*. Translated by Graham Burchell. Cambridge: Cambridge University Press, 1999.

Boschetti, Anna. *The Intellectual Enterprise: Sartre and Les Temps Modernes*. Translated by Richard C. McCleary. Evanston: Northwestern University Press, 1988.

Bourne, Joanna. *An Intimate History of Killing: Face to Face Killing in 20th Century Warfare*. New York: Basic Books, 1999.

Bourne, Randolph. *The Radical Will: Selected Writings 1911–1918*. Edited by Olaf Hansen. Berkeley: University of California Press, 1977.

Buruma, Ian, and Avishai Margalit. *Occidentalism: The West in the Eyes of Its Enemies*. New York: Penguin, 2004.

Butler, Judith. *Frames of War*. London: Verso, 2009.

Byman, Daniel, and Andrew Waxman. *The Dynamics of Coercion: American Foreign Policy and the Limits of Military Might*. Cambridge: Cambridge University Press, 2002.

Calhoun, Craig. "The Class Consciousness of Frequent Travelers: Towards a Critique of Actually Existing Cosmopolitanism." *South Atlantic Quarterly* 101:4 (2002), 869–97.

Chast, Roz. Cartoon in *The New Yorker*, 29 November 1999, 88.

Chomsky, Noam. "An Exchange on 'The Responsibility of Intellectuals.' Noam Chomsky debates with Fryar Calhoun, E. B. Murray, and Arthur Dorfman." *New York Review of Books*, 20 April 1967. http://www.chomsky.info/debates/19670420.htm.

———. *9-11*. New York: Seven Stories, 2001.

———. "Commentary: Moral Truisms, Empirical Evidence, and Foreign Policy." *Review of International Studies* 29 (2003), 605–20.

———. *Hegemony or Survival: America's Quest for Global Dominance*. New York: Metropolitan, 2003.

———. "'Exterminate all the Brutes': Gaza 2009." 19 January 2009. http://www.chomsky.info/articles/20090119.htm.

Chow, Rey. *The Age of the World Target: Self-Referentiality in War, Theory, and Comparative Work*. Durham: Duke University Press, 2006.

Cohen, Mitchell. "Rooted Cosmopolitanism." *Dissent* 39:4 (1992), 483–87.

Collini, Stefan. *Absent Minds: Intellectuals in Britain*. Oxford: Oxford University Press, 2006.

Cummings, Dolan. Review of *Absent Minds: Intellectuals in Britain*. *Culture Wars* (online, 18 April 2006).

Cusset, François. *French Theory: Foucault, Derrida, Deleuze & Cie et les mutations de la vie intellectuelle aux Etats-Unis*. Paris: La Découverte, 2003.

Cvetkovich, Ann. *Mixed Feelings: Feminism, Mass Culture, and Victorian Sensationalism*. New Brunswick: Rutgers University Press, 1992.

Derrida, Jacques. *On Cosmopolitanism and Forgiveness*. Translated by Mark Dooley and Michael Hughes. London: Routledge, 2001.

DuPlessis, Robert S. "The Partial Transition to World-Systems Analysis in Early Modern European History." *Radical History Review* 39 (1987), 11–27.

Ehrenreich, Barbara. "Maid to Order." *Harper's*, April 2000.

———. *Nickel and Dimed: On (Not) Getting By in America*. New York: Metropolitan, 2001.

Eliot, George. *Middlemarch*. New York: W. W. Norton, 1977 [1871–72].

English, James. "Hazards of the Higher Debunkery." *Journal of the History of Ideas* 68:3 (July 2007), 363–68.

Feher, Michel, ed., with Gaëlle Krikorian and Yates McKee. *Nongovernmental Politics*. New York: Zone Books, 2007.

Ferguson, James. "Decomposing Modernity: History and Hierarchy after Development." *Postcolonial Studies and Beyond*, ed. Ania Loomba, Suvir Kaul, Matti Bunzl, Antoinette Burton, and Jed Esty, 166–81. Durham: Duke University Press, 2005.

Fisher, Philip. *Hard Facts: Setting and Form in the American Novel*. Oxford: Oxford University Press, 1987.

Frank, Dana. *Buy American: The Untold Story of Economic Nationalism*. Boston: Beacon Press, 1999.

Gilroy, Paul. *The Black Atlantic: Modernity and Double Consciousness*. Cambridge: Harvard University Press, 1993.

——. *Against Race: Imagining Political Culture beyond the Color Line*. Cambridge: Harvard University Press, 2000.

Gitlin, Todd. *The Intellectuals and the Flag*. New York: Columbia University Press, 2006.

"Going Green." Unsigned editorial. *Nation*, 7 May 2007, 3–4.

Gunn, Giles. "On Edward W. Said." *Raritan* 23:4 (2004), 71–78.

Hage, Volker. *Zeugen der Zerstörung: Die Literaten und der Luftkrieg Essays und Gespräche*. Frankfurt: S. Fischer, 2003.

Haskell, Thomas L. "Capitalism and the Origins of the Humanitarian Sensibility, Parts One and Two." *American Historical Review* 90:2 (April 1985), 339–61, and 90:3 (June 1985), 547–66.

Hawley, John C., ed. *India in Africa, Africa in India: Indian Ocean Cosmopolitanism*. Bloomington: Indiana University Press, 2008.

Hazeldine, Tom. "The North Atlantic Counsel: Complicity of the International Crisis Group." *New Left Review* 63 (May–June 2010), 17–33.

Hertz, Neil. *The End of the Line: Essays on Psychoanalysis and the Sublime*. New York: Columbia University Press, 1985.

Hitchens, Christopher. *Atlantic Monthly* 291:1 (January–February 2003), 182–89.

——. *Christopher Hitchens and His Critics: Terror, Iraq, and the Left*. Edited by Simon Cottee and Thomas Cushman. New York: New York University Press, 2008.

Hobsbawm, E. J. *The Age of Extremes: A History of the World, 1914–1991*. New York: Pantheon, 1994.

Hollinger, David A. *Postethnic America: Beyond Multiculturalism*. Revised edition. New York: Basic Books, 2000.

——. "Not Pluralists, Not Universalists, the New Cosmopolitans Find Their Own Way." *Constellations* (June 2001), 236–48.

Hovsepian, Nubar. "Connections with Palestine." *Edward Said: A Critical Reader*, ed. Michael Sprinker, 5–18. Oxford: Blackwell, 1992.

Howe, Stephen. *Empire: A Very Short Introduction*. Oxford: Oxford University Press, 2002.

——. "Israel, Palestine, and the Campus Civil Wars." *Open Democracy*, 14 December 2004.

Hussein, Abdirahman. *Edward Said: Criticism and Society*. London: Verso, 2002.

Huyssen, Andreas. "Air War Legacies: From Dresden to Baghdad." *New German Critique* 90 (fall 2003), 163–76.

——. *Present Pasts: Urban Palimpsests and the Politics of Memory*. Stanford: Stanford University Press, 2003.

Isaac, Jeffrey C. "Hannah Arendt on Human Rights and the Limits of Exposure, or Why Noam Chomsky Is Wrong about Kosovo." *Social Research* 69:2 (summer 2002), 505–37.

Isenberg, Noah. "Dresden Mon Amour: Realism or Revisionism? Germans Revisit the War." *Bookforum* (summer 2005), 4–8.

Jager, Colin. "Introduction." "Romanticism, Secularism, and Cosmopolitanism." *Romantic Circles* (online journal), August 2008.

Jameson, Fredric. *Postmodernism, or, The Cultural Logic of Late Capitalism*. Durham: Duke University Press, 1991.

Jay, Paul. "Beyond Discipline? Globalization and the Future of English." PMLA 116:1 (2001), 32–47.

Kant, Immanuel. *Critique of Judgment*. Translated by J. H. Bernard. London: Collier Macmillan, 1951.

——. *Perpetual Peace and Other Essays*. Translated by Ted Humphrey. Indianapolis: Hackett, 1983.

Kaplan, Amy. "'Left Alone with America': The Absence of Empire in the Study of American Culture." *Cultures of United States Imperialism*, ed. Amy Kaplan and Donald E. Pease, 3–21. Durham: Duke University Press, 1993.

——. *The Anarchy of Empire in the Making of U.S. Culture*. Cambridge: Harvard University Press, 2002.

Kaplan, Caren. *Questions of Travel: Postmodern Discourses of Displacement*. Durham: Duke University Press, 1996.

Kendall, Gavin, Ian Woodward, and Zlatko Skrbis. *The Sociology of Cosmopolitanism: Globalization, Identity, Culture and Government*. London: Palgrave Macmillan, 2009.

Kitchen Table Cartoons. "Intimidation at the New York Times: How the Israel Lobby Silenced 2 leading Columnists." usmediaandisrael.com/?p=134, 27 February 2009.

Klein, Naomi. *No Logo: Taking Aim at the Brand Bullies*. New York: Picador, 1999.

Krikorian, Gaëlle. "A New Era of Access to Rights?" *Nongovernmental Politics*, ed. Michel Feher with Gaëlle Krikorian and Yates McKee, 247–59. New York: Zone Books, 2007.

Kymlicka, Will. "American Multiculturalism in the International Arena." *Dissent* (fall 1998), 73–79.

Leonard, John. "Motherland." Review of Amos Oz's *A Tale of Love and Darkness*. *New York Times Book Review*, 12 December 2004, 16–17.

Lindqvist, Sven. *A History of Bombing*. Translated by Linda Haverty Rugg. New York: New Press, 2000.

Livingston, James. "War and the Intellectuals: Bourne, Dewey, and the Fate of Pragmatism." *Journal of the Gilded Age and Progressive Era* 2 (2003), 431–50.

Lockard, Joe. "Chomsky on 9-11." *Judaism* 51:2 (spring 2002), 249–52.

Lodge, David. *Nice Work*. Harmondsworth: Penguin, 1988.

Loss, Jacqueline. *Cosmopolitanisms and Latin America: Against the Destiny of Place*. New York: Palgrave Macmillan, 2005.

Mamdani, Mahmood. *When Victims Become Killers: Colonialism, Nativism, and the Genocide in Rwanda*. Princeton: Princeton University Press, 2001.

Marcus, Steven. "Literature and Social Theory: Starting In with George Eliot." *Representations: Essays on Literature and Society*. New York: Columbia University Press, 1975.

Marks, Stephen P. "Access to Essential Medicines as a Component of the Right to Health." *Realizing the Right to Health: Swiss Human Rights Book*, ed. Andrew Clapham, Mary Robinson, and Claire Mahon, 80–99. Zurich: Rueffer & Rub, 2009.

McClelland, J. S. *A History of Western Political Thought*. London: Routledge, 1996.

Melas, Natalie. *All the Difference in the World: Postcoloniality and the Ends of Comparison*. Stanford: Stanford University Press, 2007.

Menand, Louis. *The Metaphysical Club: A Story of Ideas in America*. New York: Farrar, Straus and Giroux, 2001.

Michaels, Walter Benn. *The Shape of the Signifier: 1967 to the End of History*. Princeton: Princeton University Press, 2004.

——. *The Trouble with Diversity: How We Learned to Love Identity and Ignore Inequality*. New York: Metropolitan, 2006.

Minow, Martha. *Between Vengeance and Forgiveness: Facing History after Genocide and Mass Violence*. Foreword by Judge Richard J. Goldstone. Boston: Beacon, 1998.

Moody, Kim. "Protectionism or Solidarity?" *Against the Current* 87, 15:3 (July–August 2000), 34–38.

——. "Global Capital and Economic Nationalism." *Against the Current* 88, 15:4 (September–October 2000), 26–30.

Moretti, Franco. "Conjectures on World Literature." *New Left Review* 1 (n.s.) (January–February 2000), 55–67.

Morris, David. "Israel Bias and Self-Censorship." usmediaandisrael.com/?p=353, 2 November 2009.

Mufti, Aamir. "Critical Secularism: A Reintroduction for Perilous Times." *boundary 2* 31 (2004), 1–9.

Mulhern, Francis. *Culture/Metaculture*. London: Routledge, 2000.

National Labor Committee, "Wal-Mart's Shirts of Misery." New York, July 1999.

Nixon, Rob. "London Calling: V. S. Naipaul and the License of Exile." *South Atlantic Quarterly* 87:1 (1988), 1–38.

Nussbaum, Martha. *Upheavals of Thought: The Intelligence of Emotions.* Cambridge: Cambridge University Press, 2001.

——. *For Love of Country?* Edited by Joshua Cohen. Boston: Beacon, 2002.

Pape, Robert. *Bombing to Win.* Ithaca: Cornell University Press, 1996.

Parkin, Frank. *Durkheim.* New York: Oxford University Press, 1992.

Pereira, Malin. *Rita Dove's Cosmopolitanism.* Urbana: University of Illinois Press, 2003.

Pieterse, Jan P. Nederveen. *Empire and Emancipation: Power and Liberation on a World Scale.* London: Pluto Press, 1990.

Pinsky, Robert. "Eros against Esperanto," in Martha Nussbaum, *For Love of Country?*, ed. Joshua Cohen, 85–90. Boston: Beacon, 2002.

Poole, Ross. *Nation and Identity.* London: Routledge, 1999.

Posnock, Ross. *The Trial of Curiosity: Henry James, William James, and the Challenge of Modernity.* New York: Oxford University Press, 1991.

——. *Color and Culture: Black Writers and the Making of the Modern Intellectual.* Cambridge: Harvard University Press, 1998.

Rabinow, Paul. "Representations Are Social Facts: Modernity and Post-Modernity in Anthropology." *Writing Culture: The Poetics and Politics of Ethnography*, ed. James Clifford and George E. Marcus, 234–61. Berkeley: University of California Press, 1986.

Rajan, Gita, and Shailja Sharma, eds. *New Cosmopolitanisms: South Asians in the U.S.* Stanford: Stanford University Press, 2006.

Reagon, Bernice Johnson. "Are My Hands Clean?" *Sweet Honey and the Rock.* Songtalk, 1985.

Rich, Frank. "Confessions of a Recovering Op-Ed Columnist." *New York Times*, 12 March 2011.

Robbins, Bruce. "Homelessness and Worldliness." *Diacritics* 13:3 (1983), 69–77.

——. "Comparative Cosmopolitanism." *Social Text* 31/32 (spring 1992), 169–86.

——. "The East Is a Career: Edward Said and the Logics of Professionalism." *Edward Said: A Critical Reader*, ed. Michael Sprinker, 48–73. Oxford: Blackwell, 1992.

——. "Secularism, Elitism, Progress, and Other Transgressions: On Edward Said's Voyage In." *Social Text* 40 (1994), 48–73

——. *Feeling Global: Internationalism in Distress.* New York: New York University Press, 1999.

——. "Cosmopolitanism, America, and the Welfare State." "Theories of American Culture/Theories of American Studies," ed. Winfried Fluck and Thomas Claviez, REAL—*Yearbook of Research in English and American Literature* 19:5 (2003), 201–24.

——. "Commodity Histories." *PMLA* 120:2 (March 2005), 454–63.

——. "Temporizing: Time and Politics in the Humanities and Human Rights." *boundary 2* 32:1 (spring 2005), 191–208.

——. "Afterword." "Remapping Genre." *PMLA* 122:5 (October 2007), 1644–51.

——. *Upward Mobility and the Common Good*. Princeton: Princeton University Press, 2007.

——. "Progressive Politics in Transnational Space." *Radical Philosophy* 153 (January–February 2009), 37–44.

Rorty, Richard. "Human Rights, Rationality, and Sentimentality." *On Human Rights: The Oxford Amnesty Lectures 1993*, ed. Stephen Shute and Susan Hurley, 111–34. New York: Basic Books, 1993.

——. *Achieving Our Country: Leftist Thought in Twentieth-Century America*. Cambridge: Harvard University Press, 1998.

——. "The United States as Republic and Empire." Talk delivered at American Studies conference in Nepal, 19–20 September 2001.

Russell, David O., dir. *Three Kings* (1999).

Ryan, Alan. "Cosmopolitans." *New York Review of Books* 53:11, 22 June 2006.

Sahlins, Marshall. "Cosmologies of Capitalism: The Trans-Pacific Sector of 'the World System.'" *Proceedings of the British Academy* 74 (1988), 1–51.

Said, Edward W. *Orientalism*. New York: Vintage, 1978.

——. *The Question of Palestine*. New York: Vintage, 1979.

——. "Criticism between Culture and System." *The World, the Text, and the Critic*. Cambridge: Harvard University Press, 1983.

——. *Culture and Imperialism*. New York: Alfred A. Knopf, 1992.

——. *Representations of the Intellectual*. New York: Pantheon, 1994.

——. "Palestine: Memory, Invention, and Space." *The Landscape of Palestine: Equivocal Poetry*, ed. Ibrahim Abu-Lughod, Roger Heacock, and Khaled Nashef, 3–30. Birzeit: Birzeit University, 1999.

——. *Reflections on Exile and Other Essays*. Cambridge: Harvard University Press, 2000.

——. *From Oslo to Iraq and the Road Map: Essays*. New York: Pantheon, 2004.

Seabright, Paul. *The Company of Strangers: A Natural History of Economic Life*. Princeton: Princeton University Press, 2004.

Seaton, James. *Weekly Standard*, 9 October 2006.

Sebald, W. G. *On the Natural History of Destruction*. Translated by Anthea Bell. New York: Random House, 2003.

Sedgwick, Eve Kosofsky. *Touching Feeling: Affect, Pedagogy, Performativity*. Durham: Duke University Press, 2003.

Shapiro, Gary. "From the Sublime to the Political: Some Historical Notes." *New Literary History* 16:2 (winter 1985), 213–35.

Shaw, Randy. *Reclaiming America: Nike, Clean Air, and the New National Activism*. Berkeley: University of California Press, 1999.

Spivak, Gayatri Chakravorty. *A Critique of Postcolonial Reason: Toward a History of the Vanishing Present*. Cambridge: Harvard University Press, 1999.

Stanton, Domna. "Presidential Address 2005: On Rooted Cosmopolitanism." PMLA 121:3 (2006), 627–40.

Stern, Steve J. "Feudalism, Capitalism, and the World-System in the Perspective of Latin America and Africa." *Confronting Historical Paradigms: Peasants, Labor, and the Capitalist World System in Africa and Latin America*, ed. Frederick Cooper et al., 23–83. Madison: University of Wisconsin Press, 1993.

Stigler, Andrew. "A Clear Victory for Air Power: NATO's Empty Threat to Invade Kosovo." *International Security* 27:3 (winter 2002–3), 124–57.

Thompson, E. P. "The Peculiarities of the English." *The Poverty of Theory and Other Essays*. London: Merlin, 1978.

Thompson, Janna. "Community Identity and World Citizenship." *Re-Imagining Political Community: Studies in Cosmopolitan Democracy*, ed. Daniele Archibugi, David Held, and Martin Köhler, 179–97. Cambridge: Polity, 1998.

Waldron, Jeremy. "Minority Cultures and the Cosmopolitan Alternative." *The Rights of Minority Cultures*, ed. Will Kymlicka, 93–119. New York: Oxford University Press, 1995.

Walkowitz, Rebecca L. *Cosmopolitan Style: Modernism beyond the Nation*. New York: Columbia University Press, 2006.

Wallerstein, Immanuel. *The Modern World-System: Capitalist Agriculture and the Origins of the European World-Economy in the Sixteenth Century*. New York: Harcourt Brace Jovanovich, 1974.

——. *Historical Capitalism*. London: Verso, 1983.

——. "The Rise and Future Demise of the World Capitalist System: Concepts for Comparative Analysis." *The Essential Wallerstein*. New York: New Press, 2000.

——. *The Decline of American Power*. New York: New Press, 2003.

——. "The Curve of US Power." *New Left Review* 40, 2d ser. (July–August 2006), 77–94.

Wernber, Pnina, ed. *Anthropology and the New Cosmopolitanism: Rooted, Feminist and Vernacular Perspectives*. Oxford: Berg, 2008.

Williams, Alex. "Love It? You Might Check the Label." *New York Times*, 6 September 2007, C, 1, 6.

Williams, Raymond. *Culture and Society, 1780–1950*. London: Chatto and Windus, 1958.

Wolf, Eric R. *Europe and the People without History*. Berkeley: University of California Press, 1982.

Žižek, Slavoj. *Violence: Six Sideways Reflections*. New York: Picador, 2008.

Appadurai, Arjun (*cont.*)
ference in the Global Cultural Economy," 79–80, 82; *Fear of Small Numbers*, 206nn24–25, 207n40; "Patriotism and Its Futures," 16; *The Social Life of Things*, 205n17

Appiah, Kwame Anthony, 31–45; African slavery and, 198n15; *Cosmopolitanism: Ethics in a World of Strangers*, 31–32, 38–42; "Cosmopolitan Patriots," 31, 43; on cultural patrimony, 41; cultural variety celebrated by, 33; elitism in cosmopolitanism of, 199n19; *The Ethics of Identity*, 31; free-market apologetics and, 198n17; historical forgiveness and, 37–38, 40; local difference vs. relativism and, 38–39; metaphor of conversation and, 198n16; on pan-Africanism, 197n11; on patriotism and cosmopolitanism, compatibility between, 15, 31–32, 34–36, 42; on patriotism as rooted, 35, 43; patriotism vs. politics and, 197–98n13; "Rooted Cosmopolitanism," 31, 35–36, 39–40

Arac, Jonathan, 208n5

Arendt, Hannah, 203n2

Arnold, Matthew, 74, 85, 130, 143, 214n4

Aron, Raymond, 149

Arrighi, Giovanni, 194n23

Asad, Talad: *Genealogies of Religion*, 77–78; *Is Critique Secular?*, 61–64, 203n29; *On Suicide Bombing*, 58–59

Asia, 81, 83, 206n31

atrocities. *See* war, transnational aggression, violence

attachment/belonging vs. detachment: ahistorical vs. historical belonging and, 21; balance between attachment and detachment and, 29; belonging, addressing the system and, 91; belonging, definition of intellectuals and, 116; belonging, empowerment and, 28–29; belonging, remote violence and, 178;

belonging, war and, 165, 168; belonging in all cosmopolitanisms and, 53; belonging narrowly defined and, 26; belonging as normative and, 27; belonging as related to power and, 2; belonging as related to mobility and, 14; belonging to a culture and, 41; belonging vs. detachment as a cosmopolitan paradox and, 61; Boltanski on detachment, inequality and, 67; capacity for detachment and, 192n8; Collini on Said's exile from all social belonging and, 138; conflicting scales of belonging and, 169; cosmopolitanism, detachment and, 34; cosmopolitanism as gaining and losing attachments and, 11; cosmopolitanism as having multiple, overlapping belongings and, 16–18; cosmopolitanism as refusal of all belonging and, 23; detached cosmopolitan spectatorship and, 216–17n16; detachment, patriotism and, 35; detachment, secular democratic state and, 128; detachment and belonging as interdependent and, 189; detachment as Enlightenment virtue and, 131; detachment from national self-interest and, 10; detachment from nation and, 19; disinterestedness/detachment, exile and, 130; global justice reconciled with local belonging and, 194n25; imported commodities as distant belongings and, 90; intellectuals' detached view of cosmopolitanism and, 117; national belonging, atrocity remembrance and, 184–88; national belonging, double standard and, 50; national belonging in Chomsky's comparisons and, 52; national belonging vs. responsibility and, 220n26; new cosmopolitanism as detachment and, 22; rhetoric, belonging and, 71; rhetoric, detachment and, 48–49; Said's secularism, detachment and, 117–21, 127; Said's secularism, effort at self-detachment and, 132; scholarship, nonbelonging and, 62; secular and religious belonging and, 120; unconscious belonging and, 186; violent origins in word *attachment* and, 30

Aurelius, Marcus, 37

Ayer, A. J., 140, 149–50

Bangladesh Liberation War, 52–53

Barber, Benjamin, 36

Barkan, Elazar, 176

belonging. *See* attachment/belonging vs. detachment

Benda, Julien: *Representation of the Intellectuals,* 116; *Treason of the Intellectuals,* 19

Benhabib, Seyla, 198n17

Benjamin, Walter: "The Storyteller," 178

Berman, Jessica: *Modernist Fiction, Cosmopolitanism, and the Politics of Community,* 35, 197n10

Bernheimer, Charles, 217n4

Bérubé, Michael, 53

Bilgrami, Akeel, 123

Blake, Casey: *Beloved Community,* 171

blaming, denunciation: dependence on foreign products and, 6–7; forgiveness among nations and, 188–89; historical forgiveness, economic inequality and, 41; historical forgiveness, imperialism and, 37; historical forgiveness among nations and, 188–89; humanitarianism and, 203n3; by humanities scholars, 73; Israeli/Palestinian conflict and, 191n4; as multidirectional, politically complicated, 91; Said's incidental humanism and, 129; of suffering, 68–69, 86; victim vs. agent/rescuer and, 207n41; Wallerstein vs. Chomsky and, 84; world-system's relationship with, 70, 87. *See also* comparative national blaming

Boltanski, Luc: *Distant Suffering,* 67–71, 87–90, 203nn2–3, 203n5

Bongiorni, Sara: *A Year without "Made in China,"* 8

Bosnian War, 54

Bourdieu, Pierre, 74

Bourne, Joanna, 179

Bourne, Randolph, 157–58, 160, 164, 166–67, 171, 216nn10–11

Brazil, in examples, 25, 82, 205n18

Brown, John, 160–61

Brunetière, Ferdinand, 145

Buchanan, Pat, 210n16

Burke, Edmund, 39

Buruma, Ian: *Occidentalism,* 123

Bush, George W., 23, 25, 51, 135, 165–66, 194n26, 216n12

Butler, Judith: *Frames of War,* 62–65

Calhoun, Craig, 17

Cambodian-Vietnamese War, 52–54, 61, 63–64

capitalism: American hegemony, imperialism and, 90–91, 135; balanced discourse on global capital and, 24–25; commerce-centered cosmopolitanism and, 198n17; commodity histories and, 18; comparison and cosmopolitanism as assimilated to, 47; consumption vs. production domains in Eliot and, 208n9; cosmopolitan detachment and, 18; cultural transmission through, 41; decolonization and, 206n32; free trade, protectionism and, 91; free trade and, 6; Golden Rule and, 54–57; multinationals' relationship to, 107–8; "single web of trade and," 40; Wallerstein and end of, 84. *See also* world-systems theory (Wallerstein's)

Chast, Roz: cartoon about imported commodities, 94–99, 103, 111

China: blaming for U.S. dependence on goods of, 6–8, 210n16; rise of, 55–56, 82–83; Tibet and, 152–54, 214n12

Chomsky, Noam, 46–64; American-centric cosmopolitanism of, 52–54, 60; American Jewish background and cosmopolitanism of, 17; anarchism of, 58, 200n9; anthropological over normative stance of, 202–3n28; Asad compared with, 59; avoidance of, in *New York Times* Op-Eds, 151–53, 155; Cambodia/East Timor comparison of, 63–64; comparison in cosmopolitanism of, 47, 50–51, 60; consistency, hypocrisy in, 202n21; "extraterrestrial" figure in cosmopolitanism of, 48–49, 51–52, 59, 200n8, 200n12, 201n18; Foucault vs., 59, 201–2n20, 202n25; *Hegemony or Survival*, 48–49, 59; inequality of power in comparisons of, 57; international law vs. anarchist assumption of, 59–60; leverage of individuals over the state and, 60–61; Michaels compared with, 55–56; Perry Anderson compared to, 202n24; political blaming of, 73; on elite's ethical norms, 202n22; principles and proximity in cosmopolitanism of, 58; rational thought in cosmopolitanism of, 21; response avoidance by, 200n10; Said compared with, 132; on Tibet, 214n12; United States as represented by, 203n30; Wallerstein compared with, 84, 194n23

Chow, Rey: *The Age of the World Target*, 201n17

Christians, Christianity, 77, 121–22, 128, 131–34, 166, 189, 211n7

Churchill, Winston, 218n8

Civil War, U.S., 84, 159–62, 164–65, 168, 195n26, 215n5

Clifford, James, 10–12, 34, 44, 192n12, 199n19

Clinton, William Jefferson, 54, 196n32

Cohen, Mitchell, 35

Cold War, end of, 9, 215–16n9

Collini, Stefan, *Absent Minds: Intellec-*tuals in Britain, 137–55; Chomsky viewed from intellectual framework of, 155; comic voice of, 141–42; conversion of intellectuals into public figures and, 143–45; critical reviews of, 213n2, 213n8; cultural authority of intellectuals in, 143, 148; culture as world changing and, 213n4; dissidence/influence and publicness/politics in, 146–47; existence, significance of intellectuals in, 137–39, 140–41; expertise vs. public speech of intellectuals and, 144; intellectual civility suggested in, 139; intellectuals in relationship to society and, 146; intellectual status of Collini suggested in, 141; intellectuals' use of media to reach public and, 149; media as test for models of, 151–52, 154–55; nonintellectual academics defended in, 150; public authority of intellectuals in, 142–43; public-based definition of intellectuals in, 152; on Said's dialectic, 116, 138

communitarianism, 39, 193n20

comparative national blaming: 9/11 vs. Bay of Pigs example and, 195n28; Allied bombing, German civilians and, 176–77, 181, 182–83; causality tracks and, 186; China and, 210n16; China/Tibet vs. India/tribal rebellions and, 214n12; detachment vs. belonging and, 189; historical forgiveness and, 174–76, 187; "Israel street wisdom example" of, 173, 184; national memory recovery and, 184–85; "Nazi rule of thumb" example of, 173–74, 183; participation in, cosmopolitanism and, 187–88; E. P. Thompson, Perry Anderson debate and, 217–18n5; universal blamelessness and, 175; violence, technology, proximity and, 178–80

comparison: affronting function of, 181–82; of British and French intellectuals,

147; capitalist-driven analogies and, 18; China/Tibet relations vs. Western policy on religion and, 153; commensurability needed in, 199n1; cosmopolitanism as strengthened by, 65; double standard and, 6–7, 50–51, 53–54, 64; ethical invisibility of comparer and, 63–64; inequality of power and, 61–63; intellectuals and, 138–39; Israeli-Palestinian conflict and, 125–26; of literature and imperialism, 217n4; Michaels's use of Golden Rule for, 55–56; nonalignment, nonidentity of different scales and, 3, 21; Palestinians missing in, 197n10; parity and ethical value of, 201n17; selectivity in, 60; between unequal cosmopolitanisms, 49–50. *See also* comparative national blaming; *specific countries, world regions*

complacency: American nationalism and, 153; Appiah's *Cosmopolitanism* and, 32; cultural diversity celebrated and, 34; marginality and, 22; temporal cosmopolitanism and, 37

Comte de Lautréamont (Isidore Ducasse), 201n17

conservatism, social, 142, 154

cosmopolitanism, changes and tensions within: abstraction vs. actuality of, 194n25; allegiance to humanity as primary and, 15; all-inclusivity and, 200n11; attachment vs. detachment and, 121, 131; culture, the aesthetic and, 34, 197n6; descriptiveness vs. normativity and, 12, 34, 62–63, 132; global justice, multiple humanities and, 196n30; identities "lightly worn" and, 8; Žižek's version of, 152, 154; instrumental rhetoric vs. disinterested aesthetic and, 71; "international popular" as paradox in, 17–18; Kantian vs. Hegelian versions and, 19; between local and universal identities and, 193n12; mobility vs. global justice and,

11–12, 14; nationalism coexisting with, 191n8; national vs. transnational scale and, 3, 9, 154, 187; normativity without avowal of norms and, 203n29; as paradoxical or imperfect, 53, 61; refusal of political obligations, affiliations and, 11; resistance to military conflict and, 14; restriction vs. broadening and, 10–11; Said's secularist critiques and, 131; scales of loyalty colliding under, 192n11; transnationalism vs. culture mixing and, 2–3; two scales of belonging in tension in, 169; universal solidarity vs. political force and, 88

cosmopolitanism, new: as balance between particular and universal, 15; Collini's engagement with intellectual significance and, 150–51; as complacent resolution for global antitheses, 31–32; concerns over Appiah's view of, 44; "cosmopolitanism from below" and, 11, 43–44; critiques of, 193n17; distinguishing of unequal cosmopolitanisms and, 49; as historical, 19; Hollinger on, 199n20; "hyphenated heterogeneity" as focus of, 45; "international politics" and, 96–97; as messy, 44–45; multidirectional blaming and, 91; national pride, national shame and, 104; "new cosmopolitans," value-positive terms and, 33; political irresponsibility and, 22; power against violent nationalism and, 30; power inequality acknowledged and, 65; stretching of solidarity and, 19–20, 153, 155; tension of actual and normative in, 133–34

cosmopolitanism, "rooted," 31, 35–36, 37, 39, 42, 53

cosmopolitanism, term: ethical prestige of, 13, 192n8; *kosmo-politis*, 11; as piety, 31, 196–97n2; popularity of, 2

cosmopolitanism and human rights, 184–85, 187

cosmopolitan studies, 4

cosmopolitics, 3–4, 24–27; cosmopolitan theory of power and, 202n25; example strategies of, 24. *See also* political action, agency; political obligation, responsibility; power, inequality of

cultural studies, 101–2

culture: academic dependence on term, 102; the aesthetic, cosmopolitanism and, 34, 197n6; aesthetic disinterestedness vs. the instrumental and, 71; Collini's view of, as world changing, 213n4; cosmopolitanism, anthropological vs. aesthetic sense and, 34; cosmopolitanism and appreciation of differences in, 13; cosmopolitanism and mixing of, 2–3, 134; cultural heritage vs. religion and, 153; economics, world-systems theory and, 79–80; Ferguson on inequality, Africa and, 81–82; intellectuals as determined by, 143; Kantian aesthetic and, 112; as luxury, 205n17; metropolitan cosmopolitanism and, 193n14; Mulhern's comparison of action with, 108; as nationally vs. globally determined, 78–79; periphery as overlapping with, 86; as political vs. apolitical, 101; reverence for objects of, 73; traces of production and, 110–11; as transmitted through materials, 41; Wallerstein's account of 1968 and, 205n19; world-systems theory vs., 71–78

"Culture and Society" tradition, 74, 101, 108, 209n14

cultures, diverse, multiple: cosmopolitan as celebration of, 33; Dewey on U.S. internationalism and, 215n6; significance of, in Third World, 86; as systems in world-systems theory, 204n10; in United States, 14–15, 154; U.S. multiculturalism vs. minority cultures in other countries and, 193n17. *See also* culture

Cummings, Dolan, 213n5

Cusset, François, 212n14

Cvetkovich, Ann, 210n19

Debs, Eugene V., 161, 215n7

De Genova, Nicholas, 169–70

Deleuze, Gilles, 212n14

Derrida, Jacques, 134–35

detachment. *See* attachment/belonging vs. detachment

Dewey, John: America as redeemable for, 170–71; America's internationalism, cosmopolitanism and, 215n6; Bourne and, 160; decision-making process of democracy and, 172; pragmatism and pacifism and, 167; problem-solving belief of, 166; public as concept expanded by, 157; U.S. in First World War and, 158, 164–65

diasporic communities: Hispanic immigrants in cultural assimilation example and, 55; intellectual in exile and, 212n14; long-distance nationalism and, 16–17; "made in America," anti-immigrant sentiment and, 103; national belonging and, 185–86, 219n22; nationalism, detachment and, 61; "new cosmopolitans" vs. traditional, 33, 134, 197n5; North Africans in Europe as example of, 25; refugees as political agents and, 24

Diogenes, 11

Dobbs, Lou, 8

double standard. *See* comparative national blaming; comparison

Dreyfus Affair, 137, 144–46

Du Bois, W. E. B., 164

DuPlessis, Robert, 86

Durkheim, Emile, 209n14

Eagleton, Terry, 213n8

East Timor, invasion by Indonesia of, 63–64

*effort*, term, 124–26

Egypt, in examples, 5, 195n26

Ehrenreich, Barbara, 105–6, 210nn19–20

Eliot, George: *Middlemarch*, 98–102, 108, 208n7

England, Great Britain: Allied bombing of Germany and, 180, 183; Perry Anderson's French comparisons with, 218n5; Collini on 20th-century intellectuals in, 146–49; imperialism of, 37–38; memory in worldview of, 185; Orwell's Burmese comparisons with, 20; Orwell's Indian comparisons with, 90; Robbins's connection to, 186; in world-systems theory example, 82. *See also* Collini, Stefan, *Absent Minds: Intellectuals in Britain*

English, James, 141

Enlightenment, the, 10–11, 131

Enzensberger, Hans Magnus, 181

Eurocentrism, 128–29, 131–32

Faurisson, Robert, 202–3n28

Feher, Michel, 23

Ferguson, James, 81–82, 206n28

First World War, 158, 160, 164–67, 171, 178, 215n7

forgetting. *See* memory and forgetting

forgiveness, historical. *See* blaming, denunciation

Foucault, Michel, 201n17; as antiprogressive, 85; Chomsky's antistatism vs., 202n25; Chomsky's 1971 debate with, 59; Chomsky's norms compared with, 201–2n20; critique vs. sensibility and, 62; culture's advantages and disadvantages and, 74–75; ethos in, 203n29; nonpyramidal power distribution critique of, 194n23; on power distribution, 65, 134; Said's effort set against power and, 124; Said's temporal generalization vs., 122; specific intellectual, concept of, 142; on systems, 204n13

France, in examples, 16, 54, 137, 139, 144–46, 181–82

Frank, Dana: *Buy American*, 103

French theory, 19, 75, 115, 118, 124–25, 145, 147, 149, 205n15, 218n5

Friedman, Thomas, 50, 214n9

Gaskell, Elizabeth: *North and South*, 108

Gates, Henry Louis, Jr., 37

genocide, 28, 54, 60, 61, 87–88, 179, 207nn40–41

Germany: Boltanski on, 69; in examples, 50; Wallerstein on, 85. *See also* Sebald, W. G., *On the Natural History of Destruction*

Ghana: Appiah on cosmopolitanism, patriotism and, 15, 35–39, 43, 197n11, 198n15

Gilroy, Paul: *The Black Atlantic*, 72

Gitlin, Todd, 22–25, 163, 194–95n26, 195n28, 196n32

Golden Rule, 18, 49–51, 53–56. *See also* Chomsky, Noam; comparative national blaming

Good Samaritan story, 88–89

Gramsci, Antonio, 18, 96–97, 142, 218n5

Greek influences, 12, 122

Guattari, Félix, 212n14

Gulf Wars, Persian. *See* Iraq War

Gunn, Giles, 128–29

Hage, Volker: *Zeugen der Zerstörung*, 177

Haskell, Thomas, 19

Hawley, John C.: *India in Africa, Africa in India*, 12

Hegel, Georg Wilhelm Friedrich: *Sittlichkeit*, 203n29

Herman, Edward, 63

Himmelfarb, Gertrude, 36

Hitchens, Christopher, 173–74, 177, 219n15

HIV/AIDS, 25; in examples, 6, 42, 103, 196n32

Hobsbawm, Eric: *The Age of Extremes*, 178–79

Hoffa, Jimmy, 210n16

Hollinger, David, 199n20; *Postethnic America*, 14–15, 19, 35, 38, 44, 193n17, 194n25

Holmes, Oliver Wendell, Jr., 159–62, 165, 167–68, 215n5

Holocaust, 24, 174, 180, 183–84, 207n40

Honduras, 98

Honig, Bonnie, 198n17

Hovsepian, Nubar, 130

Howe, Stephen ("Israel, Palestine, and Campus Civil Wars"), 173, 206n32

Hugh of St. Victor, 120

humanists, humanism: altruism of, 102; antisystem views of, 87; Clifford on Said and, 10; comparative literature and, 217n4; disinterestedness and, 130; "liberal subject" of, 117; memory freedom and, 181; particular over general valued by, 75; Perry Anderson's anti-humanism and, 182; political power of, 129; reconceptualizing cosmpolitanism and, 8–9; relationship between power and speech and, 70; Said's effort as, 124; Said's secularism and, 118, 134; suffering and, 87; Wallerstein's anti-progressiveness and, 85; world-systems theory and, 77

humanitarianism: Appiah on, 42; blaming and, 203n3; capitalism and, 112; in Chomsky's comparisons, 52; disinterest vs. politics and, 90–91; as foreign policy cover, 26, 32; Haskell on origins of, 19; interventional, 60, 87–88; political agency of movements, organizations and, 23–25, 196n32; politicization of, 67–70; secularism and, 119; self-interest and, 130; structural absence of causality and ethics of, 71

humanities scholars: "alternative modernities" and, 81; anticomparison position

of, 174–75; antiprogressives and, 85; antisweatshop campaigns, political action and, 111; coherence of global vs. local scale and, 72; global injustice and, 82; institutional "intellectual sweatshops" of, 109, 210n21; powerlessness and, 124; pragmatism vs. pastness of, 167; Said and political power of, 129; suffering and, 86–87; Wallerstein's time scale, political agency and, 87; world-systems theory vs. antisystem and, 207n40; world-systems theory vs. culture and, 73–76, 78–79

human rights cosmopolitanism, 184–85, 187

Human Rights Watch, 23

Huntington, Samuel: *The Clash of Civilizations*, 166

Hussein, Abdirahman, 75, 125–26

Hussein, Saddam, 180

Huyssen, Andreas, 178, 188

identity: domestic cosmopolitanism and detachment from, 29; ethnic, racial, 15–16; exile and loss of, 211–12n10; humanitarian vs. sufferer and common, 67, 88; irony toward, 192n7; local, national vs. global, 8, 169; Michaels on politics of, 55–56; new cosmopolitans and blurring of, 33–34; pragmatism and racial, 164–65; Rabinow's "critical cosmopolitanism" and, 192–93n12; racial, cultural vs. national, 38; religious, 122; secularism and, 133–34; worlds-system theory, class and, 21

immigrants. *See* diasporic communities

imperialism: as agent of historical change, 85; British, 20, 37; Christianity and, 128; comparison as form of, 175, 217n4; denunciation of, 22, 37, 47–48, 54, 131, 169–70; domestic democracy as interrelated with, 169; exile and,

212n14; forgiveness of past atrocities of, 40; NGOs and U.S., 23; Orientalism and, 122; Said on collective memory and, 126; Said on literature as complicit with, 129; of U.S. and global capitalism, 135

India: in Chomsky comparisons, 52–53, 60–61, 202n24; in intellectual property defiance example, 25; in Michaels's globalization example, 55; Orwell's British comparisons with, 90; pluralizing of cosmopolitanism and, 11

indigenous peoples: Aymara Indians in Bolivia, 55; cultural production of, 41–42; identity and, 38; immigrant belonging and, 186; interdependencies and, 40; sovereignty of, 20

Indonesian invasion of East Timor, 63–64

inequality. *See* power, inequality of; world-systems theory (Wallerstein's)

intellectual property, 6, 25–26, 196n32

intellectuals: Chomsky as, 155; cosmopolitanism, xenophobia and, 145; division of labor and, 209n14; French vs. British models of, 149; historical reasons for interest in, 213n5; "homelessness" of, 117–18, 132, 211–12n10, 212n14; Žižek's version of cosmopolitanism and, 154–55; ordinariness of, 137; professional credentials for, 145; Said on vocation of, 116–17. *See also* Collini, Stefan, *Absent Minds: Intellectuals in Britain*

international law, 59–60, 175, 183, 195n28

IRA, in long-distance nationality example, 17

Iraq War: in Perry Anderson and political authority discussion, 202n24; in anti-imperialist patriotism discussion, 169–70; Appiah's notable omission of, 42; in Dewey and First World War discussion, 157; in domestic cosmopoli-

tanism contrast example, 16; irrational retribution and, 188; liberal hawks support of, 19; media depictions of first Gulf War and, 1; media double standard and, 51; in NGOs as political agents discussion, 23–24; in nonidentity of scales example, 3; remote warfare and, 179–80; U.S. nationalism and, 2; in U.S. support for perpetual Middle East conflict discussion, 5, 166

Isaac, Jeffrey C., 202n21

Israeli/Palestinian conflict, 125–28, 151, 173; American war on terror comparisons of, 191n4; Chomsky on ethical norms and, 202n22; Palestinian suffering noted in Op-Ed, 214n9; patriotism and, 35; violence against Palestinians and, 5, 50, 61–62, 89–90; Zionism and, 130, 197n10

Israelites, ancient, 179

Jager, Colin: "Romanticism, Secularism, and Cosmopolitanism," 131–34

James, William, 30, 159, 164

Jameson, Frederic: *Postmodernism, or, The Cultural Logic of Late Capitalism*, 110; on sublime and place in division of labor, 109–10, 112, 210n23; Wallerstein's influence on, 72

Jay, Paul: "Beyond Discipline? Globalization and the Future of English," 78–80

Jennings, Jeremy, 149

Jews, Judaism, 54, 58, 88–89, 122, 145, 151, 164, 174, 214n9; Zionism, 17, 35, 130, 197n10. *See also* Israeli/Palestinian conflict

justice, global: antisweatshop movement and, 107–8; Chomsky's rational-comparative view of, 200n10; colonialism and, 54; cosmopolitanism as abstract standard of, 194n25; cosmopolitanism as having universalist impulse and, 3; cultural diversity and,

justice, global (*cont.*)
34; cultural expression, silencing and, 80–81; Foucault vs. Chomsky and, 201–2n20; humanities, systems and, 82; new cosmopolitans and that of Said, 13; newer cosmopolitanism and, 45; newer cosmopolitanism as democracy between U.S. and world, 170; rooting of local vs., 39–40; secular responsibility and, 28; solidarity, distance and, 70; solidarity with the disadvantaged vs., 199n20; worlds-system theory and, 77–78

Kallen, Horace, 164
Kant, Immanuel: the aesthetic and, 71, 203n5; "Analytic of the Sublime," 109–10; comparison defied in sublime of, 178; *Critique of Judgment*, 95, 112; normative cosmopolitanism of, 19, 88; Spivak on, 111–12; "sweatshop sublime" compared to sublime of, 95–96
Keenan, Thomas, 179
Kerry, John, 216n12
Keynes, John Maynard, 140
Klein, Naomi: *No Logo*, 107–8
Korean War, 84
Krikorian, Gaëlle, 23
*Kulturkritik* tradition (Thomas Mann, T. S. Eliot, and F. R. Leavis), 101–2
Kymlicka, Will, 41, 193n17

Larkin, Philip, 141–42, 150
Leavis, F. R., 140
Lebanon, 50
liberalism: Adad and, 62–63; Žižek critiques on, 152, 154; liberal hawks and, 19; presentist impulse of, 38, 41–42; as transparency, self-effacement, 150; universalism and, 10
Limbaugh, Rush, 8
Lindqvist, Sven, 180, 183
literary criticism, 94, 96, 101, 158–59, 167

Livingston, James, 164, 215n6
Locke, Alain, 164
Lodge, David: *Nice Work*, 93–95, 99–101, 104, 108, 111, 208n7, 210n15
Loss, Jaqueline: *Cosmopolitanisms and Latin America: Against the Destiny of Place*, 33

MacIntyre, Alasdair, 90
MacIntyre, Ben, 213n2
"Made in America" campaign, 7–8, 103–4
Malik, Kenan, 213n2
Mamdani, Mahmood, 179
Marcus, Steven, 100, 208n9
Margalit, Avishai: *Occidentalism*, 123
marginality, 22–24, 26, 128
Marx, Karl, 19, 85, 183, 207n36, 210n19
Mazzini, Giuseppe, 192n8
McKee, Yates, 23
media: celebrity, antisweatshop movement and, 97–98; cosmopolitanism as depicted by, 13; intellectuals' reaching of public through, 149; international vs. national blame, forgiveness and, 176; suffering, responsibility, and, 87–88, 90; unpopular cosmopolitanism in U.S. and, 151–55
Melas, Natalie, 199n1
memory and forgetting: German memory of Allied bombing and, 177, 180–81, 183–84, 219n12, 219n18; guilt, traces of production and, 95, 110; humanities and, 86–87; mass media and, 176; political recalibration and, 38; Said on collective memory and, 125; slavery in U.S. and, 216n12; U.S. military interventions and, 16; violence, inequality and, 163
Menand, Louis, *The Metaphysical Club: A Story of Ideas in America*, 157–71; Civil War narrative in, 159; comic voice and, 141; Dewey and Debs in, 215n7; domestic democracy, imperialism and, 169; loss of belief in beliefs

and war in, 168, 215n5; loss of belief in beliefs in, 161–62, 165–66; past military violence in, 167; pragmatism, patriotism, and U.S. militarism in, 157; pragmatism and race in, 164; pragmatism and social justice in, 163; on pragmatism and the Cold War, 215–16n9; pragmatism and violence in, 160; pragmatism vs. patriotism in, 158; structural contradiction in, 160

Mexican War, 170

Michaels, Walter Benn, 166, 216n13; *The Trouble with Diversity*, 55–57

Middle East: blaming and, 6; Said's use of *effort* and, 125–26; suffering in, 90; U.S. support of violence in, 5. *See also* Iraq War; Israeli/Palestinian conflict

migrants. *See* diasporic communities

Mill, John Stuart, 37

Minow, Martha, 188

mobility: cosmopolitanism and, 11–12, 14

Moody, Kim, 210n16

Moore, Michael, 8

Moretti, Franco, 49, 72

Mulhern, Francis: *Culture/Metaculture*, 101–2, 108, 140

Muslims, Islam, 77, 122, 154, 166, 174, 189, 194n26, 195n28

Naipaul, V. S., 119

Nairn, Tom, 146, 218n5

nationalism: apologist examples of, 195n28; Benedict Anderson on shame and, 189; blaming, forgiveness and, 185–86; capitalist contradictions with, 19; Chomsky's comparison as reverse of, 52–53; contradictions within, 5; cosmopolitanism, betrayal and, 146; detachment and, 34; diasporas and, 16; economic nationalism and passive, 8–9; Kulturkritik as covert, 102; long-distance, 17, 197n5; long histories of, 193n17; Michaels on pragmatism,

patriotism and, 216n13; new vs. older cosmopolitanism and, 10, 12; of powerful and powerless, 123; pride vs. shame and, 104; Said's critique of academia and, 128; Said's dialectic of memory over territory and, 126; Said's secularism and, 21

nationalism, U.S.: American imperialism and, 169; antinationalism and, 20; antisweatshop movement and, 103–4, 109; cosmopolitanism and rise of economic, 83; detachment vs. national shame and, 189; "I'm great, you stink" mentality of, 1, 3, 4–5, 16, 18, 29–30, 39, 191n2; nonidentity of scales and, 3; intellectual property, AIDS and, 6; long-distance atrocities and, 5; new wave of, 7; patriotism, cosmopolitanism and, 35; regulation vs. welfare and, 44

*New Cosmopolitanisms: South Asians in the US* (Rajan and Sharma), 33, 197n3

*New York Times* Op-Ed page, 151–55, 213–14n9, 214n11, 217n17

NGOS, 26, 67, 87–88, 199n20

9/11. *See* September 11, 2001

Nixon, Rob, 119

*Nongovernmental Politics* (Michel Feher, with Gaëlle Krikorian and Yates McKee), 23

Nussbaum, Martha, 14–15, 31, 43, 194n25, 197n16, 199n20, 217n17

Obama, Barack, 191n4

obligations. *See* political obligation, responsibility

*On the Natural History of Destruction. See* Sebald, W. G.

*Orientalism* (Said): academic success of, 129; Ali on influence of Foucault in, 125; Anidjar on Said's secularism and, 119–20, 122–23; Clifford on Said's humanism and, 10; Eurocentrism in academia and, 128

Orwell, George, 105, 120, 143, 194n24, 211–12n10; *Road to Wigan Pier, The,* 20, 90

Palestinians: Said on nationhood of, 116, 127; Said on Orientalism and, 126. *See also* Israeli/Palestinian conflict

Parkin, Frank, 209n14

patriotism, 43; American's version of cosmopolitanism and, 16; anti-imperialist, 169–70; Appiah on cosmopolitanism, Ghana and, 197n11, 198n15; Appiah on cosmopolitanism vs., 15, 31–39, 42; choice between cosmopolitanism and, 14; cosmopolitan paradox and, 53; Gitlin's reversals on, 16; as marginality alternative, 23; in Menand's narrative, 157–58, 163; Michaels on pragmatism and, 216n13; Nussbaum's vs. Rorty's views of cosmopolitanism and, 217n17; politics vs., 197–98n13; Rorty, pragmatism and, 157; Shaw, antisweatshop movement and, 104; U.S. militarism, Muslims and, 166, 195n28; as variant of cosmopolitanism, 3; welfare state and, 44

Philippines, example of cultural autonomy and, 175

Pieterse, Jan, 82–83, 204n8

Pinsky, Robert, 14

political action, agency: analytic spectatorship and, 202n24; charitable individual vs. state and, 43; as commitment of Said, Chomsky, 21–22; epiphanies and, 103–4; forgiveness and, 188; gray area as site of, 123–24; humanism and, 102; incommensurability of scales and, 189; intellectuals as engaged in, 147; international vs. national considerations in, 109; leverage of individuals on the state and, 60–61; literary criticism and, 101; multinational corporations and, 108;

national vs. transnational interests and, 36–37; proximity and, 58, 201n16; in reaction to suffering, 70–71, 90–91; Said's effort and, 127; spectatorship, imperialist violence and, 170; "sweatshop sublime" and, 96, 97, 98–101, 106, 112–13, 208n5; Third World vs. West in Said and, 122; victim-agent-rescuer relationship and, 207n41; Wallerstein and, 87; world-systems theory and, 78

political obligation, responsibility: atrocity remembrance and, 219n22; commodities, distance and, 90; cosmopolitanism as normative and, 20; denunciation of suffering and, 69; ethics of intellectuals and, 117; Gitlin on, 23–24; historical remembering as, 181; humanism and, 102; incommensurability of scale and, 189; insight, powerlessness and, 94; as luxurious opportunity, 108–9; national debts and, 220n26; NGOs and, 87–88; *Nongovernmental Politics* on, 23–24; rooted cosmopolitanism and distant, 42–43; suffering and, 87–88; "sweatshop sublime" and, 96, 97, 98–101, 106, 112–13, 208n5; two scales of, 43

politics. *See* political action, agency; political obligation, responsibility; power, inequality of

Poole, Ross, 219n22

Posnock, Ross, 167, 216n11; *Color and Culture,* 14, 38

power, inequality of: American hegemony and, 90–91; core and periphery and, 77, 82–83, 86; cosmopolitanism and acknowledgment of, 65; cosmopolitanism of Chomsky and, 49–50, 57; cultural respect and, 81; culture's effect on, 78; division of labor and, 93–95, 96, 98–101, 105–7, 204n10, 209n14; global North and global South and, 21–22, 24, 42; housework vs. industrial labor and, 105–6, 210nn19–20; local vs. global class privilege and, 194n24; long-distance nationalism as pathology and, 16–17; maps of systemic power and, 40–41; new cosmopolitanism and antitheses of, 32–34; newer cosmopolitanism, welfare state and, 44; Occidentalism vs. Orientalism and, 123–24; politics of comparison and, 61–64; structural inequality vs. fixed global status and, 206n28; between sufferer and non-sufferer, 67; theories of class and, 80; Third World and First World and, 56, 68, 86, 112; unequal norms in comparisons and, 201n17; universal standards as compromised by, 59; violence and, 163. *See also* capitalism; world-systems theory

pragmatism: Chomsky on Israeli/Palestinian conflict and, 50; cosmopolitanism as having diverse scales and, 3; Dewey's, 157; global injustice vs., 78; historical forgiveness, present inequality and, 40–41; Menand's narrative, Cold War and, 215–16n9; Menand's narrative, patriotism and, 158; Menand's narrative, racial identity and, 164–65; Menand's narrative, social justice and, 163; Menand's narrative, violence/war and, 160–66; Menand's narrative and, 216n10; Michaels on nationalism, patriotism and, 216n13; Rorty and, 216n12; secularism, political engagement and, 128; solidarity and, 168; storytelling vs. action and, 167; violence and, 192n7; war and, 162–66

progressives, progressive politics, 7–8, 107, 132–33, 167, 207n38

public sphere: Chomsky's discounting response from, 200n10; as conversational or storytelling form, 170–71; culture and opinion of, 143; democratization of, 137; humanitarianism and, 67; intellectual authority, recognition in, 141–42, 144, 146, 150; as multiple, 145, 149; *New York Times* Op-Ed page and, 151–54; politics and, 147–48; as zone of causal connectedness, 155

Pullman Strike, 215n7

*Question of Palestine, The* (Said), 127

Rabinow, 192–93n12

race, 14–15, 38, 162–65, 177, 186

Rai, Milan, 63–64

Rajan, Gita, 33

Reagon, Bernice Johnson: "Are My Hands Clean?," 100–101, 208–9n11

refugees. *See* diasporic communities

regulation: detachment as undermining, 18; welfare state and, 44

religion: Anidjar on Christianity and, 121–22, 211n7; Anidjar on Said's secularism and, 119; Asad on world-systems and, 77–78; belonging and, 120; Jager's cosmopolitanism and, 131–34; regulation of university and, 214n11; Said's secularism and, 118, 121; war and, 165–66; Žižek on, 152–54. *See also individual religions*

responsibility. *See* political obligation, responsibility

rhetoric, rhetorical devices: aesthetic vs., 71, 203n5; for denunciation of suffering, 68; discourse of generalized presumptive forgiveness, 174; *effort* in Said and, 125–26; extraterrestrial detachment, 48–49, 51, 53–54, 59, 61–62, 64, 200n8; family anecdotes, 198nn14–15; international solidarity as affected by, 69; narrative in which inefficiency becomes irrationality, 181; narratives, storytelling as, 158–59, 162–

rhetoric, rhetorical devices (*cont.*)
63; NGO public opinion campaigns, 67;
past imperialist violence expressed
with vocabulary of sin, 170; power of
system vs. power of words and, 71;
praise and blame, 175; reconciling cosmopolitanism paradox with adjectives, 194n25; Sebald's romantic tendency as, 219n16; storytelling, war
technology and, 178; *theology* to
describe argumentation, 121; tracks of
causality, 186
Rich, Frank, 213–14n9
Ricoeur, Paul, 69
Rizal, José: *Noli Me Tangere*, 175
Robbins, Bruce, 212n14; *Feeling Global*,
159
"rooted cosmopolitanism," 31, 35–36, 37,
39, 42, 53
Rorty, Richard: on academic left and
reform, 163, 171; *Achieving Our Country*, 158; adaptability and, 167; on
American solidarity, 169; on cosmopolitanism's plurality, 192n11; Nussbaum's view of cosmopolitanism compared with patriotism of, 217n17;
patriotism and, 43, 157; pragmatism
and, 216n12; secularism of, 165; spectatorship linked to cosmopolitanism
and, 216–17n16; spectatorship of past
imperialist violence and, 170; on
storytelling, 159; "Unpatriotic Academy," 43
Russell, Bertrand, 165
Rwanda, 54, 70, 87, 179
Ryan, Alan, 44, 166

Sahlins, Marshall, 76–80, 86
Said, Edward, 115–35; Collini on dialectic
of, 116, 138; culture vs. system and, 75;
*effort* and antisystemic thinking of,
125; effort as humanist impulse of, 115–
16, 124; exiled intellectual practice of,

21; filiation, affiliation of, 29, 132; *From
Oslo to Iraq and the Road Map*, 115;
humanism of, 125; humanism vs. post-
structuralism and effort of, 134; intellectual in exile and, 212n14; on intellectuals' disappearance and betrayal,
116–17; irony of academic success of,
130; *The Landscape of Palestine* (introduction to), 126; on Op-Ed page,
214n9; on Orientalism and Eurocentrism in academia, 128–29; Palestinian
background and cosmopolitanism of,
17; Palestinian concerns, intellectual
detachment and, 127; Palestinian/Is-
raeli conflict, 125–26; on Palestinians
and homelessness, 127; political power
of humanities and, 129; spatial and
temporal totalizing of, 122; system vs.
antisystem, humanism vs. antihumanism and, 204–5n15; Wallerstein's
influence on, 72. *See also* secularism,
in Said
Said, Wadie, 115
Sartre, Jean-Paul, 144, 149
Saudi Arabia, in examples, 5, 8
scale, temporal: Ahmad on Said's view
of, 122; dissidence vs. influence of
intellectuals and, 146–47; German
civilians' memory of Allied bombing
and, 184–85; historical forgiveness
and, 37–38; memory vs. forgetting
and, 86–87; military violence in the
past and, 167; objections to cultural
program and, 3; perception of suffering and, 219n21; Wallerstein on, 84, 87
scales, geographic, 3; global access vs.
power of action and, 95; interference
between, 21; Orwell's defamiliarization
and, 20–21; proximity, physical patriotism and, 36; world-systems theory
and, 71–72
Schmitt, Carl, 59
Seabright, Paul, 198n17

Sebald, W. G., *On the Natural History of Destruction*, 176–87; Allied bombing memory vs. concentration camp guilt and, 183; author's personal connection to, 186–87; *capacity* to remember suffering in, 178; comparative national blaming and, 188; efficiency, irrationality in bombing narrative of, 181; on German silence about Allied bombings, 177–78; German silence vs. defense of the rational in, 182; Germans' silence, "poetic justice" and, 218n8; memory and shame in, 219n18; memory recovery in, 184–85; remoteness and cruelty argument of, 179–80; romantic tendency in, 219n16; time and suffering in, 219n21

secularism, in Said: Anidjar on betrayal and, 117; as against belonging, 118; effort and, 135; as exile, homelessness, 119–21, 124, 127, 211–12n10; humanism and, 134; intellectuals and, 132; Israeli/Palestinian conflict and, 128; in *Orientalism*, 123; power as encumbering, 130; revised cosmopolitanism and critiques of, 131

secularism, in Žižek, 152–53

Sedgwick, Eve Kosofsky, 130–31

September 11, 2001 (9/11), 84, 173–74, 176–77, 185, 188, 195n28, 205n19

Shapiro, Gary, 208n5

Sharma, Shailja, 33

Shaw, Randy: *Reclaiming America*, 104, 108

Singer, Peter, 42–43

Siskin, Clifford: *Blaming the System*, 70, 203n4

slavery, 84, 159, 161–64, 185–86, 195n26, 198n15, 205n18, 216n12

Smith, Adam, 40

sociology, 68–69, 90

solidarity: Chomsky, U.S. government and, 54; communitarianism and, 39;

cosmopolitanism as having allegiance to, 15; distanced vs. proximate, 88–89; division of labor and, 209n14; global justice vs., 199n20; humanitarianism and international, 69; "international-popular," action and, 97; Kant's aesthetics and, 112; long-distance violence and, 5, 17; military aggression and, 44; Nussbaum's call for allegiance to, 31; responsibility, action and, 109; Said's secularism and, 118; stretching of cosmopolitanism and, 19–20; suffering and, 67, 70, 89; war and, 168; welfare state and, 22, 169; world citizenry, 9, 11, 32

Solomon, Deborah, 151

Spivak, Gayatri Chakravorty: *A Critique of Postcolonial Reason*, 109–12, 210–11n24

Stanton, Domna, 196–97n2, 199n19

Stern, Steve J., 205n18

subsidies, 6, 42, 51, 217n16

suffering: of body in Marx, 210n19; colonialism blamed for, 201n14; compassion fatigue vs. conception of, 178; compassion vs. pity and, 230n2; disease and disgust in discourse about, 103; disinterested spectator and, 89; equivalence of all, 184; of German civilians from Allied bombings, 176; giving aid while causing, 90; obligation, solidarity and, 67; political responsibility and, 87–88; politicization of, 68; violence vs. economic, 7–8; Wallerstein on capitalism and, 85; world-systems theory and, 86

Sun, Yat-Sen, 192n8

"sweatshop sublime": action vs. inaction and, 98–101; "international-popular" politics and, 97; as shared dilemma without simple solution, 96; "sinking back" and, 112–13, 208n5; social interdependence through, 106

Taylor, Mark, 214n11

terrorism: labeling of nonallies and, 16; political stigmatization of Islam and, 194–95n26, 195n28; state violence vs., 59, 65; "war on terror" and, 5, 191n4, 215–16n9

Thompson, E. P., 147–48, 217–18n5

*Three Kings* (film), 1, 191n3

Tunisia, 5

United States, militarism: aid to Israel and, 90; celebration of multiculturalism unaffected by, 34; in Iraq War, 202n24; in mainstream media and *New York Times*, 151–52; in Menand's narrative on Civil War, First World War, 157–58; moral disaster of, 171–72; reform concurrently with, 22–23; solidarity with non-Americans and, 169; violence, foreign policy, and exportation of, 193n19; Wallerstein on, 85

United States at historical juncture: humanism and, 8; national vs. transnational scale and, 4; new wave of nationalism and, 7; rising economic nationalism and, 83; structural self-interest vs. disinterestedness and, 91; U.S. decline, rise of East Asia and, 206n31

universalism: antisweatshop movement and, 102; Chomsky's comparative blaming and, 52–53, 58; Clifford on Said's humanism and, 10–12; Clifford's critical cosmopolitanism and, 192–93n12; cosmopolitanism contrasted with abstract, 19; cosmopolitanism as having balance between particularism and, 15; historical thinking as contrasted with, 19–20; impulse of cosmopolitanism, 3; Kantian cosmopolitanism and, 88, 112; Nussbaum's cosmopolitanism and, 31; rhetoric, the aesthetic and, 203n5; thinking historically and, 20; world-systems theory and, 77

Vico, Giambattista, 118

Vietnam, 52–54, 60, 61, 63–64, 179, 195n26, 202n24

violence. *See* war, transnational aggression, violence

virtue: ecological, 8, 44; extrication of domestic democracy from imperialism and, 169–70; lack of capacity for violence as, 59

Waldron, Jeremy, 14, 38, 40–41, 198n17

Wallerstein, Immanuel, 68–87; alternative view of injustice by critics of, 81; "The Curve of US Power," 206n31; *The Decline of American Power*, 84, 205n19; on global North and global South, 21; *Historical Capitalism*, 85; *The Modern World System*, 71–72; "The Rise and Future Demise of the World Capitalist System," 73, 75, 83. *See also* world-systems theory

war, transnational aggression, violence: Allied bombing and, 186–87; belonging and, 29; bombing and forgetting and, 219n12; bombing as affecting outcome of, 219n15; boundaries of moral community and, 155; community irony about own identity and, 192n7; complicity and, 19; ethical substance of cosmopolitanism and, 14; forgetting of, 163; global democracy and, 172; long-distance (remote), 5–6, 178–79; as meaningless spectacle, 1; 9/11 vs. other atrocities and, 173–74, 176; perpetual justification of, 194–95n26; power theories and, 64–65; pragmatism and, 161–62, 164–66; technology and, 178–79; U.S. exportation of, 193n19; victimhood vs. victimizer and, 176; virtue and lack of capacity for, 59; Wallerstein on, 85; of the West toward the non-West, 119–20. *See also specific wars and conflicts* welfare state, 22, 44, 107, 169

Werbner, Pnina, 13

West, Amy, 24

Whitman, Walt, 170, 217n17

Williams, Raymond, 29, 100–101, 108, 142, 214n4; *Culture and Society*, 74

Wilson, Colin, 138

Wilson, Woodrow, 160, 164

Wolf, Eric, 206n26

Womersley, David, 213n8

*World, the Text, and the Critic, The* (Said), 118

world-systems theory (Wallerstein's): "alternative modernities" vs., 82; antisystemic power and, 206n33; "class between nations" and, 80, 82–83; coercion and, 207n36; common division of labor in, 73, 204n10; core and periphery, shifts and, 82–83; disjoining (disjuncture) of economics from culture and, 79–80; economic vs. cultural factors in, 73–76, 78; epistemology of, 207n40; global, transnational scale in, 72; inequality of power and resources in, 77; luxuries exchange in, 75; Pieterse on undertheorization of, 204n8; power distribution of Foucault and, 194n23; progressive political gains and, 207n38; reaction of humanities to, 71; Stern on local factors in Caribbean slavery vs., 205n18; theory of power and, 68; Wolf on choice of, 206n26

World Trade Organization, 98

World War I, 158, 160, 164–67, 171, 178, 215n7

Zionism, 35, 130, 197n10

Žižek, Slavoj, 151–55

Bruce Robbins is the Old Dominion Foundation
Professor in the Humanities at Columbia University.


Library of Congress Cataloging-in-Publication Data
Robbins, Bruce.
Perpetual war : cosmopolitanism from the viewpoint of
violence / Bruce Robbins.
p. cm.
Includes bibliographical references and index.
ISBN 978-0-8223-5198-6 (cloth : alk. paper)
ISBN 978-0-8223-5209-9 (pbk. : alk. paper)
1. Cosmopolitanism. 2. Violence. 3. Afghan War,
2001– 4. Iraq War, 2003– I. Title.
JZ1308.R63 2012
303.6—dc23    2011053339